A Gust of Plumes

INDIAN OCEAN

PEMBA

Tanga

ZANZIBAR

DAR-ES-SALAAM

MAFIA

Kilwa

Mikindani

R. Rovuma

Lindi

Newala

PORTUGUESE EAST AFRICA

Lushoto

Pangani

Bagamoyo

Morogoro

R. Rufiji

R. Pangani

T A N G A N Y I K A

Kongwa

Dodoma

Kilosa

Ifakara

Mahenge

Kondoa

Manyoni

Iringa

Singida

Gt Ruaha River

Njombe

Songea

L. NYASA

Tabora

Chunya

Mbeya

Tukuyu

L. RUKWA

Mpanda

Sumbawanga

Kigoma

L. TANGANYIKA

INTERNATIONAL BDYS
MAIN ROADS
RAILWAYS

N

0   100   200

A Gust of
Plumes

A biography of Lord Twining of
Godalming and Tanganyika

by

DARRELL BATES

HODDER AND STOUGHTON
LONDON SYDNEY AUCKLAND TORONTO

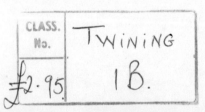

FOR MY WIFE

Contents

Illustrations

MAPS

8

Acknowledgments

MY MAIN DOCUMENTARY sources have been papers made available to me by Lady Twining and her two sons John and William Twining. They consist mainly of letters and scrap books left by Lord Twining's mother when she died in 1962, and of material accumulated by Lord Twining himself. Agatha Twining was an inveterate and for the most part a methodical hoarder, and she kept letters from her younger son and other papers relating to him from birth in bundles tied with ribbon and in carefully stitched paper folders. Some contain more than others but from about 1939 onwards she seems to have kept most if not all the letters which he wrote to her. Lord Twining did not keep many of his mother's letters but in other respects he too was an inveterate and methodical keeper of records, letters and press cuttings, and they amounted in the end to an attic full of files and of sorted and unsorted papers. Among them were the typescripts or manuscripts of some chapters of reminiscences, one called 'From Cadet to Governor' and the other 'In quest of Crown Jewels'. I have of course drawn on them both for information and inspiration but with a few small exceptions I have not reproduced them as they were apparently never submitted for publication by Lord Twining and were probably not intended for publication in the unrevised and uncorrected form in which he left them. I have also had access to letters in the possession of Lady Twining including many written to her by her husband, and to others belonging to Miss Evelyn Du Buisson.

Much unpublished material about colonial experiences—diaries, letters, note books and taped reminiscences have been collected together or located by the Oxford University

9

Colonial Records Project, and I have made some use of these. For published sources—books, official reports, newspapers and periodicals I have relied mainly on the old Colonial Office section of the Foreign and Commonwealth Office library, the library of the Institute of Commonwealth Studies at Oxford and the London Library. In all I have received much help and much courtesy from the librarians and their staff. I am also indebted to Oliver Woods for putting the press cutting archives of *The Times* at my disposal.

I have included a short list of books. It does not attempt to be a complete list of relevant publications: it is merely a note of books which I have read and found useful. I have not used the official records and files of the Colonial Office partly because the only years for which they are at present available, i.e. up to 1940, are those in which Twining was least likely to appear, and partly because it seemed better in any case not to try and use this sort of material for some chapters when it was not available for others. Histories and biographies of the Twining period based on such material will, if the thirty-year rule is maintained, have to wait until about the year 1990.

Although I have made much use of both published and unpublished documentary material, my main source of information has been the memories of persons of all races who knew Twining at one stage or another of his life or who were in the places where he lived or worked at the same time as he was there. A list of their names appears in an appendix, and my debt to them is acknowledged in the introduction. Included in the list are the names also of other persons to whom I am equally indebted for help or advice or encouragement. The only persons in this category not included in the list are my agent, my publishers and last, but certainly not least, my wife. I am also grateful to my son Nicholas for his help in reading the proofs.

Introduction

HE WAS BORN in a London vicarage in 1899, and he died of cancer when he was sixty-eight. He was an awkward little boy and a very ordinary young man but slowly and sometimes painfully, like an insect that sheds skin after skin on its way to maturity, he emerged in the end a complete, resplendent, gay and unorthodox man with a remarkable talent for extracting service and devotion from other people and for giving a special kind of pride and leadership to them. Although he was in his time and in his own field a well-known character, almost a legend, Lord Twining's name is familiar now only to those who knew him or were concerned with colonial affairs in the forties and the fifties. The case for writing a book about him rests partly on the fact that he was by any standard a distinctive and entertaining person, and partly on the interest and the comparatively unknown quality of the period in which he played his most active and leading parts. Much has rightly been written about the final stages of our colonial history—the achievement of independence by what were once dependent territories. Twining's period was the stage before this, in which the ground for independence was being prepared. In some cases it was done too slowly at first and then too hastily, with insufficient money sometimes or too little foresight, but in almost all cases it was done hopefully and with good intention. It was a period of development and welfare, or investment and training, a period above all of a curious faith when people thought they had time to do what had to be done, when they talked of multi-racial societies and believed that it might be possible after all for black and white and for governors and governed to work out a solution together. It was the last act but one of what turned out in the end in the minds of many people to be just another imperial tragedy.

Twining was in all his parts a creature of his generation, and must fairly be judged as such, as much by those who were older than he was and sometimes clucked at things he did or said, as by those who were younger and felt themselves at the end to be out of tune with the seemingly old-fashioned attitudes and loyalties which were as much part of him as his love of royalty and his romantic taste in music. There are obvious difficulties in writing a biography of a man who has only recently died, and I am grateful to his family for not attempting, when they placed his letters and papers at my disposal, to suggest what should be said or left unsaid. The views expressed and the judgments are my own. There are difficulties too when the subject is a public servant, as Twining was, because most of the documentary evidence is still barred under statutory and other rules. Against this is the advantage that so many of the people who knew and worked with him are still alive and in good memory. Finding out the facts and sorting them out and writing them down has had something, I have found, of the fascination and the frustration of investigating a complicated case, and of preparing the written and the verbal evidence for presentation to a court. I am grateful to all those who have made statements or submitted themselves to cross-examination or provided clues, and to those who have helped in other ways, and as a tribute and a record I have included a list of them, as well as a list of books and a note of other documentary sources, at the end. There are no footnotes.

I

The Background

IT WAS VERY warm in London at the end of June in 1899. The temperature at Westminster on the 28th went up to seventy-six but it was thundery and the sky was overcast. On the other side of the river at the Oval 10,000 spectators sat through the sultry afternoon held in close attention, according to the cricket correspondent of *The Times*, by Ranjitsinghi's grace and vigour while he and his partner made 325 runs in four and a quarter hours. Things were moving more slowly at the vicarage in Vincent Square where Mrs. Twining, the wife of the vicar of St. Stephen's, Rochester Row, was late with her third baby. It had even started off badly with the family doctor mistaking the pregnancy for a growth and Mrs. Twining had trouble right to the end with her eyes, for which she wore dark glasses of a curious shade of blue, and with headaches and chills—'so *very* naughty and foolish just now', as her mother told her in a letter. On top of this, the weather and the obstinate lateness of the baby made things very tiresome for everybody at the vicarage but suddenly in the evening a violent thunderstorm cleared the air and the tension, and next day, on the 29th, the baby was smoothly born. In another letter written from Hereford on the 3rd of July her mother gives us a vivid picture of a domestic Victorian birth. 'Thank Nurse Blackhall so very much for her letter which told me all I wanted. It must indeed have been very quick at last—how quick!—and I am thankful you had no chloroform. It was a blessing it was got over without a doctor and now the less you see of them the better. You really beat the record in quickness this time ... Bless you darling child,' the letter ended, 'in your new happiness—but let it be the very last!' One of her many sisters, commenting on the fact that the baby was born on St. Peter's Day and would she hoped be called Peter, said the same thing in a more sisterly way '... but my dear *don't* go in for being a mother to the twelve apostles!' It was in fact Agatha Twining's last baby. She was twenty-six. Her husband was twenty years older.

Even as babies go he was not a beautiful baby. Mrs. Twining kept the letters of congratulation she received tied up in blue ribbon and there is singular lack of comment on the new baby's looks and disposition. Her mother wrote again on the 10th of July to complain that after eleven days 'he ought to be showing his eyes and improving in his complexion'. The phrase 'a fine specimen' occurs it is true in one letter and clearly refers to the baby, but 'so pretty now and has such a lovely silky coat' turns out, like most of another sister's congratulatory letter, to be tactfully about the beauties of her new horse.

One thing most of the letters are clear and indeed firm about is that the baby ought to be called Peter, partly because of the day of his birth and partly because when he followed in his father's footsteps 'The Rev. Peter Twining' would sound so nice. Both Mrs. Twining and her husband, in so far as he had any say in the matter, appeared to have thought so too. But the folder in which Mrs. Twining kept her congratulatory letters is inscribed 'Edward Francis Twining June 29th, 1899' and Peter only appears in inverted commas below as a wistful and unofficial postscript.

One reason for this was someone known in the family as great-uncle George. He was sub-Dean of Salisbury Cathedral at the time and came up to London for the day to perform the christening. He travelled by train, first class. He was an eccentric and it was then, as now, easier and safer to be an eccentric on a private income. Even in an age when long hair was regarded as a sign of venerability or virility the length of his beard, which he wore to his waist, might have caused raised eyebrows if he had not been so well off. It wasn't however enough to excuse to some members of the congregation a habit which he had of carving pew ends and other objects during services in the cathedral in the intervals when he wasn't taking an active part. Another of his eccentricities was a strong aversion to the name of Peter. Perhaps he thought as a good Low Churchman that it smacked of Rome. Whatever the reason he refused to christen the Twining baby with that name. 'Edward Francis,' he said, 'are names enough for any man.' Mrs. Twining went to bed for the christening with a headache, as she often did when things didn't go her way, but whether this was the opportunity for great-uncle George's obstinacy or its consequence it is difficult now to say. Mrs. Twining however continued to call her son Peter to her dying day and so it seems did almost everybody else in the family. Great-uncle George may have won a battle but with a person as determined and as persuasive as Agatha Twining on the other side he seems to have lost the war.

Great-uncle George's real name was Dr. George Bourne. He was one of Mrs. Twining's relations, like most of the relations who directly or indirectly played a part in Peter Twining's boyhood and in his later life. She was born a Bourne, her father being Colonel Robert Bourne of Cowarne Court near Ledbury in Herefordshire, 'telegraph 11 miles, Burleygate Hereford' as their expensively embossed writing paper helpfully explained. The Bournes were an established country family with a comfortable lot of well-cushioned ancestors to lean against and a wide range of hereditary rents, investments and talents to pass on. One of Agatha Twining's brothers Gilbert achieved distinction as Emeritus Professor of Zoology and Comparative Anatomy at Oxford although, England being England, his son Robert became much better known by virtue of his prowess as an oarsman at Eton and at Oxford, where he four times stroked the University crew to victory in the Boat Race. But the wealth and talents of the Bournes look pale beside the attributes of the family from which Agatha Twining's mother came. Her mother's maiden name was Baker. Baker is of course a very ordinary name, but neither the sons nor the forefathers of Mr. Samuel Baker of Lypiat Park in Gloucestershire were ordinary people at all. His family tree was full of fascinating branches; a baronet who built Sissinghurst Castle in 1515 and later became Henry the Eighth's Chancellor of the Exchequer; seafaring men of Deal and Poole and Bristol where, to quote a polite Victorian biographer, 'the maritime traditions of the family were in harmony with the active life of those sea-ports' in eras when smuggling and piracy were not only profitable but patriotic; owners of sugar estates run on slave labour in Mauritius and Jamaica. It was his sons however who turned out to be the most fascinating generation of them all. As young Twining was brought up on stories of these Baker sons and lived for many years in the sunlight and the shadow of their various reputations they deserve a closer look.

Mr. Samuel Baker had five sons. One of them died young but the other four, Samuel, John, Valentine and James, lived to make their marks in different ways on the pages of Victorian history. Of the four Samuel is the best known, partly as Sir Samuel Baker, explorer and searcher for the sources of the Nile in the age of Livingstone and Stanley and Burton and Speke, and partly as the controversial and colourful Baker Pasha whom Ismael Pasha, Viceroy of Turkish Egypt, appointed as Governor General of the Equatorial Nile Basin and who was succeeded four years later in this bizarre and lucrative post by General Gordon of Khartoum. The achievements of Samuel's brothers John and James were less dramatic and on the whole less profitable but they were still remarkable. In their early twenties Samuel and John had, with the Baker flair for the uncommonplace, on the same day and in a single ceremony married sisters, the daughters of the local rector. This, some thought, meant settling down but as neither brother had the talent nor the inclination to work in a London office and as neither liked the tameness and the gallic orthodoxies of life in colonial Mauritius where they were sent to run the family estates, they chartered a ship registered as *The Earl of Hardwicke* but more generally known as Noah's Ark with enough on board in the way of human, animal and material necessities, including inevitably a pack of hounds, to establish a piece of rural England in the highlands of Ceylon. This was in 1848 before it had been discovered that the soil and the climate were good for tea. Baker's Farm consequently had its ups and downs and

Samuel left to try his hand at other things but John stayed
on until he died in 1883. The other two brothers, Valentine
and James, after a period of wild oats sown for the most part
with horse and gun, went into the Army and seemed destined for a time for careers that would by Baker standards
be somewhat orthodox; but both in the end did the unexpected. James went off to British Columbia and showed
his versatility by going into politics and becoming Minister
of Education, and Valentine became the controversial centre
of one of the great Victorian railway-carriage melodramas.
Later, 'Her Majesty having no further occasion for his services', he went on to make another name for himself, with a
resilience and a tragic courage which one cannot but admire,
in the less inhibited services of the Sultan of Turkey and the
Khedive Ismael. Annie Eliza, Mrs. Twining's mother, was a
sister to these unusual brothers, and seems to have trans-
mitted both to her daughter and to her grandson Peter not
only a wealth of family anecdotes and precepts but also
some, though perhaps not all, of the Baker qualities.

It was at Cowarne Court that the first of these processes
occurred. Agatha Twining often took her children to her
parents' house for fresh country air and food. 'I am out
nearly all day,' Peter wrote in an early letter to his father,
'and I and Betty [his sister] sleep out at night, and if it rains
I sleep in the summer house and Betty sleeps indoors;
mother feeds me up on milk, cream and butter like anything ...' Perhaps Mrs. Twining pined too for a touch of the
easy country-house affluence which Cowarne Court, in con-
trast to the gloomy vicarage in Vincent Square, so gener-
ously provided. Cowarne Court is now demolished but in
the early nineteen hundreds when Peter Twining went
there it was an enormous house in an enormous park.
Colonel Bourne is said to have paid £125,000 when he
bought it in 1876. The hall was so big that when the first war
came and coal rationing was introduced it was impossible to
keep it warm without the aid of local influence and a bit of
bucolic barter, because its area in square feet was three
times more than the maximum allowed for in the regulations. It was uncomfortable and ugly even by contemporary
standards and there were bathrooms, one regular visitor told

me, to which water had not yet penetrated. But there was a large nursery wing, a constant supply of expendable Swiss and German governesses, a wide range of animals to play with, a tennis court and always jam for tea.

It was not surprising therefore that Mrs. Twining and her children were by no means the only ones who went to stay at Cowarne Court. Agatha Twining had five sisters and three brothers and they and their families were also frequent visitors. And there were of course from time to time the Baker relations too. Colonel Bourne, who might well have served as a model for Jane Austen, seems to have taken little notice of his guests except to ask them when they arrived in a loud voice when they were going in order, or so he said, that he could tell the coachman when to be ready for the long fourteen-mile drive back to the railway station through the narrow winding Herefordshire lanes. He also presided every morning at family prayers with all the thirteen servants kneeling in a row according to their rank and station but the only other time the children saw him was at the end of dinner when some of them were allowed in briefly with the dessert. Mrs. Bourne however took all the children under her wide and generous Baker wing and summed them up and saw that they were happy. Peter Twining, she seems to have sensed at once, needed particular attention. He was a thin, plain, pale boy with a stammer and awkward limbs which couldn't throw or run fast or wield a cricket bat. He was good at charades and family plays and he had an aptitude for practical jokes and boyish mischief. It must however have sometimes seemed to him, as he watched all those other cousins, that they had an alarming, almost an unfair advantage of good looks and wealth, and of social, athletic and academic talents. He appealed to some of them, and others found him amiable but mostly they didn't notice him at all. He was often to be found alone, sulking, hands in pockets, head firmly down. 'Poor Peter' his cousins called him. Perhaps it was compassion that made Mrs. Bourne take him into her especial care. When the other children whooped off to shoot imaginary elephant 'like great-uncle Sam' or to play games with rough and accomplished ease or to make bold self-confident Baker and Bourne and Baily eyes at the nieces and the nursemaids, Peter used to help his grandmother scrape the plates and feed the proceeds to the ducks. While they scraped the plates and fed the ducks Mrs. Bourne used to tell him stories about her famous and exciting brothers. Most of the stories were about Samuel. One doesn't know exactly what stories she picked out or how far she varnished or curtailed them, but with the benefit of hindsight one can imagine which of the many Baker stories she might have told him were the ones which particularly appealed to him and stuck most firmly in his mind. Peter Twining had a dominant, strong-willed mother, a sister and more than his fair share of aunts, and it seems likely that he would have had a liking for the story of Samuel as a small boy, fair, sturdy and adventurous, as Peter would have liked to be and wasn't, planting one of his sisters up to her neck in the garden to make her grow on the principle that what was good for trees ought also to be good for girls. There would have been stories of the elephant and other game he had shot in Ceylon and Africa and of the occasion perhaps when he found himself with an empty muzzle loader and an angry buffalo and, 'hastily rolling up the small change in his pocket in a piece torn from his shirt', he rammed the packet down with a charge of powder and fired it off. The buffalo was so stunned 'by the collision with Her Majesty's features upon the coin' that the attack was repulsed and Samuel escaped. Peter Twining never acquired a taste for shooting but this was the sort of dramatic and occasionally embroidered storytelling which he liked and which he was himself later to develop into a fine art. There were tales of course about Baker's discovery of Lake Albert in his search for the sources of the Nile, and of the acclaim and the knighthood which he got when he returned to England. There is one small story about this expedition, which one suspects he also heard and noted, about how when Baker went to meet the ruler of one of the old Uganda kingdoms whom he wanted to impress, he, being in rough travelling clothes and knowing, as he put it, that 'personal appearance has a certain effect even in Central Africa', dug out a full-dress Scots Highland suit which he apparently carried about with him for such occasions and put it on for the interview, with very good

results. No doubt there were stories too of Baker Pasha and
his efforts to suppress the slave trade in the southern Sudan
but it is probable that some of these were modified or omit-
ted by Peter's grandmother as the methods which her
brother sometimes employed were even then regarded by
many as old-fashioned. It wasn't after all just to suppress the
slave trade that he was paid £10,000 a year by the Khedive
Ismael. There were indeed several things about the redoubt-
able Samuel Baker that Peter Twining certainly didn't hear
from his grandmother. And like any other boy with an enquiring mind and an extra curiosity about what is concealed
by his elders he was particularly intrigued with one aspect
of his great-uncle's life which was never mentioned. When
Baker's first wife, the rector's daughter, died of typhus in
Bagnères de Bigorre he went off to the Balkans to build a
railway. It was during this period, to quote one of his Victorian biographers, 'that his wanderings threw him into
touch with Florence von Sass'. There is an element of controversy about how Baker met his Florence but the version
which Twining preferred was that one day Baker went out of
curiosity to a Turkish slave market where, with a sort of
Victorian inevitability, a beautiful white girl was up for sale.
Baker, who never lacked the courage of his impulses or the
money to finance them, naturally bid to save her from a fate
much worse than death, and got her. Whatever the truth
Florence von Sass emerged from the hazards and uncertainties of the Ottoman Balkans to become Baker's constant and
courageous fellow traveller, companion and wife, and one of
the most remarkable women of her generation.

Another question mark hung over the stories about
Samuel's younger brother Valentine. This particularly intrigued young Twining, partly because Valentine was a
soldier, which was what he himself from an early age wanted
to be, and partly because one of Colonel Valentine Baker's
daughters was his god-mother. The question mark hung over
the division between the two separated parts of Valentine's
career—first as a brilliant and successful cavalry officer in the
service of the Queen, and then as a soldier of fortune in the
Balkans and the Middle East. No one would ever explain the
reason for this separation and change of status, and it took

young Peter Twining some years to find it out. What happened was that in 1875 Colonel Valentine Baker, having just relinquished command of the Tenth Hussars to take up a Staff appointment which would undoubtedly have led to higher things, got into a first-class carriage of a London train at Liphook. Sitting alone in the carriage was a girl of twenty-two, 'a very lady-like kind of lady' as a *Times* correspondent later put it, who eventually found it necessary to open the door of the carriage while the train was still in motion and climb out on to the footboard. The case roused the emotions of a generation which had a particular taste for melodrama, and Colonel Baker was sent to jail and dismissed from the Army. The case makes strange and rather pathetic reading now—'I felt his hand underneath my dress; on my stocking, above my boot'. Although the trial, if not the public atmosphere, seems to have been fair, and the sentence on the evidence not unjust, one wonders whether on the early part of the journey from Liphook to Woking Miss Dickinson was quite as lady-like as she made out and whether there may not after all be something, however tenuous, in the romantic theories that Colonel Baker allowed himself to be convicted in order to shield a mysterious third person travelling in that first-class compartment who had royal blood and a very gallant reputation.

Cowarne Court and the exploits and mysteries of the Baker family must have seemed a long way from Rochester Row and Vincent Square where the Twinings lived. The train that took them from Paddington to Ledbury took them away to a different world. St. Stephen's church where Peter Twining's father was curate and vicar for over forty years had been built and endowed by the rich and philanthropic Miss Burdett-Coutts in 1847 at a time when there was a shortage of churches in the slummier parts of Victorian London, 'the populous city of Westminster presenting', in the words of a contemporary document, 'not the least prominent instance of this spiritual destitution'. It is now of course a respectable and well-ordered part of London but in the early years of the century when the Twinings lived there it was still known as Devil's Acre, where policemen went about in threes and one of them was murdered one foggy night just

for the price of his boots. As a boy Peter wasn't allowed out
alone in Horseferry Road. There was a horsemeat butcher
within smelling distance of the vicarage and a V.D. clinic, for
the soldiers who came into the area every evening, farther
down the road. It is surprising at first sight that an area of
such mean tenements and rough characters should have still
survived into the early nineteen-hundreds so close to such
Meccas of respectability as the House of Lords, the Army and
Navy Stores and Westminster Abbey. In fact it was this
proximity to the Abbey which was the cause. Much of the
Rev. William Twining's parish was within the old precincts
of the Abbey which had had privileges of sanctuary dating
back to the times of the Saxon Kings and Edward the Con-
fessor, whose charter offered anyone fleeing there for any
cause 'all maner freedom of joyous libertie; and whosoever
presumes or doth contrary to this my grant, I will hee lose
his name, worship, dignity and power and that with the great
traytor Judas that betraued our Savoiur, he be in the ever-
lasting fire of hell'. Although these rights were legally ex-
tinguished by a Statute of Restraints in the reign of James
the First the habit of 'taking Westminster', as the saying went,
when one had got the wrong side of the law seems to have
persisted into Edwardian times with the result that places
like Great Peter Street and Strutton Ground, within a stone's
throw of St. Stephen's church, still had more than their fair
share of landladies who asked no questions and tenants of
both sexes who worked irregular hours. Although the vicar
also had his ration of more regular and more well-to-do
parishioners, particularly from the red-brick and neo-classical
porticos of Ashley Gardens, it was not a prosperous parish.
The vicar's emoluments were six hundred a year and that, it
seems, was all he had. It was not much on which to live in
the manner in which vicars were in 1900 supposed to live
and not much on which to bring up a family which, because
of all those relations, thought of itself, to use the jargon of
those days, if not perhaps as upper middle class at least as
middle middle class. The gaps both of economics and social
standing were bridged to some extent by the vicar's wife.
She brought to the vicarage in Vincent Square not only a
superior social status but a private income of four hundred

a year. This was just as well as Mrs. Twining liked the outward appearances as well as the indoor conveniences of having domestic servants which they would otherwise have found it difficult to afford. Agatha Twining liked to do her shopping too in stores and emporiums with well-known names, and as she always bought the best whatever the state of her finances it was fortunate that she had some money of her own.

The Rev. William Twining was not only a poor man but, according to many who knew him, a singularly unprepossessing one as well. People remember him as a tall, rather flabby man with a long bony nose, like the rector in Charles Morgan's *Sparkenbroke*. His fingers were limp and cold, 'it was like shaking hands with a dead trout' as someone who didn't particularly like him put it. He was by most accounts, at least in his later years when his children were growing up, a quiet, retiring man, 'a nice old thing', a man who in his own house seemed somewhat colourless beside the vibrant and temperamental vivacity of his wife. Indeed there were many among his wife's relations and friends who were surprised that the young Agatha, rich, well-born and charmingly attractive should have chosen him as a husband in preference, it was said, to other suitors more endowed. Her sister Ruth confided to her diary on the 18th of September, 1894:

We heard from Mother the astounding news that Agatha is engaged to be married to Mr. Twinning, the vicar of St. Stephens, Westminster! We are quite overcome with astonishment and I almost say disgust. I have never seen him but Faithy [another sister] has and she says he does not look the sort of man to be Agatha's husband and might be 40 or more. We heard that Agatha was rather weak on Twinning but then Agatha is weak on a great many clergymen, and our suspicions were never seriously aroused. It has all come about very suddenly. We know next to nothing about him, not even his name, age, or whether he has parents, brothers and sisters and what. Faithy and I kept raving and ranting about it all day and wrote rather mad letters to Mother and Agatha. Faithy declares he is like a frog—but admits he is tall and manly looking.

Her letter to Agatha was signed 'your very loving and
struck dumb with amazement Ruth'. She still hadn't learnt
to like him or spell his name properly by the time of the
wedding.

We think he is not nearly good enough for Agatha and
wish it had not been so hurried. Another pity is that he
was neither at Oxford or Cambridge, only Kings College.
He has no private means. No one knows anything about
his father. A mysterious brother of his who is not talked
about appeared in the church at the wedding service and
disappeared mysteriously afterwards.

Parsons however in those days seem to have been intrinsi-
cally attractive to young girls, particularly if they were religious, and Agatha who had a mind and a will of her own
from an early age may well have seen the more solid qualities
underneath the graceless façade which made him a good husband and a conscientious father, and a vicar who may not
have counted for much at home but who by all accounts was
very much respected and in command of his church and
parish. Organists and choir boys took no liberties with the
Rev. William Twining; he cleared the parish debts by careful management of its affairs; Working Men's Bible classes
and the St. Stephen's Temperance Society flourished under
his close direction, and he established a club for the male
employees of the near-by Army and Navy Stores which seems
to have been a model of its kind. He was a pioneer too in
establishing Boy Scouts and Wolf Cubs in London although
the popularity of the Pack which he started at St. Stephen's
may have been due, through his friendship with the Baden-
Powells, to its possession of a live wolf cub as much as to his
own enthusiasm. Peter Twining may have been like his
mother in temperament and character but the influence of
his father, though less obvious, should not be overlooked.

It comes as a surprise to those brought up when Twining's
Tea were household words to find that the Rev. William
Twining was a poor London parson. The trouble was that
he came from the wrong branch of the family if indeed there
was any relationship at all. The tea Twinings came from

Painswick in Gloucestershire whence an early ancestor moved to London in the seventeenth century to look for work when the bottom fell out of the West Country wool trade. Although the Rev. William Twining spent a lot of time and trouble with land and parish registers tracing his own descent back to Twinings and Twynnyngs and Twinninges in Worcestershire and Gloucestershire he never succeeded in proving any firm connection between the two families. Whatever the real answer is, the hard fact remained that he had none of the money or the considerable Forsyte-like position in trade and society which the tea Twinings had achieved. It is not surprising that at the age of seven young Peter, looking with envy and a touch perhaps of jealousy at his mother's relations and at his namesakes on his father's side, told his parents that one day he would put their name of Twining on the map.

It may be that this story, like other cosy domestic stories in this and other families, is quite untrue. If it is true it was not a statement which is likely to have made his parents feel any particular hope or pride. If his elder brother Stephen had said it, or even his talented and unusual sister, they might have nodded their heads and smiled: but poor little Peter, with his stammer and his awkwardness, it must have made them want to laugh, or cry.

2

School and Salad Days

IN 1908 WHEN he was eight Peter Twining was sent to boarding school. He went to The Old Ride at Branksome Park
in Bournemouth. It was a good school and an expensive one.
One suspects that it was Mrs. Twining's idea. It was con-
veniently run by one of her cousins and special arrangements
were no doubt made about the tuition and the boarding fees.
The idea perhaps was to get Peter away from the atmosphere
and fog of Rochester Row and to give him greater confidence
when he met his expensively schooled cousins in the holidays at Cowarne Court. He was still small and slight and
awkward, and he needed all the help he could get. He was,
in the words of one of his contemporaries at the Old Ride,
'a squinney, inky sort of boy' who stammered when he got
nervous or excited. 'I find Peter's stammering rather bad,'
the headmaster wrote in 1909 to his cousin Agatha, 'when
he reads aloud, especially when he reads a piece with long
words in it.' He was also 'rather inclined to sit and dawdle'.
He had no noticeable talents either in the classroom or on
the playing field and was generally unremarkable and un-
remarked. Sir Francis Chichester, who was at The Old Ride
at this time, can't remember him at all. But the few who do
remember him found him talkative and likeable, and Twining himself in the draft of an autobiography many years later
said that he was 'quite happy, very lazy and incredibly
stupid'. It is of course one of the commoner conceits of the
English who succeed to say that they were bottom of the class
at school but in Twining's case this boast seems to have been
quite justified.

In 1910, when he was eleven, Twining went to Lancing. In this case it seems that it was his father who made the choice and fixed the details. One of the reasons why he chose Lancing was that it was a Woodard school, designed originally, according to Evelyn Waugh who went there later for different reasons, to inculcate High Churchmanship especially in the education of sons of the clergy. Another reason was that it offered special terms to parsons. His elder brother Stephen had gone there at reduced fees on a choral scholarship and the persistent and resourceful vicar managed to get Peter into Lancing too on what was called a Provost's scholarship, which in those days at least were offered on the hard-upness and piety of the parents rather than on the scholastic or other merits of the boy.

Lancing was bracing both in its climate and its curriculum. Chilblains and chapel fifteen times a week were the things that some who were at school there remember best: others found the atmosphere and the isolation equally monastic. Several of the masters were in Holy Orders and unmarried, and apart from the housematrons and Sister Babcock who was in charge of the sanitorium and had a moustache (a boy who might well have been Peter Twining but wasn't once offered her a razor and was caned for it), the exclusion of feminine influence and domestic life was pervasive. There were some females of sorts who did the beds and emptied the chamber pots but they were kept well out of sight, and other menial tasks were done by youths and by bootmen, 'old, illiterate, misshapen' to quote Evelyn Waugh again, 'who lived in lightless dens, smelling of blacking and shag'. The only exception was the headmaster's wife, Mrs. Bowlby, who was kind and had boys in to tea. The headmaster himself, the Rev. Henry Bowlby, was 'a tall, lean man, distinctly handsome except when the keen winds of the place caught and encrimsoned his nose. He walked with a limp but in youth had got his blue, in a bad year, for hurdling. A fair scholar with an old-fashioned habit of introducing not very recondite classical allusions into his speech and letters, he had no particular interest in education. He hoped to become a Bishop.' One of several possible reasons why he didn't was believed to be that Mrs. Bowlby was given to innocent gaffes of speech which would be inappropriate in a bishop's wife. She kept an aviary of colourful birds like tits and cock robins, and if Twining and his contemporaries at school ran out of genuine Mrs. Bowlby stories they had little difficulty, it seems, in making up some others.

Twining didn't do particularly well at Lancing. His parents must have been confirmed in their impression as the school reports came in that their Peter was just another nice but mediocre boy. There were warnings of this too in his own letters to his mother. 'The exams are in full swing now,' he wrote in 1916; 'please don't be upset if I am bottom in every one.' It wouldn't have been so bad if he had been good at games but he was even worse at them than he was at work, and he had to fall back for schoolboy status on the success of his Bourne cousins on the river and of other cousins at cricket. One, Robin Baily, played for Harrow and Cambridge, and another, R. H. Twining, claimed for the purpose as a cousin though the relationship was in fact tenuous to the point of uncertainty, did the same at Eton and Oxford and went on to captain Middlesex. The best that Twining himself could manage in the way of athletic attainments was to be spare man to the school cross-country running team. The small unmodest pride with which he recorded his determined training and his thin successes—'went for a five mile run', 'came in fourth'—in a pocket diary for 1916 make one feel for him over the other sadder entries—'played footer (remnants)', 'watched house match v. Olds.', 'played cricket Fields III v. Heads III. scored I.'.

He may have been mediocre but he wasn't commonplace. Canon Adam Fox, who was his housemaster for most of the time he was at Lancing, had this to say of him over a generous tea ('people don't seem to *eat* tea nowadays') of sandwiches, scones and three varieties of cake in the quiet bachelor cloister where he lives in the shadow of Westminster Abbey. 'He made no special mark at first. He ran quite a normal course, and on reaching the appropriate standing became House Captain and then School Prefect; he was also a Sergeant in the Officers Training Corps, quite a good one as far as I remember.' He paused. His blue eyes smiled as his mind went back over the cloister years as master and warden, fellow and professor, preacher, chaplain and canon, and came to rest on 1916 when 'I ran the Corps, you may be surprised to learn'. He had been Professor of Poetry at Oxford 'by accident' he explained and 'for some reason or other' they had given him the James Tait Black Memorial Prize for his biography of Dean Inge. He was eighty-six. Although he sometimes forgot the names of people he had met the day before his memories of nearly sixty years ago were sharp and clear. 'But although Peter did nothing specially distinctive at school that doesn't mean that he was just ordinary. He was large, and by no means silent. He was enterprising, and took his own line, and was often found to be a leader. But I do not recall any notable sayings, and I did not discover that he had any particular gifts of administration, but this,' Canon Fox added, 'may have been from want of opportunity. It did not cross my mind that he would ever adorn the House of Lords.'

'He was large and by no means silent.' Peter Twining had lost his stammer by the time he went to Lancing except for his first year or two in moments of special stress. Some of those who were at school with him remember him as a good talker and as having a fluent and original way with words, but almost everyone, boys and masters alike, who knew him well remember him better for his friendliness and for his sense of fun. His sense of fun was often sharply pointed and was mostly at the expense of masters who were pompous or who had bubbles of conceit. There was one occasion at least, however, when it was directed at a visitor. A bishop came one day to stay at the school and preach. They were used to that of course at Lancing but this one was not only excessively boring but he also stayed too long. Until Twining, who was then sixteen and a sacristan in the chapel, put on top of the next sermon's text a time-table with the trains back to Brighton marked in ink. The man who told this story was in the chapel at the time as an assistant sacristan and vouched for the truth of it. He also had another story which has an authentic Twining ring. Someone was getting at the Communion wine but they couldn't nail the culprit until Twining hit on the idea of putting red ink in the bottle instead of wine. The culprit thus indelibly discovered was asked to leave, 'but he is nevertheless' my informant said with a quick look round at the very lean or very portly figures sleeping in their leather chairs, 'a member of the Athenaeum.'

Although the story about the trains to Brighton has been given as an example of Twining's sense of fun it is also an indication of his sense of protest. He had grievances and bellyaches like any other schoolboy but instead of just talking about them he had an urge, often an uncomfortable urge, to do something about them too. Writing to his mother when he was seventeen he burst out 'There are a lot of silly rules all of which I am going to break about the trains we are to go by. We are going to be told what trains to go by but I am not going to be dictated to by anybody I am going by the first train I can catch.' Another subject he felt strongly about was the food. As the war went on it not unnaturally got worse and worse until Evelyn Waugh, who also had a sense of protest, said that it 'would have provoked mutiny in a mid-Victorian workhouse'. Here is Twining on the subject, again to his mother.

The food at the beginning of term was much better but during the last fortnight the meat has been unsurpassable, in fact one helping I had might have been put on show for the Red X, I almost sent it to you in an envelope but on second thoughts I found I had more respect for your nasal organs. But it is no use the parents complaining, the only thing is for us to complain on the spot, which we are beginning to do with quite satisfactory results.

The letter ended, as all his subsequent letters to his mother ended, 'your very loving son, E. F. Peter Twining'.

In 1917 Twining sat his entrance examination for the Royal Military Academy at Sandhurst. It wasn't just the pressures of the war or his apparent lack of equipment for any other occupation that made him do so. He had wanted to be a soldier, as other boys want to be an engine driver, since he was small. He used to say that it was because he had been taken for a walk every day as a child to watch the Changing of the Guard at Buckingham Palace: but perhaps he remembered too that Colonel Valentine Baker whom he so much admired had been a soldier and that even the great Samuel had always regretted, even when he was rich and famous and esteemed, that he hadn't been one too. 'It gave one a status,' he said, 'in society': and status was something, one suspects, that Peter Twining, a poor relation in a rich galaxy of cousins and namesakes, and a nonentity at school, very much wanted to have.

His parents didn't want him to take up the Army as a career. His mother who was a devout and later an almost fanatical churchwoman wanted him to be a parson. His father, who had a very practical turn of mind particularly when it came to money, saw that when the war ended and soldiering became, as he imagined it would, an expensive social game again, an officer even in a county regiment wouldn't be able to live on his pay, and he of course was in no position to provide Peter with a private income. He wanted both Peter and his elder son to go into Twining's Tea Whether or not the two families were in fact related, it was generally believed at that time that they were, and they treated one another for the most part in a cousinly manner. The Rev. William Twining also knew that, owing to a tendency to produce daughters rather than sons, the tea Twinings were running out of Twinings. He was hopeful therefore that they would oblige him by offering suitable openings for his sons. He had been in the timber trade before he went into the Church at the age of twenty-nine and he had some knowledge of the Victorian world of business. He had the additional advantage of a friendship of long standing with an elderly tea Twining spinster who shared his interest both in Twining ancestry and in ecclesiastical and social problems. Louisa Twining, the daughter of the second Richard of the tea dynasty, had been born in 1820 and she was therefore well over eighty by the time the Rev. William Twining started the habit of crossing the Park on Wednesday afternoons with his daughter and two small sons for tea. Peter might have found these visits, with their interminable talk of Poor Law reform and early Christian symbols tactfully interlaced with genealogy, less memorable had it not been that Aunt Louisa provided very good muffins with the bread and butter and the tea. The results achieved by these relationships however were not perhaps as good as the vicar had hoped. Although the elder boy Stephen was taken into the firm when he left school it was as an office boy at ten shillings a week rather than as one of the family. It may have been this as much as his dislike for sitting at a desk that made Peter reject a similar opportunity when it was offered to him. It was, as it turned out, a wise decision. Twinings tea refused to take Stephen back into the firm when he returned from the war even with a well-won M.B.E. and he had to buy his way into the organisation again by paying a thousand pounds, put up by his mother's family, for a travelling salesman's area.

So the Army it was, and he went into the entrance examination it seemed with confidence. He had after all done quite well in the O.T.C. and he had started belatedly to work in the Army class in his last year at school: there was in any case a war on and there were three hundred vacancies that year at Sandhurst. His name however wasn't in the list of successful candidates which appeared in the morning papers for all his schoolfellows and his relatives to see. His rank in order of merit, according to Table of Marks of the Army Entrance Examination in July 1917, was 315. Although he got enough marks in English, English history and geography, elementary mathematics and French to scrape into the section headed Unsuccessful Candidates who have on this occasion Qualified in all Four Obligatory Subjects, his total, including 0 out of 2000 for German and 60 out of 2000 for Science, was 4161 out of a possible 12800 which must have looked sadly thin to his hopeful parents and his less hopeful masters at Lancing. In the end, however, he got in, by the narrowest of squeezes, because a sufficient number of the academically more successful candidates failed the medical examination or had for other reasons to withdraw. He received his congratulatory letters nevertheless with pride, but as he looked again at the table of marks before, with an early sense of history, he filed it and the letters away, he must have felt, like John Updike's hermit, that something he 'could not quite believe was as simple as stupidity clouded his apprehension'.

It was probably in fact nothing more complex than laziness and a daydreaming lack of concentration. I had sat one summer evening talking to a man who had been at Sandhurst with Twining and who had taken the same exam. He had been among the first dozen in order of merit with almost twice as many marks as Twining, and I wondered what he was thinking as we sat talking about the early military career of Lord Twining of Godalming and Tanganyika in that small semi-detached bungalow on the outskirts of the sort of Wiltshire village to which obscure and hard-up army officers retire.

Twining went to Sandhurst in September and left it ten months later with a commission and with some of his romantic ideas about the glamour of a military life slightly dented by early-morning parades in the winter and the somewhat old-fashioned consequences meted out to gentlemen cadets who were caught sleeping when they were meant to be working or who failed, through ignorance or lack of money, to slip a fiver to the staff sergeant. He had been posted to K Company which had been the cavalry company in easier times but any ambitions he may have had of following his great-uncle Valentine into the 10th Hussars were blunted by the discovery that neither Twining nor horses liked one another very much. He failed to become even an infantry lance-corporal, and the only lesson he seems to have learnt at Sandhurst was that if you can't come top it's better, if you want to get on, to be bottom rather than to be lost and unnoticed in the middle. This didn't present any difficulty to Twining at the end any more than it had been at the beginning, and in August 1918 he passed out two hundred and ninety-sixth, four men having failed to stay the course. He always said afterwards that he went to Sandhurst green and callow and came out a man. He had, it is true, grown in confidence and in size while he was there but according to some of his contemporaries he still in some respects had a long way to go.

Apart from his connections through his mother with the Welsh border counties his own branch of the Twining family had ancestors from Wyre Piddle and other villages and towns in Worcestershire and it was to the Worcestershire Regiment therefore that he asked to go. He was gazetted a second-

lieutenant on the 21st of August but instead of going straight
to France as he had hoped he was sent to a conscript training
camp near Lowestoft, and by the time he crossed the channel
on the 20th of November the war was over. This was a great
sadness to Second-Lieutenant Twining both then and afterwards. He wasn't a particularly martial character, but he like
anyone else would have liked to be able to say afterwards
that he had been there: and he would have liked to have
had a medal.

The next two years must have made Peter Twining wonder if he had been right in choosing the Army as a career.
The end of a war and demobilisation are not a time, as a
general rule, when soldiers and soldiering are seen at their
best. In moments of stress, and there were many in Second-
Lieutenant Twining's military career between 1918 and
1920, older soldiers were apt to remind those who had not
seen any fighting of what they had missed and even to suggest
sometimes that it hadn't been entirely accidental. The dis-
illusion was tempered to start with by the interest and the
excitement of being abroad, first in France and then in Germany. He had four months with the army of occupation on
the Rhine at Wermelskirchen and at other places near
Cologne and though he found his regimental duties dull and
burdensome and the arrogant and unrepentant attitude of
the Germans rather tiresome at first, he acquired on his visits
to Cologne a taste for music and for opera which was to
remain with him for life, and an interest in the romantic,
royal castles of the Rhine which was to bear fruit later in an
unexpected way.

Going to the opera was of course conduct becoming to an
officer, provided one didn't go too often, and Wagner was
acceptable too in small doses, but Twining's enthusiasm for
César Franck and Berlioz and his interest even in the history
and the interiors of castles caused him to be regarded in the
officers' mess as something of an eccentric. Although he had
been abroad once before, to Normandy when he was a small
boy, he had been insulated then against any possible foreign
contagions by the cotton-wool presence of his very English
family. These months on the Rhine were therefore his first
real experience of Europe and of the importance which

people, quite ordinary people, attached to things like music and food and wine. Although his seeming inability then or later to master any foreign language limited his contact with other peoples, his inherent volubility and his open friendliness went a long way towards offsetting this lack and as time went on he came to like the Germans and to achieve a sort of happy understanding with them. A fellow officer of the Worcesters who knew him well at this time says that he was an unusual and rather baffling mixture, a cross, as he put it, between Winnie-the-Pooh and Eeyore. The likeable, cheerful extrovert Second-Lieutenant Twining might easily in one mood have said, 'If I know anything about anything that hole means Rabbit, and Rabbit means Company, and Company means Food and Listening-to-me Humming and such like': and in another mood, introspective, solitary and lugubrious, he might have been the old grey donkey who stood by the side of a stream looking at his reflexion in the water. 'Pathetic,' he said. 'That's what it is, pathetic. As I thought,' he said having crossed to the other side. 'No better from this side. But nobody minds. Nobody cares. Pathetic, that's what it is.' Other people too of course were a mixture of this sort but few perhaps looked so exactly like it.

He was posted back to Britain in April 1919 and for the next eighteen months he found army life either distasteful or extremely boring. He must have realised by now that regimental soldiering was not his forte and he did all he could to get away from it. He tried for one brief afternoon the excitements and glamour of the Royal Air Force, and he applied unsuccessfully to get to India. In Dublin, where the situation when he first went there was comparatively quiet, he got himself away from his disgruntled anxious-to-be-demobilised platoon and what he regarded as the petty formalities and futile banalities of the officers' mess by doing the less ordinary and less exacting duties of a railway transport officer. Whether these duties were meant to include driving the engine is problematical but this predictably was his interpretation and resulted in his being sent back within a matter of weeks to his battalion. Discouraged by his apparent lack of success in any military field Twining claims to have put an advertisement in the personal column of *The*

Times offering his services on sugar plantations in Cuba about which he had heard good reports. Hearing that on the basis of the replies he had received to this advertisement Twining was thinking of sending in his papers, the adjutant, who was a particularly capable and sensible officer called Sammy Gabb, sent him off on a junior commanders' course at Strensall. The change from Dublin's heady air to the more down-to-earth and practical Yorkshire atmosphere and the fact that for a change he got a good report made him think, as was no doubt intended, that there might be a future for him as a soldier after all. Despite two further setbacks to his self-confidence and his military reputation in two highly unsuccessful courses in Messing and Machine-guns, or perhaps because of them and as a last resort, he was appointed battalion intelligence officer at the end of 1920. He was twenty-one, a full lieutenant now, at thirteen and sixpence a day. It was, so to speak, the end of the First Act of Peter Twining's life and the beginning, without any interval for pause or readjustment, of the Second Act. Throughout the First Act he had been a boy of different qualities and shapes, and though he had of course gradually grown older he was still in most respects a boy, awkward, unsophisticated, inexperienced and callow. The events that followed in Ireland were sharp enough to kill the boyish element in most ordinary men. But Peter Twining was not an ordinary man, and while two years of Ireland in the troubles had a lasting effect on him, even they failed, as those who knew him later know, to make him entirely and prosaically grown up.

3

Ireland

THE ENGLISH AND the Irish have always brought out the worst in one another, and the three and a half years between the middle of 1919 and the end of 1922 when Twining was in Dublin were no exception. The history of Anglo-Irish relations during this period is complex, harsh, highly temperamental and, viewed now that the heat from that particular phase of it has largely disappeared, often quite incomprehensible. It is not an easy period to summarise, and generalisations are made difficult and dangerous by the fact that policies and attitudes were extremely and bitterly controversial, not only in England as between Liberals and Unionists, but in Ireland too where the differences of approach were by no means confined to the easy distinctions of north and south and of Protestant and Catholic. And just as in England attitudes were determined as much by the tortuous exigencies of domestic politics as by the merits of the opposing arguments, so in Ireland they were shaped as much by personal rivalries and antagonisms as by the requirements of political and religious principles. The Irish seem to have a centrifugal tendency to quarrel among themselves, even in the face of an external threat, and it was this as much as English obduracy that made an acceptable solution so difficult to achieve.

To understand the situation that existed when Twining took up his duties as Battalion Intelligence Officer at the end of 1920 it is necessary to go back a few years. The question of Home Rule for Ireland had been a major issue in British politics for several decades before the 1914 war but by the

time that a realistic Home Rule Bill had become a political
possibility at Westminster under Asquith's Liberal Government in 1912 it was already ceasing to be regarded by the
bulk of the Irish people themselves as a satisfactory solution.
It didn't go far enough for the south: and the north didn't
want Home Rule at all. When the war broke out in 1914 an
attempt was made to put the Irish question into cold storage
by putting the Home Rule Bill on the Statute Book but
with its operation postponed for the duration of the war.
Redmond, the Irish Nationalist Party leader, accepted this
and it seemed at first as if one could count on a period of
peace or at least suspended animation in Ireland. But Redmond's acceptance of this compromise, his willingness to co-
operate with Britain in the prosecution of the war and the
absence of many moderate-minded Irishmen in the British
Forces played into the hands of more extreme groups like
Sinn Fein which wanted something more independent, more
united and more romantic than was implied in the Home
Rule Bill of 1914. These groups believed that the only way
to get what you wanted out of the English was by the use of
force. In support of this exciting and emotionally satisfying
argument they quoted the experience of the Irish tenants in
their dealings with their English landlords and the success
achieved by the Ulster Volunteers in blocking Home Rule
for Ireland as a whole. On this premise, and on the Jesuitical
argument that the end justifies the means, Sinn Fein and
the Irish Volunteers, who had been formed to counterbalance
their Protestant namesakes in the north, staged the Easter
Rebellion in 1916 with the moral and material support of
the Germans and, some believe, of anti-British elements in
the United States as well. The rebellion was a failure,
partly because many Irishmen thought it premature and in-
judicious and refused to support it, partly through bad management, unpunctuality and indecision, and partly because
the British forces were better armed and more efficient.
Many of the leaders were rounded up and shot but an exception was made in the case of a young man of American birth
and Spanish descent called De Valera. One of the reasons
for making an exception was that he had an American pass-
port and the British Government was anxious, for obvious

reasons, not to upset an otherwise friendly American administration which relied in some eastern States on a large and vociferous Irish vote.

As an act of force designed to establish an Irish republic the Easter Rebellion was a failure. It nevertheless spurred the British Government to make another attempt to get a settlement acceptable to both Ulster and the south and, with the help of appropriate political oils and emetics, by a majority in the British Parliament. Lloyd George proposed a compromise—Home Rule for the south, no change in the status of Ulster, and a continuation of full Irish representation at Westminster—which many Irishmen and most Englishmen thought fair and realistic, but extreme elements both lay and clerical in Ulster and the south competed in excesses of action and language to defeat it. In May 1918 most of the Sinn Fein leaders, including De Valera, were imprisoned in English jails.

The result of all this was that in the elections for the British Parliament which were held soon after the end of the war Sinn Fein won nearly all the southern Irish seats. They refused to take their places at Westminster but proclaimed themselves Dail Eireann, the parliament of an independent Irish Republic with De Valera as President. De Valera's escape from Lincoln jail was organised in a bizarre but ultimately successful way but instead of staying in Ireland to run the new government and lead the fight against the English he perplexed his followers by going off to America to raise funds and support and to quarrel violently in the process with almost all his friends. In Ireland itself it was left to men like Griffiths and Michael Collins to try to undermine and eventually to destroy British authority by acts of violence and sabotage, and by intimidation and other social pressures designed among other things to make recruitment and day-to-day life impossible for the locally staffed Royal Irish Constabulary on whom the burden of maintaining law and order under the British administration still fell. As a result the Royal Irish Constabulary had to be reinforced by the creation of two special bodies both recruited, for the most part, from recently demobilised officers and soldiers of the British Forces who were unemployed and who found readjustment to civilian life difficult or dull. One of these bodies was called an Auxiliary Division of the R.I.C., and the other became known because of its black belts and khaki uniforms as the Black and Tans. These special forces became involved in a violent and bitter struggle with the Irish Republican Army as the militant wing of Sinn Fein was now called. The units of the British army stationed in Ireland were not at first directly involved in these civilian exchanges but as time went on they too became a target for attack and more and more concerned not only with their own defence but with aiding the civil power in maintaining law and order.

While the fighting went on the coalition of Lloyd George Liberals and the Conservatives which had formed a government after the 1918 election made a further attempt to reach an acceptable compromise on Ireland. The 1920 Government of Ireland Act provided for two Irish Parliaments, one for the south at Dublin and another for the north at Belfast with a Council for Ireland to encourage those who still hoped for eventual unity. Both parts were to stay in the United Kingdom and to go on sending representatives to Westminster. Sinn Fein and the Irish Republican Army, which did not always operate in unison, both rejected this Act because it partitioned Ireland and kept the association with the Crown and the British Parliament. Not all southern Irishmen agreed with them but by this time violence and intimidation had virtually brought the exercise of normal human rights and democratic processes to a standstill. The British forces, by a variety of methods, were gradually wearing down open manifestations of Irish resistance, and this, coupled with a growing tiredness and revulsion on both sides of the Irish Sea and the pressure of Commonwealth and international opinion, opened the way for secret negotiations first for a truce which was concluded in July 1921 and then for a treaty. The compromise which in the end Lloyd George persuaded all the plenipotentiaries and his own supporters to accept was the creation of an Irish Free State with Dominion Status from which Northern Ireland would be free to withdraw, which of course it immediately did. In the light of the bitterness and intransigence of the southern Irish, the people of Ulster and the English in the previous seventy-five years, it

was perhaps a remarkable performance to have achieved a
settlement at all. It was however inevitably a compromise,
and within a matter of weeks Griffiths and Collins, who had
negotiated the treaty as plenipotentiaries of De Valera, found
themselves disowned by their unpredictable and quixotic
leader and many of their colleagues, and involved in a civil
war in southern Ireland of an even greater bitterness and
violence than all the fighting against the English.

When Twining first went to Ireland he, like most other
soldiers, didn't concern himself with the intricacies of Anglo-
Irish relations or with the rights and wrongs of the situation
there. He just did what he was told and let it go at that. He
lived in barracks, and although officers and men of the British Army could move about Dublin and the rest of Ireland
quite freely then he had no real contact with Ireland or with
the Irish. What he did see made him very English. 'As the
boat enters Dublin Bay at six o'clock on a summer morning,'
he wrote, 'the first impression is that Ireland is a delightful
place. But if the observer has to walk two miles through the
Dublin streets he is soon disillusioned. If a city is judged
by its dirt and muddy appearance Dublin would rank among
the first cities of the world.' In James Joyce's time Dublin had
more pubs, pawnbrokers, whores and slums per head of population than anywhere else in Europe. This seems to have
been Twining's impression twenty years later too. It was
sordid but from a soldier's point of view it was reasonably
quiet: few of them seem to have taken Sinn Fein very seriously then. They were just a lot of wild men, 'Shinners' who
did peculiar things. It wasn't until the 21st of November,
1920, a few days before Twining became Battalion Intelligence Officer, that this attitude sharply changed.

The 21st of November was a Sunday. At that time many
British officers lived quite happily in private houses and
hotels in various parts of Dublin and its outskirts with their
wives and families. Early that Sunday morning fourteen of
them were attacked in their beds by organised parties of the
I.R.A. and killed in what the normally staid *Times* described
as 'circumstances of revolting brutality'.

The effect on the British Army in Ireland and on public

opinion at home was electric. Nerves jumped and muscles twitched, and the familiar meaningless conditioned reflexes of speech and attitude were released in the Press and Parliament. 'We will never,' they said, 'give way to force.'

Twining's own reactions at the time, recorded later without apology or pride, were probably typical of the feelings of most English people on the spot.

It was then and only then [he wrote] that anyone began to take the Sinn Fein movement seriously. It was only then when a number of officers who one knew personally had been brutally murdered in front of their wives with a savagery that could only be expected of barbarians that the real motives of the rebels were brought home to me. And one was filled with such horror that one loathed everyone who had anything to do with this revolting movement, and one felt the desire to kill anyone of them that one could meet. But in spite of that feeling there were no reprisals. Croke Park was not a reprisal in the real sense, the troops were fired on and they fired back in self defence.

Croke Park was the scene of a Gaelic football match between Dublin and Cork watched by fifteen thousand spectators that same Sunday afternoon. Who fired first and why were inevitably controversial matters but the result was that ten Irishmen were killed by bitter and angry British machine-gun fire and many more were hurt. The 21st of November was known as Bloody Sunday after that, though of course for different reasons, by both the Irish and the English.

For the next eight months no holds were barred by either side. British Army wives and families were sent back to England and the officers moved into barracks; a curfew was imposed and military patrols moved about Dublin in lorries and armoured cars by day and night with powers to arrest anyone carrying arms and to search anyone who looked suspicious. Raids were carried out to look for arms and for anyone belonging to the I.R.A. The I.R.A. responded with attacks and ambushes on the British and on other Irishmen who didn't agree with them, and with money and supplies that came in mainly from America they were not lacking in arms and ammunition.

As Intelligence Officer Twining found himself directly involved in this situation. He was concerned not only with trying to get information, which was not easy in a city where the population either sympathised with the I.R.A. or had been intimidated by it, but also with enforcing the curfew and carrying out patrols and raids. For week after week he was up all night, sometimes raiding as many as fifteen houses between dusk and dawn. He found it not only physically very tiring and unpleasant, because of the dirt and the squalor and the smell in many of the cellars and tenements he had to search, but mentally and emotionally as well. 'It was worse for the officers,' a man who was there as a private soldier told me, 'because they had to go in first, and because they were responsible for what happened to us.' It wasn't as dangerous as the trenches but the strain and the tension, in his opinion, were worse. You never knew what was round the next corner or who your enemy was. 'Men would look away when you passed them but you knew that when your back was turned their eyes followed you as you went on down the street.'

Twining threw himself into his new duties with tremendous energy and concentration. It was as if he, like others of his vintage, was imposing it on himself as a penalty, a sort of compensation for having missed the war. The strain was worse for him perhaps than for many others because he discovered early on that underneath his shell of zest and anger he had a soft and sensitive core.

On one occasion [he wrote in a record of his time in Ireland] we had information about an important meeting in a house. We found the meeting in action but a man climbed out of a window and although I got my revolver ready and reached the back door when he was a sitting target on top of the wall of the backyard I just could not get myself to pull the trigger. This was very unmilitary no doubt but I felt that it was too much like murder.

He was ambushed once in Harcourt Street. He and another officer called Gregory were travelling in front of an armoured lorry fitted as all army lorries then were with wire-netting to deflect the bombs, a device which the I.R.A. later countered by attaching hooks to them. It was eight o'clock in the evening and the street was crowded. A newspaper report of the incident gives a vivid picture of what happened when the I.R.A. carried out an ambush in the middle of Dublin.

At the corner of Harcourt Street and Harcourt Road a cart was seen standing, and a man talking with the driver. The man took cover behind the horse, and deliberately threw a bomb at the lorry. At the same time on the opposite side of the road—the railway station side—four or five men, with their bodies protected behind the stone pillars of the station, fired at the lorry with revolvers. One of them, with a large automatic pistol in each hand, was firing both weapons simultaneously.

Heavy fire was also opened on the lorry from the roof of the station, and at least one bomb was thrown. The soldiers on the station side of the lorry opened rapid fire on this man on the roof. Further fire was then opened on the lorry by two men who were taking such cover as they could behind a lamp-post standard, and also by one man who fired from a doorstep.

The man at the door was killed by the first volley from the lorry, and the two men behind the lamp post also fell. The lorry, unable to pull up, continued its journey until it was able to turn and return. Some unarmed troops went to the assistance of the man who fell wounded behind the lamp post. One of them, who was only slightly wounded, thereupon fired again with this revolver, and also rolled towards the lorry a bomb, which on its explosion injured the officer in charge. A volley was thereupon fired at this man ... Among people attracted to the scene were a number of officers from Portobello Barracks near at hand who, hearing the firing while they were at dinner, ran out and did a good deal to quell the intense excitement and terror caused to the many civilians, including women and children, who were in the neighbourhood at the time. The terror of these people was greatly added to by the stampeding of the horses of the hackney cars which were standing outside for hire on the rank outside the station.

Five people were killed in this affair. Three of them were passers-by. Several more were wounded, and one of them was Gregory. Twining's parents saw a report of the ambush and an unnamed wounded officer of the Worcester's in the London *Evening Standard* the following day, and Peter had to send a hurried telegram and two letters to allay their anxieties and explain why he hadn't told them about it straight away. 'I am very sorry,' he wrote, 'to hear that you were upset about the ambush ... but you really need not get so worried. If it had been me you would have heard about twelve hours before you read about it in the papers.'

The I.R.A. were not of course the only people who resorted to desperate measures. Excesses bred excesses on both sides, and anger and frustration led to the adoption by the British of methods that were often very harsh.

We curfewed until midnight [Twining recorded] then we raided half a dozen houses, arriving back at barracks at about five a.m. At seven a.m. I was woken up with a message to the effect that I was to report to 2nd Royal Berkshire Regiment at eight on a special job. This I did and I was handed orders to the effect that I was to superintend the destruction of Cullenswood House in order to render it uninhabitable. It was a beautifully fine morning and our procession of lorries greatly disturbed the people who were hurrying to mass. The neighbourhood round Cullenswood House was cordoned by 100 men of the Lancashire Fusiliers, and the streets were patrolled by two armoured cars to ensure that we would not be disturbed. My party consisted of fifty men of the Royal Berks armed with picks, shovels and crowbars.

Cullenswood is a large house previously used as a school, and several wooden constructions with glass roofs had been added to the house at the back. There was every reason to believe that in some of these rooms the wooden walls had been so constructed as to enable arms to be hidden behind them. We therefore commenced our work in the wall and

soon found a revolver, some ammunition and some papers
behind a false partition. In a room upstairs a lady with
marked Republican tendencies was living. The night before she had assured us that the place was never used by
the rebels but this was soon disproved because we found
some letters signed by Richard Mulcahy [the rebel Chief
of Staff] which had not been there the night before. We
also found the remains of the evening meal and the traces
of him having slept in the house. As we had left only one
hour before curfew hour and had arrived in the morning
about one hour after curfew, we had just missed him.
When we had opened the walls in all the places where
arms might be hidden we commenced to destroy the house
methodically. The windows were smashed and the window
sashes were thrown out of the windows. The wall and ceilings were pulled out, the floors were pulled up and the
big fireplace was hacked out of the walls and thrown into
the garden below. The furniture we burnt in the garden,
and presently the fire brigade turned up: thinking they
might be 'Shinners' and up to no good we placed them
temporarily under arrest.

While we were working a small group of women, who
stayed in the house sometimes, came and watched the destruction; one of these was Mrs. Despard, the sister of Lord
French, who was at that time Lord Lieutenant of Ireland.
Mrs. Despard appeared to be very annoyed at the brutal
British soldiery and tried to address some remarks to me
on the subject but I was in no humour to argue with her.
During this time the good rebel lady upstairs refused to
move, and I decided to leave her room intact. I tried to
persuade her to leave but she still refused. The men were
now taking off the roof. Although we did not touch the
good lady's room we pulled the staircase down. How she
got down I never heard.

Later the I.R.A. started to hold up soldiers in the streets
and strip them of their belts and boots. This was countered
for a time by intensive patrols but

soon afterwards the rebels continued to hold up unarmed

soldiers and one night stripped a number of them of all their clothing. An unofficial reprisal was organised. About 200 men went out in gangs of a dozen armed with pokers, hammers, razors and other weapons. Eleven civilians were stripped, their clothing was burnt in the streets and seventy civilians had their boots removed. The boots were cut to ribbons by the razors and thrown into the canal. There was only one complaint and it was a very long time before any man in the battalion was again held up.

This doesn't make pleasant reading: but it is always easier to criticise than it is to say what exactly one would have done oneself in the same situation. Anger, fear, tension and physical exhaustion make all of us do things we would not ordinarily do: and it is noticeable that those who are most ready with their criticism are often those who have not experienced situations of this sort and who do not know therefore how they themselves would have acted. Twining at that time was twenty-two.

Dublin was divided into sectors for intelligence and patrol purposes. The area with which Twining was concerned ran from the sea up the River Liffey to Capel Street. It had a perimeter of five or six miles, and it contained the docks and some of the worst slums in Dublin. It also included the red-light district. Although Dublin was still legally part of Britain then, and subject to British laws and practices, the local police tolerated brothels and indeed encouraged them for purposes of control provided they were confined to one area, the Nighttown of Ulysses, where they carried on, according to the *Encyclopaedia Britannica*, 'more openly than in the south of Europe or even Algiers'. It was an area which Twining got to know very well.

In James Joyce's time each street in the area had its own specialised character and its own specialised sort of clientele. At the upper end of Tyrone Street the Georgian houses had a certain *passé* elegance; the girls were paraded in landaus in the mornings in the more prosperous parts of Dublin, and at night they wore formal evening dress; and there were owners who sent their daughters to the most expensive English convent schools. There were other streets where the

girls stood outside the doors in raincoats which they flicked
open to attract passers-by, and inside the rooms there were
leaden coshes hidden behind the religious pictures on the
walls. In 1921 however most of the customers were soldiers
or men in uniform; and it was not only the Black and Tans
and the soldiers of the British army that the brothels catered
for. The I.R.A. went there as well.

Twining found patrolling these streets and searching the
houses in the area the most unpleasant of all the many unpleasant things he had to do. Brothels, one suspects, were new
to him, certainly brothels in which there were four or five
beds to a room. So too were women who screamed obscenities
and spat in one's face, who pretended to have fits and tore
off all their clothes. The only redeeming feature of this part
of his duties was the acquaintance he made and the practical
arrangements he came to with a woman called Becky Cooper.
Becky Cooper was the Madame of the Mesdames of the red-
light Dublin streets: and she ruled it, by all accounts, with
a rod of iron. One night Twining came across an empty
British armoured car parked outside a house in Amiens
Street. This was more than he had bargained for and he
didn't quite know what to do. It was then that he first met
Becky Cooper. She said she would accept responsibility for
the safety of the armoured car and for its officers and crew;
and she showed him their revolvers which she had carefully
labelled and locked up in her safe. After that he worked in
league with her. Although she would never give anyone
away she guaranteed that her British customers wouldn't be
molested or robbed on her premises, and Twining in return
accepted her word if she said she had no one from the I.R.A.
that night.

On the night of the 19th of June a young and much liked
officer of the Worcesters named Brieze was killed by the
I.R.A. He had been out to lunch in the country outside
Dublin and was picked up on his way back and taken to a
lonely road where his face was blown away in front of the
girl he was with. This made the British forces as a whole
and the Worcesters in particular very angry. On the night
after the funeral when tempers were running high Twining
was told to do a raid on a house in Mount Merrion Avenue.

His orders, laid down by Brigade Headquarters, were quite clear. He was to raid the house at a specified time, search for arms, ammunition, explosives and seditious literature, and 'if any found arrest all male adults implicated'. He expected the raid to be a waste of time, like most of the others ordered by Dublin Castle whose information he had found in practice wasn't very good. The report of this raid which he made at the time was brief and dry with expurgation and understatement, unlike some of the versions which he improvised later when he was in an anecdotal mood.

Yesterday at 21.45 hours I raided the above house on instructions from 25th (P) Inf. Brigade. My party consisted of three officers and eight Other Ranks, in two armoured Ford cars.

There are two entrances to this house, each leads to the front of the house by a drive about seventy yards long.

One officer and two men left the cars at the entrance in Mount Merrion Avenue and cut across a field to the back of the house. The two cars were driven up the two drives to the front door, the house being immediately surrounded. The Officer and the two men in the field saw a man in the garden run into the house. I also saw this man run into the house.

The door was answered by two ladies. I went into the sitting room with them on the ground floor, and the other officer and the two N.C.O.s went into the other rooms. I asked the ladies the following questions, and received the following answers:

Q. What is your name please?
A. That is for you to find out.
Q. You must please tell me your name.
A. Why did you not find out before you came here?
Q. If you do not answer my question I will have to arrest you.
A. Search the house and see if you can find out that way.
Q. Are there any men in the house?
A. Perhaps.

This was repeated twice with the same reply.

Q. Who was the man I saw in the garden?
A. Go and find out for yourself. Who have you come here for? I am not going to tell you anything at all, if you want to know anything you can search the house and find out for yourself.

At this point the man came down from upstairs where he had been found by one of the men.

Q. What is your name, and what is the lady's name?
A. My name is Hayden, and the lady is my sister.
Q. How long have you been here?
A. Not very long.
Q. Exactly how long have you been here?
A. About three weeks I expect.

I asked this question again later on, and he said six weeks. I then said please tell me exactly how long you have been here as you have told me different each time.

A. I have answered this question five times and I am not going to answer it again.

At this point I sent the second lady, who answered to the name of Macken, down to the castle to be searched. The house was then searched from top to bottom, and a number of letters addressed to the President were found. When Miss Macken returned from the castle I arrested the truculent woman and the man. The woman was sent to the Bridewell and the man brought to Portobello Barracks. In the guard room I asked another officer to ask the man his name as I thought that he would give a different name. When asked his name and address the man said 'I am President De Valera of the Irish Republic. My home is Craigleigh, Greystones, but I do not live there. The lady you have arrested is my secretary. Will you please try and get her released as I hold myself responsible for everything you found in my house.'

Orders had at this time been in existence for six months

that if found De Valera was not to be interfered with. The reason for this was that Lloyd George was already involved in secret negotiations with him for a truce and a treaty. De Valera had been accidentally picked up several times by over-enthusiastic military and police patrols and raiding parties and immediately released. Twining knew about these orders but although he began to have his suspicions when he looked at the papers he had found in the house—which included a list of the President's washing—it wasn't until he got back to barracks that he knew for sure what he had done. The Adjutant asked what the devil he meant by disobeying orders, and when they rang up Dublin Castle to tell them what had happened the effect was considerable. 'Cope, the Under Secretary for Ireland, and all his satellites,' Twining recorded afterwards with a certain compensatory satisfaction, 'were tearing their hair with rage.' The military and the police however were glad that De Valera had been captured, especially so soon after Brieze's killing, for which they not unreasonably held him responsible, and an officer had to stay with De Valera for the night to prevent him from being molested while instructions were sought on what to do with him. The next day orders were received for his release, and Twining was cruelly but not perhaps inappropriately told to see him contritely and safely off at the barrack gates. De Valera shook hands and said goodbye without any sign of ill-will. Two days later Lloyd George invited De Valera as 'the chosen leader of the great majority in southern Ireland' to attend a conference in London to explore the possibility of a settlement. Just over two weeks later a truce was signed.

Unofficially the army made no secret of its disgust and disagreement with De Valera's release, and even in its carefully drafted official communications managed to convey satisfaction at his capture without actually saying so. 'The G.O.C. quite realises that the Battalion may be disappointed at the release of De Valera especially under the circumstances of the time,' and the Colonel Commandant in another letter trusted 'that the decision of H.M. Government, for whatever may be their reasons, will be accepted loyally...' In military and police circles therefore Twining was reckoned to be something between a hero and a martyr, and his stock went

very high. In a personal letter written to his mother after the
truce the C.O. of the Worcesters spoke of Twining's capture
of De Valera as 'a very fine piece of work', and referred in
glowing terms to his performance generally as an intelligence
officer. 'He is perfectly splendid and I have the greatest admiration for him. He has carried out his duties, which require very special qualities of intelligence and courage, in
such a way as to win the admiration and praise of all the
highest authorities.' Some months later Lieutenant Twining
was promoted to be Intelligence Officer at Brigade Headquarters, and for his work in Ireland generally between 1920
and 1922 he was soon afterwards awarded the M.B.E.
M.B.E.s are not won easily by subalterns. As an intelligence,
if not as a regimental officer, Twining had at last arrived.

    Peter Twining left Ireland at the end of 1922, with the
last of the British forces. He left Ireland with mixed feelings.
Up to the time of the truce and even until the signing of the
treaty at the end of 1921 had been a period for him of considerable physical and emotional strain. He was not a natural
soldier or a martial character. The sort of courage that is
needed for military activity did not come to him easily: he
had to will himself each time to face the hazards. Nor was
he the sort of man disposed to accept orders and attitudes
without question. He had his doubts about many things that
were done in Ireland: not least about the things done by
the Black and Tans in the name of the same Crown and Government that he was supposed to serve. In his last year when
it was mostly the Irish who were fighting one another and
the British forces were only there, so to speak, to hold the
ring, he got to know many of the people against whom he
had been operating before the truce. He was naturally talkative and sociable, and he talked to them a lot in bars and
restaurants and got to know something of the way they
thought and the reasons for what they did. He had hated the
Irish in his time and done, as part of what he saw as his duty,
several harsh and unpleasant things. Yet he was sorry to leave
Ireland and the people of Dublin when it was time to go and
when he had learnt to understand something at any rate of
their case. There were some things and some lessons he was
not to forget. One of them perhaps was the point made by

Stephen Gwynn in his book on Ireland in 1924.

It must be recognised that where such a situation exists as existed in Ireland for three centuries at least, a diseased psychology results. If power and privilege are confined to a minority of the people, those who possess the power and privilege will justify to themselves their situation by claiming a special fitness in themselves, and alleging a special unfitness in the under-privileged. More than that, their position with its advantages may often produce on the average a real superiority. But in all cases the degree of arrogance which an ascendency displays is certain to exceed its justification. As equality is extended or privilege disappears the truth of fact will always tend to gain acceptance; yet the last stages of the struggle will always be embittered by the rankling in ungenerous natures of an angry contempt which easily engenders an answering hatred.'

There were other lessons to be learnt about the closing stages of a colonial relationship. In less than a year from the signing of the 1921 treaty both the Irish moderates who had signed and accepted it had disappeared. Griffiths had died from the strains and stresses of fighting his own countrymen and Michael Collins had been killed by them. On the other side Lloyd George too had been driven from office. De Valera, the extremist who wouldn't compromise, was the one who survived. He remained in the political wilderness in Ireland opposing the treaty which accepted partition and the British connection until his party Fianna Fail was returned to power in 1932, and then bit by bit he managed to achieve the revision of all those parts of the Treaty, except partition, to which he had originally objected.

4

The King's African Rifles

LESS THAN A year after his return to England Twining went
off to Africa. The Battalion had been posted to Dover when
they came back from Ireland, and he found Dover and peace-
time soldiering both dull and tiresome. He also found it expensive, and unlike many of his fellow officers he still had
no money of his own. He didn't spend money on girls or on
riotous living of the bosom and bottom variety but he liked
to eat and drink well and he liked the comforts and the outward appearances of prosperity—good seats at the opera,
taxis, travelling first class. He was twenty-four. On top of
this the Geddes axe which cut down the number of battalions
of the Worcesters from four to two seriously diminished his
chances of promotion. A visiting officer on secondment from
the King's African Rifles regaled the mess one night with
stories of the excitements and the financial and other advantages of Army life in East Africa, and despite the advice of
his colonel, who thought it would be bad both for his military career and his health, he applied for a secondment too,
though he didn't tell his parents he had done so. It was only
when, after months of waiting, an offer came and had been
accepted that he wrote to his parents. His letter is worth
quoting in full if only as an early example of the private
precept which he was later to propound and act on as a public principle—always present them with a fait accompli.

My darling Mother and Father, I am afraid I am going to
disturb your quietude with rather a bombshell which may
not be to your liking.

Two or three days ago I received an intimation to the effect that the War Office were enquiring of the Battalion if I would accept employment with the King's African Rifles in East Africa.

I had only a day or two to make up my mind and after due and careful consideration and with the advice of one or two pre-war officers whose opinions I value, I said that I would accept the job. I have been medically examined, found fit for service there, have been recommended by the C.O., and the reply should come back from the War Office any day telling me to go on two months leave immediately prior to embarking. These are the facts. You may approve or disapprove. I hope it is the former, and I am sure you will when you have read my discourse on the advantages and disadvantages. At any rate there can be no turning back now. I have committed myself and must see it through.

In weighing up the advantages of being in a job like the King's African Rifles (henceforth in the document to be styled the K.A.R.) one must take into consideration the advantages or disadvantages of the position one would alternatively occupy. In my case it would be wasting my time in Dover for an indefinite period, getting into a rut, doing myself and nobody else any good, and not really enjoying oneself. To be a success in Dover, you must be a social success; the local interpretation of which is to be ordered to attend dances, tennis parties, amateur theatricals and other nonsensities, and to generally make a fuss of and kow-tow to the wives and daughters and other skirted monstrosities of serving and retired Colonels and Majors who think that just because their male relatives reached a respected rank in the army they can order subalterns about like puppy dogs. Some of them who have met me have received rather a shock. And I must be the most unpopular man in Dover among these impecunious and vulgar snobs who form the local society.

Those officers who have joined the army to get well paid for doing no work and all play are a great success. For my part I have not wasted my time here, I have learnt not a little during the training, I have passed the 1st part of my promotion exam, and I have had six months useful experience at doing rather difficult accounts. In fact I have learnt all I can in a place and at a life like this, and I am only too anxious to get on and get as much experience as possible at a job where the financial aspect is much better.

With the present rage for economy there are no jobs available in England. And the K.A.R. is a job which is considered one of the plums abroad.

The K.A.R. are distributed throughout Zanzibar, Uganda, Nyasaland, Kenya Colony and Tanganyika or German East Africa, in all a country about the size of Europe. The climate is quite good and it is considered to be a white man's country. The tour of duty is 18 months to 2 years and in certain exceptional cases $2\frac{1}{2}$ years. The normal tour is 18 months after which you get 3 months leave on full pay, and then you have the choice of another tour or of rejoining your regiment. You lose no rank or seniority in your regiment by going to the K.A.R. and the experience of a tour is considered by the War Office to be a great asset when they later consider your name for any other job. The pay for a subaltern is £450 a year without income tax and the living is cheap (my pay now is £290 a year less income tax). You also get £30 outfit allowance on 1st appointment.

Promotion in the K.A.R. is by selection which means that with a bit of common sense those who take it seriously get on. For instance all Battalions are commanded by men who in their own regiments are only Captains.

So much for the advantages. I have been trying to find some disadvantages but the only one I can find is that I won't see you for 18 months, but then it will be all the more pleasure to see you again.

I took your point of view into consideration and in the end I felt that although you would probably not want me to go, I know that you want me to get on and as this is a big opportunity I feel sure you will be unselfish. No one has ever got on in the army by staying at home and drinking tea with the local cats. Very best love.

Your very loving son E. F. Peter Twining.

Another thing Peter Twining didn't tell his parents was that he had originally been posted to the Camel Corps in Somaliland, which was something he didn't particularly care for and which he guessed his parents would like even less. However in the end the posting was altered to the King's African Rifles in Uganda. As a part of it was Samuel Baker country it could be presented to his parents and particularly to his mother in a more favourable light and in the end he got their blessing and even, when it came to shopping for outfits for the tropics, a certain compulsive co-operation. Samuel Baker, Mrs. Twining knew from what she had heard and read about her famous uncle, had always gone on his travels very well equipped, and she became more and more determined as she thumbed her way through the catalogues and saw the fascinating things that tropical outfitters stocked that her Peter shouldn't lack anything that he might conceivably need—cholera belts, guns, spine pads, rolls of lavatory paper by the gross, boxes lined with tin to keep out the white ants and carefully sized to make up a carryable porter's load. The only thing she forgot, as other mothers had done before her and others were to do afterwards, was that Samuel Baker was a rich man and that all her son had for equipment was thirty pounds. She tried to touch a relative for a loan but he reminded her a little tersely that there was a more general kind of uncle who, for a consideration, gave assistance of this kind. In the end she just ran up a bill which she and Peter between them paid off bit by bit in the course of the next two years. At last everything was ready, and on the 26th of September, 1923 Lieutenant Twining left London by train to join a French ship at Marseilles for the east coast of Africa.

At Marseilles he got a telegram to say that his father had died. It was sad but it was not unexpected. His father had been ill for several years and had some time previously had to give up his church and the vicarage in Vincent Square. Although the elder son Stephen was still in England and was on hand to keep an eye on things, it was at this time when his father died that Peter seemed to have started writing longer and more regular letters to his mother. He went on doing this until she died in 1961, when she was eighty-nine, and he had already retired. His mother kept all these letters and apart from some written between 1925 and 1939, while he was in Uganda, they have all survived. His letters are full of the sort of details that mothers want to know; what he ate, where he lived, what he did, whom he met and where he went, and he took the trouble to provide her with maps so that she could follow him on his travels and share the atmosphere of the distant places that he visited. Mrs. Twining was a traveller *manqué*, as one would expect from a person with her Baker blood, and one feels that she soon forgave Peter for leaving her in the pleasure his thoughtful and entertaining letters gave her and the satisfying wealth of material they provided, with a little embroidery of her own, to pass on to her relations and friends.

Another reason why he took so much trouble over his letters to his mother at this time was that a few years before his father died his only sister had also died in tragic circumstances after a short and somewhat tragic life. Betty Twining died of meningitis at the age of twenty-four. She was an unusual girl with a varied range of interests and enthusiasms which she touched in turn with talent but which because of illness or accident she never quite managed to shape or finish. Some, like the violin and a passion for animals and birds, were conventional in her generation. So perhaps was writing verse and a three-act play of which S. P. B. Mais said 'There is no money in it, but it is Art'. Others like dairy farming and reading for an external degree in English literature and philosophy at London University were not. She was a strange girl, given to inner conflicts and changing moods of ecstasy and intense depression. Peter was very fond of her but from an early age she had for various reasons spent little time at home, and there is no evidence to show that she played much part in his life or that she was an important influence on his actions or his thinking. She was a girl who walked alone.

With her husband and her daughter dead and her younger son abroad, Mrs. Twining began with characteristic determination to make an opportunity of her losses and her widowhood. She threw herself into church activities with such effect and zest that there was a question at one time of making her a deaconess. Peter didn't like the idea of having

a deaconess for a mother at all: not for the first time, or the
last, he tried to get his own way by flattery. 'I always did
think you were a wonderful woman and that it would have
been a thousand pities for you to narrow your scope by being
a deaconess. As plain Mrs. Twining you seem to have
achieved wonders at your work; but the very name deaconess would have put off half your friends. It may be unpala-
table but it is true.' He seems to have made his point. His
mother started devoting some of her energies instead into the
researches into the history of Westminster Abbey and its
monuments which were to bear fruit some years later in the
shape of several small booklets for visitors and children. They
also perhaps acted as an example and a spur to her unschol-
arly younger son to embark on researches of his own into
another subject later on.

At this time Mrs. Twining was living at Kingston-on-
Thames with her elder son who was making his way by
application and investment, and without the benefit of any
noticeable cousinly affection, up the ladder of Twining's tea.
He had been a gentle boy and had become a quiet but determined man. Mrs. Twining's two sons were, according to
one observer who knew the family well, like two different
sides of her own competitive and complex nature; they were
as different as lettuce and tomato and yet they went well
together, and remained close friends. Peter's letters during
this period when he first went out to Africa were addressed
as much to his brother as to his mother; and they were designed, with a nice blend of family feeling and self-advertise-
ment, not only to please but to impress them both.

It was some time however before Lieutenant Twining had
much to write home about. He had imagined, like most
others who did the journey for the first time, that the trip
across France to Marseilles and the voyage through the Suez
Canal and the Red Sea to Mombasa would be full of excitage
(a word invented and much used by himself) and adventure
and exotery (another Twining word). But much of it was
disappointing and one by one many of his illusions disappeared. 'I had no difficulty with the customs,' he wrote
sadly in his first letter home, 'on production of my passage
ticket they didn't require me even to open anything. I had

lunch on the station at Calais.' They touched Paris at nine and left again at nine thirty-five. Marseilles struck him as being 'a horrible place with a very cosmopolitan population'. Even the boat was disappointing.

It is so small. When they say it is 10,000 tons that is not meant in the same way as we talk of tonnage i.e. displacement. Its displacement is about 4,500 tons which is about as big as the Holyhead–Dublin boats.

He tried hard to paint what he saw and the people he met with a Baker brush but the brush kept slipping through his fingers and falling with a plop on to the cabin floor.

We left Marseilles in perfect weather. Not a ripple on the sea, which was a real Mediterranean Blue. Marseilles from a distance looks quite picturesque. I tried to get a bath last night but the bath had been newly painted and my foot adhered to the bottom so I gave up the attempt and had a good wash. I have quite settled down into a sort of routine now. I get up at 7 a.m. and have a bath, I then go for a mile walk (15 times round the deck). Breakfast at 8, and then another sharp walk before the deck gets crowded. From 9 until 10.30 I write my letters and my diary, and from 10.30 to 11.30 I have a stroll and a chat with somebody. At 11.30 we have a nine-course déjeuner which lasts an hour. In the afternoon I have a nap and read one of your three little books which I am enjoying. At 4 p.m. we have tea. From 4.30 until 5.30 a walk and a talk. From 5.30 to 6.30 Pickwood, Monckton, Mackenzie and I usually have a couple of rubbers of bridge. Then a wash and brush up for 7 o'clock dinner of 11 courses.

After dinner they strolled about and amused themselves watching various named East African worthies trying to court a nursing sister and a girl of fourteen who in an earlier letter he had noted, with his usual air of detachment in such matters, as the only interesting forms of female life. With one of their bridge four thus otherwise occupied, 'Mackenzie,

Pickwood and I play patience until 10.30, then after a breath of fresh air, bed'.

He was of course writing to his mother. Unfortunately he didn't keep his mother's letters so there is no knowing what she thought of this routine or whether she knew or guessed that some of the time listed as taken up with exercise and talk and observation was in fact devoted to drinking gin.

I believe [he concluded, to lay perhaps a false scent] that on most boats there are always plenty of amusements, deck games, dancing and music. Here there is nothing. There are nearly 50 1st-class passengers but no games, no dancing, no music. The Messageries Maritimes are so stingy that they have not even a Marconi licence, so we get no wireless news. We are thinking of suggesting that 2 courses should be knocked off the déjeuner and with the money saved each passenger should be provided with 1 piece of soap per week, also 2 courses knocked off dinner and a Marconi licence taken out.

Port Said however had its points.

It was a most extraordinary place, and the thing that struck me most was the look of amazement on the faces of the Europeans who were seeing it for the first time. I had made up my mind to be surprised at nothing so I hope I did not look the same.

The Red Sea was hot, and even a day at Djibouti, which wasn't a place that everybody went to, failed to relieve the feeling of sweatiness and apathy and boredom. He was glad when the voyage was over.

Mombasa [he wrote] is a curious sort of place, a very straggling town with all sorts of houses and huts and bazaars ancient and modern in stone, wood, tin, and mud and wattle, and between and around the houses what the guide books describe as 'luxurious tropical vegetation' ... [The hotel where he stayed was] quaint in the extreme.

All the bedrooms have 3 or 4 doors which you never shut, if you feel modest you draw the curtains when you are dressing ... At night lizards run about the walls and ceiling, and the white ones are poisonous and the black ones are not, but everybody encourages them to stay as they eat the mosquitos. And this morning before I could dress I had to massacre a family of ants that had invaded the precincts of my flannel trousers. To the unsophisticated such things sound almost alarming. But this is Africa and one learns to take things as they come, and I am just telling you the little things as they happen; and I think that I like Africa.

The thousand-mile journey by train and lake steamer and road to Bombo in Uganda confirmed this first impression. He had his first tentative taste of the sights and smells and sounds of Africa that draw ordinary English people back there in fact or in memory again and again, like insects to a light, however much they are bruised or bent—the sight of impala and giraffe and zebra on the Athi River plains, the smell of dry earth when it is first touched by rain, the feel of the clean, unused, early morning air at six and eight thousand feet, the people who 'got more natural' as one left the coast and the shanty towns, people dressed in skins with 'great holes in their ears and slashes on their cheeks'.

Uganda is a country three times as big as Ireland. It had a population in 1923 of about three million. It had been a British Protectorate since 1894, that is to say our right to be there and to rule it was based in law not on conquest or annexation but on treaties or other less formal kinds of agreement ('he sucked my blood and I sucked his and we lived happily together until the others came...') with the African rulers of the various and for the most part quite unrelated areas which for our own purposes or convenience we lumped together into one administrative unit and quite erroneously called Uganda. The only military force which we kept in the country to preserve this unnatural unity and to maintain law and order was one battalion of about 700 men. Most of the officers and a few of the N.C.O.s were British, seconded like Twining from their regiments: the rest, local officers, N.C.O.s and all the soldiers, were African. Although they were drawn mainly from the physically tougher and less sophisticated peoples of the north and from the progeny of Sudanese soldiers who had settled there, they were all recruited from inside Uganda, and not, as the French did with for example the Senegalese, from other more detached and unrelated peoples.

Most of the battalion was kept in Buganda which was the most densely populated area where the administrative and commercial centres were. One company however was always stationed at a place called Kakamari, in the far northeastern corner of the country, to protect the people who lived there from Ethiopian raiders who came in search of cattle, unhindered at that time either by their own authorities or by those of the Sudan, through a remote and unadministered part of which they had to pass. The reason why troops were stationed there by the pragmatic and hard-up British administration was not so much concern for the local inhabitants as a realisation that if they lost their cattle they would, in order to survive, have to raid their neighbours in Uganda and take their cattle: and this of course would set off a chain reaction which it would be more difficult and expensive to contain.

Twining hoped that he would be sent to Kakamari. He liked—or so he told his mother—the idea of its remoteness and its isolation; the feeling that he would be almost on his own, away from tiresome pettifogging majors, and far removed from the social obligations, the tennis parties and the dances and the At Homes that seemed to go with ordinary regimental soldiering in Africa just as much as Dover. In Kakamari too he would be, if not exactly in Samuel Baker country, at least in something near and like it. That, he knew, would please and impress his mother, who, he knew too, could be relied upon to pass on the news with relish to all those superior aunts and cousins he had met at Cowarne Court. 'Following in Uncle Sam's footprints, is he?' he imagined they would say, 'How perfectly splendid', and 'What a jolly good show'. In fact he spent most of the time to start with in the cantonment environment of battalion headquarters at Bombo and in the suburban atmosphere of Entebbe.

Life here [he told his mother] is really quite similar to that at home. We get up a little earlier and go to bed immediately after dinner, and rest from 2 p.m. to 4 p.m., the hottest part of the day. But otherwise there is little difference ... [Entebbe was] an awfully pretty place rather like a beautiful suburban garden suburb but with the extra fascination of the lake, the tropical plants and the natives. Unfortunately it is very official, being the seat of Government, in fact the Bank manager is the only civilian in the place; from what I can make out there is a good deal of backbiting and snobbery, God preserve me from this! I have every intention of telling all the gossipy old women that they should be ashamed of themselves.

Another thing Twining found very tiresome was the perpetuation in Entebbe of calling-habits which were already on their way out in England before the war. He had been given a list when he arrived of the people on whom he was supposed to call, and had pruned it so drastically that some of the stumps never put out their social shoots in his direction at all. The process of calling was accomplished in those days by the caller putting a card (one for a bachelor, two for the married) on a tray, usually of cheap Benares brass, which the callee had put out for that purpose on a table by the door. Originally the object had been to call on someone when they were likely to be at home and only to drop a card, to use a technical expression, if they were out so that they would know that you had been. The custom had degenerated through wear and tear and excessive use in India and other places into a performance, like ritual copulation, in which both parties vicariously took and gave without seeing one another at all.

I actually paid some calls last week [Peter told his mother] but of course I took jolly good care to see that all the inmates of the house I went to were out. It's a funny business calling. There being no bells, you shout 'Hodi?', and

praying that there will be no answer, you tip-toe in, drop a
card and run as fast as you can.

There were other social obligations just as burdensome to
be avoided. 'The bachelors (other than myself) gave a ball
at the Club on Saturday. I played bridge all the time.'
He found his military duties just as boring—training,
parades, 'shooting for some beastly cup', guard duties, running the mess, looking after the library, 'doing all the work
that Quartermaster Sergeants did at home which meant a
lot of office work after the day's parades were over'. The
only consolation was the African soldiers who were 'always
happy and smiling' with a great sense of humour and strong
feelings of loyalty and service to officers they liked. 'Some of
them,' he wrote to shock his missionary-minded mother,
'have rather a large number of wives. One Effendi (native
officer) has 18.'
He also ran a school for the African soldiers' children, and
he ran it from all accounts very well. As there was to start
with only one text book, round which all the pupils had
to gather, some of them learnt to read sideways or upside
down and had to turn other books or newspapers to the
same angle before they could decipher them. One of his
African assistants in this venture wrote the following letter
to Mrs. Twining.

Madam, though this is the first time and first opportunity to write you, yet I feel very happy in learning of
you from time to time by mean of your son, Lieutenant
Twining under his control and inchargeship I am protected
very safely. And it was he who gave me this your address
though it would surprise you to find out who he is that has
written you.
I am native, a Muganda; and I am Schoolmaster of Military School over which your son is Principal, or Officer-in-
charge. He is very good to me. And I always call him my
father. For being fatherless therefore I name him and
respect him as a father. He has done his best to help me
growing and keeping me in the best respectful way. I
thank him. And now I am feeling very happy when I write

you this letter hoping that you would do the same. He
has and is always giving me The Times newspaper to read
as to help me in studying of English. I have so lot to
appreciate him. But being a first time to write you these
few remarks will probably do...

I send my heart salute to you, Madam, waiting your lovely
reply. I beg to remain, Madam, yours black son,

L/Corpl Reuben S. S. Mukasa Sparta.

Running this school was it seems the only military duty
in Uganda which Twining performed up to then with any
enthusiasm or success. Consequently it wasn't just that Twining was dissatisfied with routine soldiering. One at least of
his company commanders was equally dissatisfied with
Twining. Apart from his unconcealed lack of interest in his
ordinary military duties and in the things which proper
officers and gentlemen did in their spare time—shooting and
playing games and going to parties in Kampala—Twinks
('Goodbye, Mr. Twinks' a deaf or absent-minded visitor had
once said and the name stuck and spread) didn't even look
like a soldier. 'He was thin and sallow and looked as if he
never brushed his hair.' He had bags under his eyes, and
worse than that he was eccentric. He collected match-box
tops and butterflies, he read too much, he was contrary in
his opinions. One way and another his company commander
was glad to be rid of him.

He got rid of him because once more Peter Twining
achieved his desire for a change by making himself dispens-
able. Less than a couple of months after his arrival in Uganda
he got himself, by a judicious mixture of charm and self-
propulsion, nicely into line to fill an approaching vacancy
in the post of Intelligence Officer; as much one suspects because he wanted to get away from the routine and the commonplace as for the positive and familiar attractions of the
post itself. When he had the job firmly under his belt he
set out the pros and cons of having it in a typical Twining
letter of this period.

My darling Mother [he wrote in January 1924] I have
some very good news for you. I returned here on New

Year's day, and on the following morning the Colonel sent for me and told me that he wanted me to take over Intelligence Officer, which I promptly did. There are many advantages and a few disadvantages.

—DISADVANTAGES—

1. As long as I hold the job, I will not be on my own in some out-of-the-way place.
2. There is no extra pay attached to it.

—ADVANTAGES—

1. I now have work which really interests me, and which I have an aptitude for.
2. I am my own boss.
3. I will have to tour about all over Uganda.
4. It goes down on my record and gives me more experience.

Of course I have been given the job entirely owing to my having had previous experience at it which is shown on my record of service. The work in many ways is rather different although the same principles hold and of course it is not so exciting. But the scope is infinitely greater as instead of having a sector of Dublin with 200,000 people to look after I have to do the work for the whole of Uganda which is twice the size of Great Britain and is bordered by 5 other countries viz. Sudan, Abyssinia, Kenya, Tanganyika and Belgian Congo all of which I have to take a considerable interest in. And where I only had social unrest I now have to dabble in Botany, Veterinary, Forestry, Geology, Anthropology, Entymology and a number of other ologies which I can't spell.

The first thing I have to do is to supply the information to the War Office in order that they can compile a handbook of Uganda embracing everything that anybody might possibly want to know if there was ever a war here; I have an office and no clerk, the former is in the H—— of a mess, and there is a nice new Corona typewriter and dozens of instruments such as Boiling point thermometers, clinometers, barometers, rain gauges, none of which I know how to use; and enough graphs, drawing paper and instruments to help me draw maps for the rest of my life.

However I am getting straightened out, and I have every intention of drawing as few maps as possible as I am not very clever at that line of business. However the whole thing should give me a very wide experience at the line of business I have a liking for and as my work in Ireland led to this, this ought to and I hope may lead to something better still.

There is also a paragraph at the end of the letter which suggests that Mrs. Twining may have been somewhat overstating to her sisters the dangers of life in Africa for her Peter.

But for goodness sake let Aunt Mill know that I am 10 yards from several white men, not 100 miles, and that I am in no immediate danger of being gobbled up by lions; there are none within 30 miles and these run away when they see you.

After his appointment as Intelligence Officer life as a soldier in Uganda was much more fun. The information wanted by the War Office had to be supplied in the form of half-yearly intelligence reports, and this gave Twining the opportunity to travel about the country as much and as often as he liked and to talk to the people who were concerned with the wide variety of subjects he had to cover. He already had a talent for getting on with people and, to encourage them to talk and to give him the sort of information he wanted, he borrowed from his father the habit of reading up other people's subjects in the *Encyclopaedia Britannica* in advance. This, he found, worked very well. People are always inclined to talk more and to talk better about their subjects if there is some informed response, however contrived or bogus it may be, and Peter Twining became very accomplished as time went by in this encouraging form of deception. One suspects from the varying style and the expertise of certain sections of the reports that he even persuaded some of his informants to do the drafts themselves.

Some of the *obiter dicta* however have an unmistakable Twining touch. 'Intending travellers to Uganda should on no account read the list of diseases they may be liable to get.' Under the heading of Accommodation—'Visitors are strongly advised to make their own arrangements. Most officials are extremely hospitable, but their hospitality has so frequently been abused that they are now forced to curtail it. One can readily understand how annoying it is to return home after a hard day's work and find 3 or 4 uninvited strangers in one's house drinking one's whisky.'

The results in any case were very satisfactory. The first half-yearly report was 258 pages long; it is informative, well set out and alternatively, depending on who wrote it, scholarly or entertaining. It brought a slightly surprised letter of appreciation from the Army Council which, in his early enthusiasm and burning desire for recognition in high places, Twining thought meant that it had been seen and blessed by people of more exalted rank than he later found out was in fact the case. 'Just the sort of letter they send to everyone, and it doesn't mean a thing,' he sadly admitted later to his mother who had at first been led to believe that it was half way to a general's baton. He may have over-estimated the impact of his report at first but he was wrong if he thought that it had gone unnoticed. It hadn't; it turned out a few years later to have been one of the most important stepping stones in his career.

He wrote a lot of letters to his mother at this time. His earlier letters had been full of escapist talk about his pets (Samuel Baker had always kept monkeys in his retinue and Twining did the same) and about his hobbies—match-box tops, stamps and butterflies, although perhaps their money-making possibilities as well as a collector's zeal had led him to amass them. 'Apparently,' he told his mother, 'a good collection [of butterflies] is quite valuable. One man who had a very good collection sold it for £750.' Now as Intelligence Officer his letters were mostly about his travels and the interesting people he met. Another thing which occupied his mind and filled his letters at this time was the choice of the route he would follow when he went home on leave. That was still some way ahead but he was already devoting a lot of time and thought to it. He went into the details and the cost of the various ways he could go with thoroughness and care. He wanted to see as many new places as possible; and he also wanted to be different. He had a deep and not particularly silent contempt for people who always travelled by the same easy and conventional sea route, Mombasa to Tilbury and back again. He was also trying to decide whether to go back to his regiment or do another tour in Uganda.

I am so glad [he wrote] that you approve of my scheme for doing the return journey from Uganda by a different and more interesting route. Thank you so much for writing to Cooks and seeing the other firm for me, they have not written yet but I expect to hear from them by the next mail.

You ask when are you to expect me home? Well this is really rather an important question as so many things are wrapped up in it, and it is coupled with another question, i.e. am I going to return or not (to Uganda).

The thing really boils down to this. An officer is not allowed to be away from his regular regiment for more than 5 years at a time, after being away five years he has to do at least two years regimental service with his real regiment. Secondly it is more advantageous to the K.A.R. if officers do their five years with them (in two tours, totalling 4 years residence in the Uganda Protectorate, 4 months on the voyages backwards and forwards, and 8 months leave). The establishment of officers is only 21, and there are always a certain number on leave, so sometimes they are very short.

Now we must look at the question as it affects me from every point of view. The pay is good and will be better if I stay on, I get £450 per annum now, in August by virtue of having 6 years total service I will be getting £500 per annum, if I come back I will almost certainly get a temporary captaincy at £550 a year as second in command of a company, and with any luck I might get a company which means £600 per annum. The climate suits me, at least so far I have been very fit; so long as I am I.O. my work amuses me, and I like the people here, but of course as soon as one really gets to know them off they go and some new ones arrive.

If I only do one tour I will go back to the regiment, probably at home but possibly in India, I should get my permanent captaincy with pay of £400 a year, in two or three years time; here there is not quite the same regimental spirit that you get at home as everyone regards himself as a bird of passage. One also has the feeling here of being rather out of it, in fact as though one has been sent off on an errand and forgotten, and I do not think being away for a long time does one much good professionally. Five years is undoubtedly a long time, especially when in what is really only a one-eyed place. I like variety, and I am temperamentally rather restless. I am not in the least sorry that I came here, it is a very great experience, and one's outlook on everything not only is broadened but undergoes an immense change. You cannot help it when you see millions of people emerging from a state of savagery and governed by a handful of Englishmen with tremendous success. This is rather wandering from the point. To resume, I am very doubtful at the moment whether I shall return here for a second tour. It is no use asking anyone here what they would advise, they are either in no better position to advise me than I am myself, or they are old stagers who have spent a long time here already and have no ambition to go anywhere else or do anything else, they have irretrievably come under the very strong fascination of 'Africa'. At the same time I have no particular desire to soldier in England, or in India for any length of time. I do not like being in a place too long, I think that two years is ample. To put matters plainly, I am in an agony of indecision about the matter. I have a very good mind to go to the Egyptian and Soudanese Army, but then everyone here says it's a rotten show (personally I believe it's only jealousy and the Egyptian Army would and do say that the K.A.R. is a rotten show). If I do decide to try for the E.A. the best thing I think would be to say that I did not think that I was coming back for a second tour, and then when in Khartoum on my way home go to the War Office there and make arrangements to go to their army.

The devil of it is that one is supposed to state before leaving here whether one is coming back or not.

At any rate I have more or less arranged it that whether I come back or not I will now do a tour of 24 months. That would mean leaving here in either September or October of next year, arriving home in the middle of November or just before Xmas 1926, it sounds a long way ahead, but I have today completed the first six months of my tour leaving only 18 months, which is really nothing.

Now to get down to further business, I have more or less decided to make the route home as follows—The Nile to Khartoum, thence to Cairo, (stop 2 nights), thence to Jerusalem, (1 night) thence to Damascus (1 night), thence to Allepo (1 night), thence to Constantinople by the Baghdad railway, staying two nights in Constantinople, thence by rail to Buda Pest, thence by Danube steamer to Vienna (2 nights), thence home by the quickest possible way; Balders who spent two years in Palestine is very keen to do the journey with me; the mileage is actually very little more than by Mombasa. The govt give you £110 instead of your passage, they send your heavy kit (1000 cubic feet) home by sea, and give you a free ticket on the train and boats in Uganda, the Sudan Government give a concession of 50% off the railway and steamer fares in Sudan, and 20% off dining car accounts. So that is all a very considerable help.

Next week or the week after I will send you a rough copy of the itinerary and cost as far as I have worked it out roughly. By the time I have corresponded with Cooks and the other firm and got the final details, it will be quite this time next year, and I will have to put in my application for permission to go and get all the visas next April if I go in September 1926, or May if in October.

It is very nice of you to think of meeting me at Frankfort, but I expect that by the time I get there I expect I will need a little quiet at home for 2 or 3 weeks, and I have had in mind for some time, that when I have sufficiently recovered from the journey!!!!! I would take you to some nice place abroad perhaps, Montreux or

Lucerne! But perhaps you would not agree.

When he had finished the first of his intelligence reports he was sent up at last to Kakamari. Kakamari was just a military post, the country was Karamoja. For once reality was up to expectation. He was only there for a few months but it was in many ways the happiest of all his time as a soldier. It was pleasant country, a high plateau of short-grassed plains and hills teeming with amiable, eatable and easily shootable game, and peopled by the sort of earthy, cheerful, naked Africans that Twining liked. A remarkably tall fine race of excellent physique, an earlier observer had called them, 'frank and outspoken ... the most honest race of savages I have ever dealt with in Africa'. European observers often forgot the disease and the hunger and the fear and the sudden death which permeated their existence but to the people themselves these things may well have seemed a fair price to pay to be left virtually untouched by the corruptions and the restrictions of other peoples' civilisations, whether they were European or African or Arab. They were a separate sort of people and they wanted and still probably want to be left alone. The King's African Rifles wasn't there in any case to govern or to civilise; it was there to keep the peace and to protect the people and their cattle from their neighbours' raiding parties. Something of Peter Twining's uncomplicated pleasure in this assignment and the sort of life it meant comes out in the combined journal and family letter which he kept on his journey back when he was recalled to finish off his intelligence reports. He did the journey on foot because he wanted to and he did it in easy stages—about 250 miles in fifteen days—but it was quite a journey none the less.

In many ways [he wrote at the end of the second day] I very much regret leaving for Bombo. This life is full of incident and varied interest and one feels and breathes African. I much prefer a tent to a rest house, all the porters light fires in a circle around the tent about 30 yards away where they jabber and gnaw raw bones most of the night. It gives me a feeling of cosiness and security.

He was shooting for the pot as he went along, mainly for the porters, but he didn't particularly like it. He wasn't a good shot, and he didn't often hit his quarry where he meant to, in the heart or in the brain, with the result that his killing wasn't particularly quick or clean. On top of this he had this awkward soft centre which made him feel a brute when he saw at close quarters afterwards what he had done. He was especially upset when he was persuaded by his hungry and more hard-hearted African following to shoot small and delicately boned animals like dik-dik.

I can't see any point in ruthless and unnecessary slaughter of beautiful animals, although it may be the thing to shoot a lot. Tomorrow [he noted a week later with a touch of relief] will be my last day of shooting. I must say that this Big Game Shooting is rather an over-rated pastime. Perhaps the dangerous game is more exciting but even with buffalo, the most dangerous of all, most people seem to climb up a tree to shoot.

Two days later he was back in settled country again with roads and cotton fields and villages where small tin shops sold 'Austrian writing paper, German beads and trinkets, Swedish and Italian matches, Dutch tobacco and Japanese cloth, Indian cotton goods, American lamps, Czecho-Slovakian cooking pots, Swiss watches. In fact the only English things were soap and cigarettes.' 'Heartrending' he found it. Now that he was back in civilisation he insisted, to keep up appearances and as a change from his exiguous Karamoja diet, on having a five-course dinner every night in pyjamas outside his tent. He listed the menus for his mother.

Dinner. Chicken broth. Tinned salmon or whitebait. Roast chicken. Custard pudding. Chicken on toast. *Breakfast.* Grape nuts (excellent food). Grilled chicken. Omelette. *Lunch.* Chicken broth. Stewed chicken. Custard pudding (that tasty baked variety). Please don't give me chicken as a treat when I am on leave.

He concluded his journal two days later.

By the time I have arrived in Soroti the sum total of my

peregrinations since I left 3 months ago will be over 300 miles on my flat feet which is not bad going. I must say that I am a little tired of walking at the moment, but it has all been well worth it. Karamoja is real Africa. Bombo etc is suburban. Even though I may not return it will always be a very pleasant 4 months to look back on. Full of unusual incidents, frequently in a momentary dilemma, sometimes tired and sometimes very thirsty, but always enjoying it. I do not know whether I should like to be stuck up there for a long time, I don't think I would, but I think that I have kept myself contented by having many interests—my London *Times*, work for my promotion exam, doing a little work at Swahili, and working out the plans for my journey home. The result has been that on arrival in camp I have always had something to do and it has kept away any feeling of loneliness and boredom which gets on so many fellows' nerves when they have 7 or 8 hours a day with nothing to do and a fierce sun to keep them indoors. I am also convinced that it is essential to keep pets under such circumstances. The dogs and monkeys have been almost worth their weight in gold to me. As it happens all my interests have come to an end today, the last day. This afternoon I finished the last of the *Times*, the final chapter of Callwell's *Dardenelles*, the last Swahili exercise, and I have put my signature to my letter to Thos. Cook and Sons. I have certainly made great strides in Swahili and have a vocabulary of over 500 words, but my grammar is deplorably weak, but as no one understands you if you speak grammatically it does not matter a great deal.

You must excuse this almost unbearable scrawl, and all the spelling mistakes, but it has been written usually under trying conditions, either in the full glare of the sun, or by the dim light of a miserable lamp, sometimes in the most uncomfortable of seats or sometimes in the most comfortable lie-down chair, but as I possess no box or chair which will sit me at a convenient height at my table it has always been written on one or both of my knees...

Soon after he got back to Bombo he had what he described

to his mother as 'something wrong with my tummy' and what his army medical sheets recorded more bleakly as diarrhoea. What he had got in fact was dysentery and he spent the best part of three months in hospital before he was invalided home. Although he had to give up his carefully prepared plans to go home up the Nile and across Asia Minor and Europe by train he did manage to persuade the doctors that a long sea voyage round the Cape would do him good; and he thus added Zanzibar, Dar es Salaam, Mozambique, Beira, Lourenzo Marques, Durban and Cape Town to his growing list of places visited. His diary however discloses nothing about this voyage except the number of miles travelled each day; the only exception is an entry for the 13th of April, 1925. 'Fancy dress. Went as Col. Gout and won 1st prize. 60 votes for Best Gents brought on board and 10 for best sustained character.'

He spent the next six months in England, some of it in the Officers' Convalescent Home at Queen Victoria's old house at Osborne in the Isle of Wight which he thoroughly enjoyed. Despite the amenities and the free and easy regulations which allowed one to go away for the weekend to London or to Brighton whenever one liked, the commandant apparently had difficulty in keeping it full, except of course in Cowes Week; and fearing that it might be closed down and that he might lose his job he tended to hang on to his customers for as long as he could. In the end however Peter managed to get away to Europe for a month visiting some at least of the places he had meant to go to on his way back from Africa. He went by train to Prague and Vienna and Budapest and back by way of Salzburg, Innsbruck, Zürich, the Rhine and Paris. There is nothing in his diary or his letters to throw any light on what he did on these journeys but it seems clear, reading between the lines, that this sort of travelling was for him one of the best things in life. To travel alone from place to place in the middle parts of Europe; the solid comforts of medium-priced hotels, eating meals in trains, the names of romantic-sounding places strung out like geographic washing above the windows of the railway carriages, wine that was as cheap as beer and beer that was as cheap as wine, cigars and sticky liqueurs, long leisurely meals that could be studied and planned with care from enormous bills of fare at the table or on the menus written in green and purple ink outside the door; the smell of trams and urinals and market stalls. Talking too to everyone he met, in English if he could but if need be in his atrocious French and German aided by smiles and gestures and his compelling friendliness; seeing the sights (he had borrowed all his mother's Baedekers), and, more and more important as time went on, going to the opera and listening to music. He had begun his musical education on the Rhine in 1919; now he began to widen the foundations of his tastes with Verdi and Puccini, and all the classic operas in the continental repertoire. He made an experimental note in his diary of Saint-Saëns and Rimsky Korsakov opposite Gounod's *Faust* and *Carmen*. When he got back to England he bought himself a portable gramophone and albums of records in blue and red and yellow. They went with him afterwards almost everywhere he went. Porters carried them through river reeds and up narrow hippo-trodden tracks. They went in canoes and paddle steamers and in ships, in box-body cars and diesel lorries, and in the end in special trains and private aeroplanes.

He went back to Uganda in October. He had decided after all to do a second tour in the K.A.R. Again he went by a different route, in one French boat this time from Marseilles to Constantinople via Naples, Malta and Athens, and then down through Smyrna and Rhodes and Cyprus to Port Said, where after a quick look at Cairo he caught another French boat to Mombasa.

He returned again to battalion headquarters at Bombo, and continued his work as Intelligence Officer, concentrating this time on the second volume of a military report which dealt with routes and itineraries. This was of course absolutely Twining's métier and gave him an excuse to go over any route by river, lake, road or track that might conceivably be used for military purposes: for good measure he extended his scope outside the territory and did annexes on the Cape to Cairo route, the cross-Africa route and the Costs of the Nile trip. Once more he made a very thorough job of it, and once more he was commended.

Soon after he got back to Uganda his fellow officers at Bombo were surprised when, apparently out of the blue, two young women came to visit Twinks. One of them was tall and handsome, intelligent and quick, with a deep voice and a hearty laugh, both in constant use. Her name was Evelyn Du Buisson. The other had blue eyes, fair hair and a determined mouth. She had a quiet voice and a quieter smile. She was a doctor, serious and shy. She was known as May, though her real names were Helen Mary. The two girls were cousins. They had come up from Northern Rhodesia, where May Du Buisson had been in the government medical service and Evelyn had a farming brother, to stay with a Kenya uncle. 'Friends of the family,' Peter Twining told his fellow officers, 'met them by accident in Mombasa on my way through.' He had in fact met them by design and had invited them to stay. They had at first refused, pleading lack of funds. But when life with uncle on a remote Kenya farm began to pall the funds were somehow found.

Remembering how he never went to dances, and played bridge whenever he could at cocktail parties, his fellow officers were both concerned and intrigued about what exactly their Twinks planned to do with his female guests. What he did in fact was to take them off to the Mountains of the Moon, the cool, snow-capped range that lies between Uganda and the Congo. In less than an hour after they started they were back at their starting point, the car, all twenty-five pounds-worth of it, abandoned in a roadside ditch, and the Du Buisson cousins thankful, apparently, that it was and that they would never have to drive in it again. Someone else kindly drove them to their destination in a commercial van. Sometimes Evelyn sat in the back with Peter Twining, and sometimes it was May. Whichever it was got covered in fine red dust. Evelyn got extracts from *Aida* in an enthusiastic but rather throaty voice. May eventually got not so much a proposal of marriage as a suggestion that the matter might be discussed. Later in the hotel where the two girls were staying there was a somewhat general discussion about the sort of items on which negotiations might be commenced, existing commitments, nature and location of future occupation, capital and income, and other incidental matters like the number and sex of children. Evelyn suggested that she should leave them and was told very firmly that she should stay. It was not a sudden or a whirlwind courtship. It took more than two years of correspondence and indecision and discussion, in which it seems Evelyn continued to play a part, before they finally made up their minds to get married.

It was not of course the first time they had met. The Du Buissons and the Bournes, Peter's mother's family, were old Herefordshire acquaintances. They were the sort of families between which, in England, marriages are frequently arranged. They were both well established and well-to-do with roots that went down far enough to conceal the elements that fed them and gave them substance—the hard work, the shrewd and frugal husbandry, and the hard bargaining over soil and property and trade. The Bournes' roots were embedded perhaps in finer and more English clay: the Du Buissons' perhaps were better nourished. The Bournes had Cowarne Court and the Du Buissons had an estate in Carmarthenshire. Peter and May had first met there when he was eleven; a pale rather towney boy, she thought him. She was a country girl. She taught him to milk a cow; and one day they went to Carregcennen Castle and dropped a bent pin together into a wishing well . . .

The Du Buissons were Protestants who had fled from France in 1684 after the revocation of the Edict of Nantes. In England they allied themselves in business and blood with another family of refugees. Both had a tradition and a talent for survival, and a certain dedicated obstinacy of nose and mouth that just would not be defeated. They have traded together now for 300 years of ups and downs: there is hardly a country in the four continents where Peter and May Twining were to live and serve in which the firm of Henckell, Du Buisson and Co. hadn't at one time or another made an enterprising profit or an enterprising loss.

Although Twining spent another two years in Uganda to complete his attachment to the King's African Rifles he was beginning to get more and more concerned with the problem of his future. With the possibility of marriage in mind he discovered that you couldn't draw marriage allowance in the Army until you were thirty-five. He was twenty-six. This was

one of the factors which made him start to wonder all over
again whether the Army was really the right career for him.
Another was the fact that after ten years service he was still
only seventeenth in order of seniority in his regiment as a
subaltern. To make matters worse he had failed his examination for promotion to captain; and there were senior officers
under whom he had served who found his obedience to command and attitude to superiors less commendable than some
of his other military performances. Even if he had wanted to
stay in the Army his prospects of advancement were therefore pretty thin.

He was far from sure however that he wanted to stay in the
Army anyway. The prospect of going back to the sort of
peace-time regimental soldiering that he had experienced at
Dover appalled him; and though he was an inveterate grass-
is-greener-in-the-next-field man he wasn't encouraged much
by reports he had received from Army friends who had actual
experience of these supposedly greener fields. One of them
wrote from Singapore that 'in a soldier's life in the Far East,
tea parties, the set of your tie and the fall (good expression
that!) of your trousers are the most important events. Everyone who doesn't live for such matters is looked upon as a
backwoodsman.' And May Du Buisson had made it clear
that she didn't particularly like the idea of being a soldier's
wife. One way and another Twining seems to have made up
his mind about the middle of 1927 to try for something else.

The first thing he tried was the Department of Overseas
Trade in Nairobi. There were no vacancies and nothing came
of that. He tried, through family influence, to get an intelligence post in the Sudan but without success and it wasn't
until he got back to England and had at last brought his
negotiations with May Du Buisson to a conclusion and had
discussed the matter in length with her, that he decided in
the spring of 1928 to see if he could get into the Colonial
Administrative Service.

He may indeed have had this as a possibility in the back
of his mind for some time. In the course of collecting information for his intelligence reports and his military handbook
in Uganda, Twining had got to know a lot of Administrative
Officers and had liked and admired them very much. He

The Rev. William Twining.

Agatha Twining with her three children, Stephen, Betty and Peter, aged five months, in 1899.

E. F. Peter Twining.

As second-lieutenant in the Worcestershire Regiment in 1918.   At his marriage to Helen Mary Du Buisson in 1928.

envied them the variety and the satisfactions of the job they had to do and the large responsibilities they were given from an early age. The work was so constructive, he told his mother, compared with the basically destructive nature of a soldier's job and in the Army one had to wait years before one got anything like an independent command. Another thing he envied was the Mandarin-like status which Administrative and Political Officers were accorded in the Sudan and East Africa and in other places he had visited.

At that time recruitment for the Administrative Service in the colonial territories was run by a man called Ralph Furse. He was working very hard and with considerable imagination to attract into the service the cream of the sort of people in the universities who cultivated what he regarded as a proper balance between brain and brawn. If he couldn't get men with a First and a Blue, a Second and a certain competence at games (or, some said, a Blue and a certain competence at work) would do. At first sight Temporary Unpaid Captain E. F. Twining, who was hopeless at exams and even worse at games, wasn't a very likely starter; but Furse kept some vacancies open deliberately for older men from the Armed Services with slightly different qualities. He was looking for men who had a proved talent for leadership and for getting things done. The men who interviewed Twining at the Colonial Office and went through the reports of his referees and sponsors, knew what Furse was looking for and came to the conclusion that Twining came into this category. His Uganda intelligence reports and the way he had set about getting his information and arranging his material had impressed a number of people both in Uganda and in the Colonial Office, and this was used in Twining's favour to offset his lack of academic prowess. He had got married on the 21st of July, 1928, and the offer of a post as a Cadet Administrative Officer in Uganda came to him when he was on his honeymoon in Europe.

Agatha Twining thoroughly approved of her son's marriage and his choice of bride. Apart from her new daughter-in-law's own distinctive merits of which she had for many years been well aware, she knew that May Du Buisson came from what she regarded as a very good family with enough money, as one of the Du Buissons put it, to be secure but not enough that they didn't all have to work. Soon afterwards her elder son Stephen made an equally satisfactory marriage to a girl called Georgina Gaskell who was well endowed with charm, wealth and relations, one of whom later become Lord Llewellin and Governor General of the short-lived Federation of Rhodesia and Nyasaland. There had been some who had thought that because of her compelling and dominating personality Agatha Twining would be the only woman in her two sons' lives. There may indeed have been times when both the new Mrs. Twinings thought so too. However they both had considerable powers of persuasion and strength of character, and in the end they managed to be not only indispensable wives but indispensable daughters-in-law as well.

5

The Colonial Service

'CANDIDATES PROVISIONALLY SELECTED for Administrative and Secretariat appointments in Tropical Africa are required,' the official Colonial Office handout said, 'to undergo a course of instruction in this country before embarkation on first appointment. The course commences in October and extends over the autumn, spring and summer terms at either Oxford or Cambridge University.' Twining was sent to Oxford. The course of instruction covered a lot of acreage and almost every field of it was new to him. 'Criminal Law, Procedure (Civil and Criminal), and Evidence; Tropical Economic Products, vegetable and mineral, their occurrence, nature and uses; Elements of Islamic Law (Maliki and Shafai Schools); Elementary Surveying; Anthropology; African Languages and Phonetics; Tropical Hygiene and Sanitation,' and in case this display of virtuosity and capital letters wasn't enough 'such other subjects as the Secretary of State may from time to time approve.' 'Candidates,' the handout concluded, 'will be required to give careful and intelligent attention to the instruction on the various subjects, and to pass the prescribed examinations. They will be subject in all respects to the usual University discipline.' No wonder Twining kept his name on the Army half-pay list as a precaution.

Peter Twining claimed in later years from the safe vantage-point of success that he did no work at all at Oxford and that he failed in every subject except forestry. In fact he seems to have worked quite hard and the only examination he failed to pass was the one on Civil Law. He took a leading

part in the affairs of the Colonial Service club and finished
up with a report of the Quite Satisfactory type. For a man
whose philosophy was Top or Bottom it was a skeleton in
his cupboard which he did his best to conceal.

Outside the limited confines of his course however, Oxford
seems to have passed him by. Not only did Twining make
no mark on Oxford but Oxford seems to have made no mark
on him. Part of the trouble was that he was attached to St.
Catherine's which in those days was an unlovely and somewhat unfashionable and rudimentary college. Consequently
he had nothing to do with it and claimed not to have entered
it or even seen it all the time he was there. He was married
of course and lived in rooms in north Oxford. And he was
twenty-nine. Not unnaturally he found undergraduates and
the University disciplines of the nineteen-twenties rather
puerile. 'My wife is a midwife' (which she wasn't), or 'My
wife is pregnant' (which she was), were the excuses he gave
when he came in to his digs after hours or was caught by
the Proctors drinking in a pub. In 1928 and 1929 these were
both unusual things for a junior member of the University
to say, and no doubt he got away with it.

The only mark which Twining seems to have made on the
Oxford scene when he was there was his capacity for ordering and eating unusual meals. He was reasonably well off as
a result of his marriage and one of his favourite eating-places
was the Spread Eagle at Thame. John Fothergill, in knee
breeches and buckle shoes was running the Spread Eagle
then as a gourmets' rendezvous, and in his Innkeeper's Diary
he noted that 'three lads, Mathew, the K.C.'s son, Twining
and Simpson dined here because they are soon all to go off
to various parts of Africa. I think it was about the best dinner we've ever built up.' After dinner they had iced lager
which was criticised as an epicurean solecism by the people
at the next-door table who had been following their neighbours' choice of food and wine with fascinated interest.
Fothergill approved the choice of lager though partly, he
admitted, because they had previously had Tokay. Twining
hadn't travelled the middle parts of Europe for nothing.

In July of 1929 Peter Twining left for Africa. He went by
the direct sea route this time because his passage, like that

of the other Administrative Cadets who had done their apprentice courses at Oxford and Cambridge, had been booked in advance by the Crown Agents who arranged journeys in those days on the same principles on which they ordered paint for public buildings; repeating the same dose over and over again was less trouble and much cheaper. He also travelled without his wife. She had produced a son while they were on the Oxford course and it was decided that she should stay behind for a month or two to, so to speak, run the new baby in.

When he arrived in Uganda, Twining found that he had been posted to a place called Gulu. A few weeks after he got there he sent some notes to his wife, with copies to his mother and his mother-in-law, to give her an idea of what to expect. They were headed 'All about Gulu or an appreciation of the situation'. They started off with *'Position and Climate'*.

Gulu station is in Northern Uganda about midway between the Victoria Nile and the Sudan Border. The Albert Nile is about 50 miles to the west.

Great Uncle Sam Baker passed through the District on both his journeys and built a permanent camp at Fatiko about 20 miles away. Fatiko Hill can be seen from the houses.

The station is 3700 feet above sea level. At the end of the rains in November it gets very hot (95 degrees in the shade by day, 69 degrees at night). A constant strong hot wind makes it reasonably cool for the rest of the year.

The station itself is not unhealthy but a lot remains to be done to improve it. There are mosquitoes but they are said not to be infected with malaria.

The greater part of the district has been depopulated owing to sleeping sickness, and is now closed to all except elephant which abound. The populated part lies only 15 miles on either side of the motor roads.

Part of the district lies on the Western side of the Albert Nile and there is a sub-station there named Moyo. Moyo lies in the hills overlooking the Nile valley and is healthy but most of the sub-district is hot and low lying and much is uninhabited owing to sleeping sickness.

Communications

These are bad, very bad when compared with the rest of Uganda. The nearest Telegraph is Masindi 110 miles away. Telegrams can only be received and despatched once a week and then on foot to Masindi. They may take anything up to a week to get there. Nearest telephone Kampala 300 miles away.

Letter once a week by runner. Parcel and Paper mail once a fortnight by steamer to Atura Port. It takes a month between ordering and receiving goods from Jinja or Kampala.

At Moyo there is a weekly mail steamer from Butiaba on Lake Albert. There are no motor roads. No telegraph. In fact one is completely cut off for a week at a time.

Personalities

Natives. The tribe is the Acholi. I am well acquainted with them as my K.A.R. Company was almost entirely composed of them. They are perfectly delightful, cheery, intelligent but rather backward owing to their geographical situation.

Most of the peasants wear no clothes whatsoever.

They are very pleasant people to work for as they are very keen to progress in the right direction. They are easy to manage but require firmness. They are comparatively free from disease and are increasing at a tremendous rate, but unfortunately the infantile mortality is very high, largely due to trying to feed 12 months old babies on meat and maize.

In the Moyo sub-district there is a different tribe, the Madi who have a number of things in common with the Acholi, but are not quite so attractive.

'They are very pleasant people to work for...' The last word of this phrase is one that as a soldier Twining is less likely to have used. A year's course at Oxford in the semantics and the philosophy of a new kind of colonial policy, based on the dictum that African interests were to be paramount, had produced a noticeable change of attitude and style. He went on in the same vein to describe the small town and the work and the way of life, though he still contrived to end it on a more familiar and characteristic note that neither Oxford nor any later experience quite managed to eliminate.

The Station

Gulu really sits in the middle of the wilderness, bush, jungle or whatever you like to call it. It was established in 1911. Until 1926 there were only mud and grass buildings, but now there are two permanent European houses, a permanent Office or Boma, 3 Asiatic houses and about a dozen Indian shops or dukas. There is a temporary native hospital, two temporary European houses (one which I am now in is semi-permanent and quite good), a Rest house, Police lines, Prison, Cemetery with one grave in it, and various miscellaneous stores and huts. The township extends for a two-mile radius from the Boma and has been laid out on a generous scale as though one day it will be a great City. It is probable that it will grow a little in the next few years and we hope that next year they will build two more European houses, a permanent Rest house and a permanent Hospital.

The two existing houses are quite good. They are the type that I made a plan of before I left, except that the verandas are open and have no mosquito netting. They possess a fair amount of furniture, such as tables, chairs, side-board, chest of drawers, cupboard etc. and can in fact be made comfortable. They stand in uninteresting gardens, but there is a good view extending to the Agora Mountains 50 miles away on the Sudan border. People usually keep pretty fit in the district in spite of the many disadvantages and the isolation.

Unless a doctor comes we will get one of the permanent houses. If a doctor comes we will have to argue about it and may have to live in the semi-temporary house which is 3 roomed, concrete floors and is made of sun-baked bricks with proper ceilings and a thatched roof. There are mosquito-proof windows and doors, a bath room and two

store rooms. The disadvantage is that it is rather dark.
Many people however, prefer it to the permanent houses,
why I don't know. If two more houses are built they will
be bigger than the existing ones. Simpson has kindly said
that when his wife and family go home in the spring, we
can have the new District Commissioner's house if built.

Recreations and Amusements
  1. *Walking.* Usually with a view of inspecting the
station and noting things that need improvement.
  2. *Tennis.* Hard court. The Simpsons play, so do the
C.M.S. [Church Missionary Society].
  3. *Gardening.* Possibilities absolutely limitless. Most
things will grow only too prolifically.
  4. *Badminton.* This would be an excellent way of taking
exercise when only 2 or 3 people in the station, but cannot
be played between November and March owing to the
wind.
  5. The Acholi constantly bring in baby wild animals and
at present the station is well stocked with pets. 3 Persian
cats, Fowls. 2 Monkeys. 1 Baby Oribi Antelope and 1 Reed
Buck.

Food and Cost of Living
  Local foodstuffs are plentiful and cheap. Imported foods
are expensive owing to the transport charges.
  Local prices are as follows: N.B. 1/- = 100 cents

Eggs 2 cents each	Chickens 20 cents each
Milk 14 cents per bottle	Sheep 10/- each
Bullock 30/-	Milch Cow 70/-
Potatoes 2 cents per lb.	Monkey Nuts 10 cts per lb.
Meat 3 lbs. per 1/-	Rice 20 cents per lb.

Bananas 40 cents per bunch of about 50
  Sim Sim (which gives a very excellent cooking oil) 10
cts. per lb.
There is a station shamba (vegetable garden) and I am
going to make one of my own when my seeds arrive. Toma-
toes grow like weeds. A certain amount of fruit, oranges,
paw-paw, mangoes etc. grow, but the seasons are short.
  I am arranging to have a supply sent up by the fort-

nightly boat regularly. Butter, cheese and bacon comes every fortnight by boat to Atura from Jinja. The water supply is quite good but could be improved. Filters are provided. We might keep chickens as a hobby.

Work

Actually I am supposed to do all the petty work, minor court cases etc. and to listen to the hundreds of natives who bring their troubles to one every day. In addition I am in charge of the station labour, i.e. 80 porters who fetch water and fire wood, cut the grass, build the roads and buildings and generally keep the city going. I am also in charge of the Police and Prison. The Prison is rather comic.

There are about 60 prisoners and the Prison compound is so dilapidated that it would be as easy to escape as to walk out of the garden. But the Acholi consider it dishonourable to escape. The prisoners too go out to their work in charge of a senior prisoner, who considers himself a very important person. I really think they quite enjoy themselves.

Then there are a thousand and one things to see to. Taxes to collect, accounts to supervise, the constant checking and revision of cases tried by the chiefs' courts, roads to repair, outbreaks of rinderpest to deal with, supervision of cultivation of food and economic crops, births, marriages, divorces and deaths to register and regulate and hundreds of returns to send into H.Q.

The district is quite a busy one, cotton, sim-sim, ground nuts and hides being the chief exports, about £60,000 finding their way into native pockets every year. There is little serious crime, mostly domestic troubles.

At the moment the pièce de résistance is a campaign to instruct the natives how to cultivate more scientifically. Government has provided £750 to be spent on clearing and stumping ground, the purchase of ploughs and the training of oxen and demonstrations.

I am to do this on 100 acre plots in the three counties, so I will get plenty of safari. It is literally true that I am turning my sword into a ploughshare.

Nothing that I was taught at Oxford will help me in this. I should imagine that the natives will teach me a good deal more than I will teach them.

The new Mrs. Twining had of course already had a taste of Africa and this was the sort of stuff to make her mouth water, though more as a wife and a doctor perhaps than as a mother. The baby however was 'delicate' and Gulu clearly had its limitations as far as hygiene and medical facilities were concerned. So he was left behind with May's mother, Mrs. Du Buisson. A few weeks after his wife arrived and had begun to settle in at Gulu, Twining was sent off to the sub-station at Moyo a hundred miles to the north on the other side of the Nile. May Twining, of course, went too.

Moyo was in a sense Twining's first independent command; it was the first time that he had been entirely on his own. Although he was nominally under the District Commissioner at Gulu, the lack of communications and the detachment of his D.C. gave him the appearance and to some extent the reality of being his own master. It was a pleasant feeling, and he made the most of it.

Moyo wasn't much to look at but it was home. Their house when they arrived was, in the husband's words, 'little better than a broken-down cow-shed'. His wife writing to her mother described it in more practical detail as

a single room surrounded by verandahs, on one side the verandah was converted into a bathless bathroom and on the other side into a store. The front verandah which had a low wall was the living room, and the back one housed household equipment, the primitive kitchen was some yards away, no stove and we cooked on stones with a fire of wood and used a petrol tin oven. Sanitation was a pit latrine in the garden ... We had at the start a very little Public Works Department furniture, the rest we made out of packing cases. Later on the Powers that be began to send us furniture and the first to arrive on a porter's head was a municipal type dustbin. It made an excellent water filter. Refrigerators were unknown in small stations in those days and our weekly butter ration which travelled with our mail 100 miles on porters' heads from Gulu had generally disintegrated into an oily stream by the time it arrived; doubtless the porters' hair and skin received much needed nourishment. We lived on the country as much as possible, meat was unobtainable unless one bought an entire animal but skinney chickens were only 2d. each, and these with vegetables and fruit from our garden were our staple diet.

If he had still been a bachelor Twining would probably have installed a large staff of servants, a multitude of monkeys and other pets, a portable gramophone and plenty of gin, and would hardly have noticed his surroundings. But he wasn't, and within a few months a new room had been added of their own design and specification. The framework was made of mud and wattle and the walls were plastered with cow dung.

The cow dung smelt rather when first applied but was very satisfactory when dry and kept out the ants, but it needed replastering every three months or so. The roof was beautifully thatched in the local manner and soon became the home of numerous snakes which most disconcertingly would drop onto our beds or the floor with a horrid plop. We killed over ninety during the time we were there. We were told they were harmless which they were when dead but they had their uses as they kept down the rats and other vermin.

Peter Twining and his wife were very happy there. There were in the nineteen-thirties few better foundations for a lifelong partnership than sharing a house like this and sharing the life of a District Officer in a remote part of Africa. Mrs. Twining, being a doctor, was soon taken on the strength as a temporary Medical Officer, and immediately plunged into a variety of activities some of which, like running the small local hospital and doing sleeping-sickness control, could be described as medical, while others were of a kind which are now generally classified as social welfare. Some of these duties brought her into positions of official confrontation with her husband. He, for example, was responsible for the prison: she inspected it for health and cleanliness. The ups and downs of this functional relationship provided Twining when it came to writing his reports with opportunities of which it seems he did not fail to take advantage. Bland reports of the state of relations between the Administration and the Medical Department in the small sub-station of Moyo may have provided amusement at the time both for those who wrote them and for the few who read them but it seems unlikely that they had any influence on E. F. Twining's subsequent career. What interested his family however was his frequent absences. He often had to go away on his own, travelling in his parish or visiting his neighbours both in Uganda and in the Sudan, and although May Twining herself, fully occupied as she was with her own official duties and a constant stream of visitors, didn't seem to mind, her husband didn't have much difficulty in persuading his in-laws that it was bad for a white woman to be left on her own in the middle of darkest Africa. There were some missionaries near-by but for various reasons, personal and doctrinal, they didn't count. The result of this anxiety was, as was no doubt intended, that May's cousin Evelyn Du Buisson, who had been with her on her first trip to Uganda in 1926, was sent out to stay with them. She stayed for nearly a year. Peter Twining's stock went up in the eyes of his African subjects, the Madi. It was not every Administrative Cadet who could afford to have two wives, and for years afterwards his successors at Moyo had to listen to Madi stories of the Bwana who would have his camp bed put out, as was proper, in the middle of the rest house verandahs with one bed on the right and in line for his first and senior wife, and another on the left and a little bit behind it for the second one.

The Madi were different from the tall slim nilotic Acholi whom Twining had so much liked and admired at Gulu and in the ranks of the King's African Rifles. They were more negroid: thick-set and black and naked except for occasional tufts of grass and aprons made of hide for ornament or modesty. 'An idle race, riddled with disease,' he called them, 'eking out a somewhat precarious existence with recurring famines.' Twining got to like them very much; they had a sense of humour not unlike his own, earthy and uncomfortably based sometimes on the infirmities and misfortunes of other people. When Twining punished a minor peccadillo by putting Eno's Fruit Salt on their hair in the rain they thought it funny; the Acholi, who had a stronger sense of dignity, did not. One thing the Madi had however was a talent for laconic description. Twining may still have been Twinks to other Europeans but to the Madi he was *goi goi* —the goat who will never follow the herd, who just has to go his own different way.

Whatever the original reasons were for Evelyn Du Buisson coming out to join the Twinings she soon made herself indispensable. Demands for her assistance and attention came from several quarters, and she soon found herself in a potentially exploitable position.

It does not appear [she wrote home soon after her arrival] that I am in the least likely to find time heavy on my hands—the only difficulty appears to be whether the administrative or medical department had prior claim on my services. I have meekly awaited the issue and worked for the winner—but think of replenishing my depleted purse by selling my services to the highest bidder! Peter was very cock-a-hoop having the resources of the local revenue collector behind him but May has just received an enormous bag of undescribably dirty money from the medical department so he may not have it all his own way, and I see the path to riches opening before me.

It wasn't only in the District Office and the hospital that her seemingly inexhaustible energy and enthusiasm were of value. She supervised the planting and the running of the garden which Peter was happy to leave in her hands once he, like a general or a governor perhaps *en herbe*, had composed the general planning and the strategy. She looked after the pets and the domestic animals—'two black colubus monkeys, 1 red colubus monkey, 2 grey monkeys, a baboon, a small buck, 3 sheep and 3 lambs, 1 goat and 2 twin kids, about 12 fowls and a civet cat'; and in the evenings when

May was tired and had gone off to an early bed she shared Peter's love of opera and requiems, and his passion for verbal argument. 'Both of us,' she says, 'were uneducated but quick.' They argued about almost anything, not so much to impress on the other their own point of view as to release mental energy. They would often end up defending the positions which they had originally set out to attack. It ended occasionally in tears or sulks but for the most part it was a good-humoured and satisfying exercise which, like a nightcap of brandy or Ovaltine, set them up for a good night's sleep. 'He was sometimes infuriating but he was never dull.'

He also made the most of his opportunities as far as anecdote and description were concerned when anything out of the ordinary came his way. One such opportunity was an unexpected encounter with the then Prince of Wales who was on a hunting and sightseeing expedition to East Africa.

I fear [he wrote to his mother in March of 1930] that all our little local news must suffer this week in order to give you a full account of our great thrill i.e. the unexpected arrival of the Prince of Wales. We had made the most careful enquiries as to his movements which were being kept quiet, and the Game Ranger and the Head of the Uganda C.I.D. both of whom were accompanying the Prince had assured us that there was no chance whatsoever of the Prince coming anywhere near us. His plans were to stay on the S.S. *Lugard* and to make trips into the interior some 50 miles down and to disembark at Rhino Camp on the 21st, and motor through the Congo...

On Wednesday evening (by which time we had entirely forgotten that the Prince was even in Africa) we played deck tennis, and at 6.30 knocked off rather exhausted. As we approached the house, two bicycle runners arrived a little breathless. They handed me a very rough scribble from Salmon the Game Ranger, to say that the *Lugard* with the Prince on board had arrived at Laropi, and that he would wait dinner for me (in shirt sleeves) until 8 p.m., that they very much hoped I could get down, and would I bring the cycle runners down as the steamer was leaving at 11 p.m., when it had finished fuelling. There was a vague reference to May, hoping that she might get down too.

We were all rather bewildered, to say nothing of being thrilled to the marrow. It had been raining heavily, and there were ominous clouds about; it was clearly impossible to get down to Laropi and up again that night, in fact the risk of getting stuck on the road in the dark going down was considerable. It therefore meant taking camp kit. There was no invitation for Evelyn, and we could not leave her behind, if May went down, and to add a further difficulty, the two cycles had broken down. May was also very tired and so, after a short discussion, we decided that I should go down alone with the two runners. They changed me, packed me, and helped me with the car in a few minutes which seemed like a few hours, and at 6.45 I started off with a full carload just as darkness was setting in. The road was soft, but my lights were good, and I covered the fifteen miles in thirty-five minutes at the expense of breaking several culverts and ploughing up the surface. I had rather mixed feelings whilst driving down. One had read and heard so many contradictory things about the Prince, and I conjectured what I would find him really to be like. I was rather afraid that I would be disappointed. However before I could come to any conclusions about how I was to behave or what I should talk about, I found myself pulling up at the pier, where I was met by Salmon and a boy with a lamp.

Salmon I knew well before, and he took me straight up on to the deck and introduced me to the Prince, who said, 'I expect you want a drink after driving down that hill; we have been watching your lights for some time. Come and sit down,' which I did while all the others stood up, which rather threw me out of my stride. However he put me at my ease and asked me whether I was at Sandhurst with his brother, and talked about the Army, the K.A.R., and Africa, until dinner was announced.

Knowing that the Prince dislikes being looked at out of curiosity, I was careful not to look at him more closely than I would look at any one else I was talking to, but he gave me one very good searching look which I met with an equally searching one, and I drank in all the little points that I knew I would be expected to recite to May and Evelyn on my return.

He is not noticeably little, but actually is not very tall and of slight build but well proportioned and with a distinctly active look about him. He has most attractive hair and eyes, and I would describe him as very nice looking. He was extremely fit after his strenuous time and was on the top of his form.

He was wearing a pink tennis shirt (as worn in Kenya) but without a tie, a sweater with the Guards' Colours, khaki corduroy shorts, check stockings which were too big for him, and brown shoes...

In the dining room I tried to sneak down to the far end of the table but he called to me to sit beside him. We had a good dinner and he ate and drank sparingly. He joined in the conversation with everyone else, which was general. The conversation veered round to local history, and he turned to me and said, 'Have you by any chance got Baker's books, I hear they are first rate and I have been unable to get a copy anywhere.' I told him I had the ones concerning this part of the world, and would send them through to meet his safari by special runner. He said, 'I would be most awfully grateful if you would, and I will be sure and let you have them back.' He talked about Uncle Sam with much enthusiasm. Salmon let out that I was his Grand Nephew and he was most interested and asked me to put him right as regards the dates of his two expeditions.

After dinner we went and sat on deck and he again made me sit next to him. The conversation was again general, extremely informal, in fact it was difficult at times to remember one was talking to the Prince. He talked about his experiences in Uganda which had evidently been very exciting. He had not tried to shoot anything in Uganda but had merely taken cinematograph pictures of game including charging Rhino and Elephant at very short range. When the conversation veered round Home topics and particularly the dole, he displayed an extraordinary knowledge of the intricacies of the subject. I was quite sorry when at 11 o'clock I took my leave, he was charming and thought-

The Twinings' house at Moyo in Uganda.

St. Lucia: Government House, Castries.

North Borneo: Government House, Jesselton.

Government House, Dar es Salaam.

ful and made the Captain switch the searchlight on to my
car to help me turn round, and sent a nice message up to
May, saying how sorry he was she had not been able to
come down, and hoping she liked the place and her work.

Altogether it was a very pleasant evening and a red
letter day in my life. I came away quite an enthusiast
about the Prince, who struck me as being a most charming,
natural and unaffected man without the vices rumour
sometimes paints him with, but with a healthy and sport-
ing outlook and any amount of pluck. There was no doubt
that he was the dominant personality, or that he would
make his mark anywhere; he appeared to be very intelligent and quick and to be very well informed. It was a rare
opportunity and I was too sorry for words that May and
Evelyn were not with me.

I motored back early next morning and at once sent off
Baker's books which I hope he will enjoy.

At Moyo and in the country of the Madi the Twinings' life
was dominated, as District Officers' lives in remote areas of
East Africa often were, by the presence of certain insects. In
their case the insects were the mosquito, the tsetse-fly and
the locust. The country along the line of the Nile and its
various tributaries was thick with Anopheles, the species of
mosquito that carries malaria. They didn't make the swamps
and the valleys uninhabitable but they were the physical
cause, as much as anything else, of the Madi's idleness and
apathy, and one of the main reasons why it was difficult for
the Twinings to induce them to improve their health and
their economy. The tsetse-fly was an even more serious menace as one species carried human sleeping sickness which was
not only very debilitating but often fatal as well. Another
species caused trypanosomiasis which had a similar effect on
cattle. The result was that large areas of the Madi country
were left untenanted and empty, and it was hard work for
the Administration and the medical and veterinary authorities to stop the tsetse-fly from spreading, and to keep a careful watch on both human beings and cattle to check that
they had not been infected. There were about 25,000 people in
the Madi area and they were all, men, women and children

screened every three months to see if they were clear. It meant a lot of rough travelling, hard work and persistence with little help in the way of money and equipment. But the worst menace of all was the locust. In the middle of 1931 they appeared as hoppers on the east bank of the Nile moving forward slowly in a dense mass about three or four thousand yards across and about forty miles in depth. It was an awe-inspiring sight for anyone; for the Madi who lived on the margins of existence without any reserves of food or cash it was quite terrifying. Locusts exist as hoppers, that is to say, as rudimentary insects without the ability to fly, for several weeks; and it was in that period, in the days before spraying from the air, that people had their only chance of destroying them. Twining had to mobilise the whole population to dig ditches in the path of the locusts and along the edges of the cultivated fields so that the locusts could be driven into them with sticks and branches and there beaten or trampled to death. The sight and the stench were sickening. Millions were killed in this way but it was like trying to stop a river with a bucket and spade. The hoppers came to the bank of the Nile and started to move across the surface of the water. Fish came and birds swarmed to eat them as they went across the sluggish, slow moving water but they made no more impression on the mass of hoppers than the ditches and the sticks. The hoppers moved up the west bank of the river and went on eating every green thing in their path. More ditches were dug and another million or so locusts were killed until one day the hoppers hung themselves up on the bare stalks and branches of the things they had stripped and shed their hopper skins and emerged new and shiny and slippery with wings. When their wings were dry they rose from the ground and flew off to bring famine and disaster to another country and another people. The Madi shrugged and smiled, and waited for the government to bring in food. It came in sacks and tins, and they survived. 'God is merciful,' they cried, 'it only happens once in six or seven years.'

Twining didn't like his office much or the work he was supposed to do in it, and he left most of it in the hands of two Acholi clerks named Paulo Odong and Antonio Opwa 'a

tall and very striking-looking young man with charming manners'. He used them and often overworked them but they
were willing and devoted instruments, and although he was
sometimes inclined to take the credit himself for things that
they had done, he was quick to defend them against criticism
or attack and he did everything in his power to help them
afterwards both in their private troubles and in their careers.
He didn't forget people he liked and who served him well,
and many years later Antonio Opwa and his wife for instance
were invited to stay at Government House at Dar es Salaam.

With his rear so to speak secured by the competence and
loyalty of his subordinates and by the lack of communications with his superiors, Twining spent as much time as possible on tour. And when he toured, he toured in the grand
Samuel Baker manner with an army of retainers and a battery
of equipment—tents, field kitchens, gramophones, guns
(which he rarely used) letters, bicycles, monkeys, goats and
pussy cats. His wife went too with her own array of medical
and hygienic supporters and equipment, and of course there
was Evelyn too. They usually started off at dawn with a cup
of tea and sent the cook off in advance with bacon and eggs
and marmalade so that a proper English breakfast would be
ready for them at nine o'clock after they had progressed
through the countryside in a stately manner on foot, or on
bicycles if the going was good, with a line of porters strung
out behind them. There were chiefs to be talked to, and
exhorted to plant more cotton, grow more trees, collect
more taxes and, if May was there, to dig more latrines. There
were murders to be investigated, missionaries to be out-
flanked and witchcraft cases to be listened to.

On safari at Adgugopi [he addressed a letter to his
mother-in-law]. When we left we were informed that a very
good Chief near Moyo and five of his people had been
poisoned and one had died. The poison was some extract
of a snake and herbs powdered and dangerous when in-
haled. There were no further deaths and we are hunting
for the perpetrator but of course it is difficult to find them.
I have however sent for a witch diviner who is said to be
expert at smelling them out. Following this we heard of

four little boys who had run away from school and whilst crossing our formidable Aigugi river one was drowned. The victim's brother, a R.C. mission teacher, swore that it would never have been drowned if a witch had not cast a spell on the child. Nothing would convince him otherwise —so much for his Christianity. The final straw was when May was sent for to help the 15th and favourite wife of the President of East Madi. Twins were born but the wife died. All the 14 others have been accused of witchcraft. Perhaps [he went on] the cases have come at an opportune moment as they may stimulate my interest in law for my final exam in December. I fear I cannot take much interest in the legal side of my work. It is too cumbersome for a situation when arbitraryness alone is understood. Some people too become so frightfully pedantic having gained a slight knowledge of law, and progress gets held up owing to a wrong legal interpretation or quibble.

The law and particularly examinations in law were a bore and a burden to Twining; and so were languages and examinations in languages. They were a burden and a bore but one couldn't, Twining knew, get anywhere in the administrative service in Uganda without them. Having failed the first of his law examinations and having failed after nearly ten years in East Africa to achieve more than a smattering of Swahili he started to think about a change of scene and occupation.

The other day [he told his mother-in-law half way through his first tour in Uganda] I saw in the *Times* a summary of the Palestine Report and the recommendation that the Intelligence Service should be enlarged. After consideration I put in a wholesale but guarded application to be considered for any vacancy of an Intelligence Appointment in any Dependency under the Colonial Office. I added a rider to the effect that my application was in no way prompted by any dissatisfaction with our present lot ... Of course it may come to nothing and if so no harm is done as we are quite happy here but one's first love is always one's best love and it is a good thing to have irons in the fire to improve one's position.

The answer to this application was discouraging. In those days when gunboats were still in fashion and trouble in the colonies was rare, Intelligence Officers were, in the eyes of the Colonial Office, all right for the Army perhaps but not the sort of things one wanted or needed to have oneself. 'Intelligence Officers?' they said when they saw Twining's application. 'We don't stock the article.' Twining however was determined to get on and if he couldn't do it by moving sideways into intelligence then it would have to be done by moving towards the centre. So he started to tug amiably at strings on various local networks to get himself nearer the seats of power. The first of these moves took him in 1932 into the Provincial Commissioner's office in a dog's-body sort of job which was known generally as P.C.'s pup; and the second a few years later took him to what the cynical or the envious called bottle-washing in the central secretariat.

They were humdrum jobs in humdrum places, first in Kampala and then in Entebbe, the colonial suburbia which he had despised as a soldier in the K.A.R. He didn't enjoy them much but he put up with them because he thought they might do him some good in his career. He was not however in temperament or in talents an office or a subordinate man, and his performances in the provincial office and in the secretariat only served to underline these facts. The result was that he was used more and more on extraneous duties, and it was on these and in particular on one of them that he found an opportunity to make his mark. Most people liked him in Uganda, though there were some men and several senior wives who were not amused by his sense of humour, but few took him very seriously or rated his chances of success very high until he was given an important part to play in arranging the local celebrations for the Coronation of King George the Sixth in 1937. By a combination of geniality, unorthodoxy, good organisation, persuasiveness, and tremendous drive and infectious enthusiasm he made what would otherwise have probably been a somewhat pompous and stereotyped event into something that was both entertaining and impressive. The press reports and the programmes and

the letters of congratulation which Twining received afterwards show clearly how well it was done and what a success
it had been but perhaps the best and certainly the most
evocative account is the one he himself sent to his mother.

Now [he wrote] I must tell you something of our show.
For three or four weeks before I was working night and
day, for it was only by the utmost attention to detail that
we were able to get anywhere.

As far as I was concerned our celebrations began on
Sunday 9th, when the delegation of six Naval Officers
headed by the Captain of H.M.S. *Enterprise*, arrived by air.
On Monday and Tuesday we were busy rehearsing the
various ceremonies with the participants. On Monday the
700 Chiefs, 1500 Boy Scouts, 300 Girl Guides and a small
party of School Children arrived. The Chiefs were either
billeted out or accommodated at Makerere College. The
Boy Scouts built their own Camp and the Guides and
School Children went to various Missions. The Messing
and transport arrangements were very complicated, the
latter necessitating the chartering of special steamers, trains
and buses.

Wednesday began with a tremendous storm which made
it necessary to postpone the parade for an hour. The sun
came out, and at 10 we had the Trooping of the Colour.
The Kabaka (the King) accompanied by his ministers and
Chiefs first arrived in procession. Then the Governor with
a large suite, including the Naval Officers and three other
officers in full dress specially attached. The parade went
off perfectly and the enormous crowd were delighted. (I
had issued 7,000 tickets and provided seats for that number alone.) We then went to Government House where we
held a Levee, which was attended by 530 people. The
Kabaka (who got a K.B.E. in the Coronation Honours)
presented a loyal address, the Governor then held an
Investiture and presented a fine piece of plate to the
K.A.R.

In the evening we had the combined Tattoo and Firework Display which was very much my own personal show
having invented it, trained 2 of the items myself, organised

the whole, built a stand, sold all the tickets myself, and finally directed it, both at the rehearsals and the full performance at which I had loud speakers and was like a B.B.C. announcer. It was all rather fun, but very tiring. We had a good audience, the 1,200 seats were sold out and about 1,000 paid to stand.

Before the Governor arrived we had community singing. The Governor on arrival pressed a button which did nothing actually, but pretended to set off a maroon which in turn set off an enormous bonfire across the lake which in turn set off 50 rockets. The Buglers then sounded Retreat in the dark and then on went the 40 odd spot lights, flood lights and foot lights, and the band and drums beat tattoo and the audience settled down to enjoy themselves. More fireworks followed and then some Boy Scouts did a single stick turn. More fireworks and then some schoolboys did the Parade of the Toy Soldiers. I got the particulars of this from the Duke of York's School at Dover, and adapted it to local conditions. The boys wore white trousers, red tunics and white pill box hats, the officer a bearskin. They were excellent, and fairly brought the house down. Immediately afterwards was the scoop of the evening—H.M.'s speech. Nobody knew we were to have it except me. I had a wireless set with an expert hidden in a room just behind me and he signalled that now was the time. The boys were just off the arena when out blared the National Anthem, followed by the Speech, every word of which could be heard by all present. The Tattoo then proceeded. Fireworks. A musical P.T. Display. Fireworks. A War Dance by 120 warriors in Leopard Skins, Ostrich feathers and Spears and shields. Then from Savage to Soldier, showing the process of turning native warriors into real soldiers. Fireworks. A torchlight march and then to grant finale. All 400 performers formed up and presented arms. The lights went up, and the band played God Save the King, while in the background were firework portraits of the King and Queen, and finally a volley of 100 rockets. The audience who beforehand had been inclined to scoff and had complained at having to pay for their seats were literally staggered. The Governor was astonished and delighted. Everything had gone without a hitch and without any delay and most amazing of all no European had been on the arena the whole evening. So ended a very successful day...

Friday was a very strenuous day. At 10 a.m. we had a parade of 5,000 Boy Scouts, Girl Guides and School Children which went off most successfully, and in the afternoon we had the Ceremony at the High Court which was to have been held on Thursday. This was also my invention and it turned out to be a most dignified ceremony. First the Kabaka arrived in procession and was given his salute of 9 guns. Then the Governor and suite arrived and was met by the Judges in their robes, the Bishops in their pontificals and Executive and Legislative Councils. They all proceeded to the High Court Terrace below, on which were a Guard of Honour of K.A.R., the visiting Chiefs and an audience of 6,000 ... That evening there was a State Ball at Government House. I left in the middle to get a little sleep.

On Saturday it was of course raining, but it cleared up a bit and the Governor drove in state through the decorated streets of Kampala to pay a ceremonial visit to the Kabaka. The streets were lined with troops and there were the usual guards of honour, salutes of guns, investitures, speeches and replies. In the afternoon there was a Pageant of Native History, and in the evening a repeat performance of the Tattoo at Kampala. The ground had been under water in the morning, but with 100 tons of sawdust we managed to dry it out although it was very muddy. Everything went excellently before an audience estimated at 10,000, and all were delighted.

On Sunday at 11 a.m. we had the great Thanksgiving Service in a packed Cathedral. First a Procession of 200 Chiefs in their richly embroidered robes. Then a procession of the 2 Bishops, the Governor and the entourage, the judges and members of Council. The service was magnificent and most inspiring and left a deep impression on all present. So ended our celebrations.

I have been simply inundated with congratulations. I enclose a few for your perusal, which I would like back. It has all been very gratifying and success lay in the preliminary attention to detail, and the whole-hearted support I received from my 120 co-workers.

I could not get to Ceylon but am having a short holiday here and at the Coast.

P.S. Incidentally I got a Coronation Medal which was nice.

Sir Beresford Craddock, who is now an M.P. but who was then working for a cotton company in Uganda, once went to dinner with the Twinings at Kampala. After dinner instead of the usual gossip and dirty jokes and charades, Peter Twining produced, as he often managed to produce, something unexpected. He announced that he was going to give a lecture on crown jewels. The lecture was illustrated with slides and facsimiles of famous diamonds and royal crowns. Craddock found it absolutely fascinating. Exactly when or why Twining got interested in the subject is to some extent a matter of speculation; but by 1937 his interest was sufficiently established and well-known for the Kabaka of Buganda to seek his advice on the choosing of a new crown. He seems to have started when he was at Moyo but it wasn't until he went home on leave in 1932 that he began to take it seriously. He had always been a firm believer, as we know from his letters to his mother when he was in the K.A.R., in the importance of having hobbies to fill up the empty hours and to keep himself from getting stagnant. He had been through butterflies and stamps and match-box tops, and although he continued to collect and buy stamps as an investment, what he was really looking for was something more distinctive, something that other people didn't do. He came on crown jewels by chance through reading a letter in *The Times* about the Holy Crown of St. Stephen. He was intrigued, and as so often happens a casual interest was fed by an apparent series of coincidences, references to the subject in books and papers which would otherwise have gone unnoticed, the discovery that someone he had known for several years belonged to a family of crown jewellers. His interest grew and grew and soon he was conducting a correspondence with museums and chanceries all over Europe: he had realised that if he extended his interest to the crown jewels of the whole of

Europe this would give him the opportunity and the excuse to wander about Europe when he was on leave in search of evidence and material. He paid two fairly lengthy visits to Europe when he went on leave in 1932, and he did further trips in 1935 and 1938. They had a second son in 1934, and Mrs. Twining stayed at home.

Apart from his absorption in crown jewels and his brief period of enthusiasm and glory over the Coronation celebrations the years between 1932 and 1938 were dull and rather barren ones for Peter Twining. He had neither the unobtrusive temperament nor the talent for detachment needed in a secretariat official and his value as a district officer was limited by the fact that he couldn't pass the statutory examinations in Swahili. The result was that he was given the sort of odd jobs that no one else particularly wanted to do. He was film censor for a time and had some difficulty with the owner of one cinema whose experience of censorship up to then had been limited to putting his cap over the projector to cut out the bits that the authorities or the bishops didn't like. He was asked to revive an organisation called the Uganda Literary and Scientific Society, and did it very successfully; and in 1938 he was sent on an attachment to the B.B.C. in London so that he could start up a Government broadcasting service in Uganda when he got back. The trouble was that the authorities in Uganda and the Colonial Office didn't quite know what to do with him. They recognised his energy and his ability and enthusiasm when it came to organising something that he liked; but because of his failings over languages and office work there was really no niche in their normal establishment where he could fit. And he was getting on for forty. The result was a compromise. He was offered a transfer to another territory in a different kind of job. The post which was offered to him eventually was that of Deputy Head of a new Department of Labour in Mauritius. Having himself sought a move, he accepted it with pleasure, and with relief. It wasn't in truth a well paid or particularly impressive post, but as usual Twining was determined to make the most of it and to regard it as a challenge to the potentialities and the sense of purpose which he knew that he possessed. Writing to his mother on the 19th of December, 1938, a few days after he had been offered the Mauritius post, he said

What really pleases me about this Christmas is that a new vista is revealed to me. No longer must I work up an interest in things that do not interest me. No longer have I got to follow a routine. I left the Army because I felt the work was destructive rather than creative. I can look back on my ten years in Uganda with certain achievements. Not worldly achievements but having done something towards the construction of a better life for the people one has to guide. I know that I have contributed something towards their happiness and towards the sort of life which Christ would have had them have.

But this 10 years has been my apprenticeship. Now I am starting an entirely new chapter. The possibilities are limitless. To start with they are, it is true, limited to a comparatively minor problem. A problem of half a million Indians and others living an existence of poverty and squalor, without spiritual or material hope ... The cynics merely look at the material benefits to myself. Certainly they are great and will increase with the success which I cannot fail to achieve. But that is merely by the way and I feel inspired in my new work and if it at times conflicts with the dogmas of the Church it will not conflict with the teachings of Christ which I regard as of far greater importance.

He was of course writing to his mother who was very religious and whom he liked to please. Twining was not a religious man though he went regularly to church: that is to say he went once a month, one Sunday in four or, with a bit of luck and as a sort of bonus, one in five. But he did have a noticeable sense of purpose, a sort of crusading zeal. He liked to do kindnesses and to help other people, particularly people who were underdogs or who were in trouble. It earned him many firm and lasting friendships. Lord Tweedsmuir who was in Uganda then as an Administrative Officer counts Peter Twining as one of half a dozen men to whom for help and kindness he is most indebted.

Twining's sense of purpose in this respect coupled with his resilient and instinctive feeling that he was destined to succeed took him to Mauritius in a mood of hope and optimism that few men at the age of forty would, on the evidence, have dared to have.

6

Mauritius

TWINING SET OFF for Mauritius by sea from Mombasa on the 21st of February, 1939. He went on board in high spirits. He had had a happy grass-widower send-off from Uganda and there were convivial people he knew in Mombasa. The ship was Dutch with standards of service, comfort and cool cleanliness that made one wonder how the Union Castle and the British India ships of those days got any passengers at all. The only trouble was that the ship was so popular that he had, as he told his mother, 'the ignominy of sharing a cabin with another, and large though the cabin may be I have not the slightest intention of doing so. I always have a cabin to myself.' His wife had stayed behind in England with the children. The elder boy John was nine and going to boarding school. The younger boy William was four and due to come out to Mauritius with his mother and a Norland nurse in a month or two.

In Mauritius they say 'God made our island first and Paradise afterwards'. The evening Peter Twining arrived it started to rain. It was still raining when he wrote to his mother a week later. It was some time before he saw anything beautiful or paradisical about Mauritius.

This place [he wrote] is certainly unique—it is quite astounding! Although the island is well equipped with the amenities of civilisation such as tarred roads, an efficient and comfortable railway, water, drains, electric light and cinemas, the atmosphere and mental outlook belong to the eighteenth century. There are some 10,000 pure bred

French, many of whom are the descendants of old noble families who fled during the French Revolution. They are charming, though haughty and aloof, and belong to a world that is no more. There are 250,000 Indian coolies, 200,000 coloured people, many of them half breeds, 10,000 Chinese and 500 British including 200 Tommies.

Port Louis is hot, dirty and the smelliest town I have ever set foot in. Every shop seems to keep dried shark and a selection of coffins as their normal stock in trade . . . Now I must stop. The rain is pouring, literally pouring down. Everything is damp and humid. In fact I expect mildew or even fungi to grow on my forehead and on this paper at any moment. But do not worry. This is a pleasant spot but already I have determined to get a transfer to something better in 3 years time.

When the rain stopped and the sun came out he began to see that Mauritius had a certain charm. Up in the hills 'where the whites live' it was beautiful and cool; it reminded him in parts of Scotland. He had rented a house at a place called Phoenix not quite as high up as Curepipe where most of the well-to-do French lived, but the rainfall was less, and so was the rent. He paid six pounds a month for it. His office was down on the coast at Port Louis. He went down to it every morning, to his surprise and constant amusement, by the nine seven train. The carriages were like boxes on four wheels with a large 1, 2 or 3 painted on each door. 'One would not have been at all surprised,' another observer said some years later, 'to see a sheep knitting at the window of any one of them.' As the train went down the hill past railway stations with names like Quatre Bornes, Beau Bassin and Richelieu the guard made his way along the running board and checked through the windows that the passengers had their tickets. When the train arrived at Port Louis the passengers went off to their offices and shops. Office hours, the story goes, were from ten till four. One first read the local papers to keep abreast of events and gossip (ten to twelve); then there was lunch, taken at a little restaurant around the corner (twelve to three); a few letters to sign, *un coup de telephone,* and then back to the hills by train again before the mosquitoes started to appear.

Port Louis was like the setting for *A Street Car Named Desire*.

> The section is poor ... but it has a certain raffish charm.
> The houses are mostly white-frame, weathered grey, with
> rickety outside stairs and galleries and quaintly ornamen-
> ted gables to the entrances of both ... The sky that shows
> around the dim white building is a peculiarly tender blue
> almost turquoise which invests the scene with a kind of
> lyricism and gracefully attenuates the atmosphere of de-
> cay.

Tennessee Williams was writing of course about the *vieux carré* section of New Orleans but the two places had a lot in common. They were both settled by the French, within three years of one another, early in the eighteenth century; they had both acquired with time a population richly varied in colour as well as race, and they were both touched periodically by hurricanes.

The combination of a French community and a British colonial hierarchy which both tended to look for inspiration to the past, produced a social life in the appropriate season that was somewhat out of date.

> It began on Saturday [Peter Twining told his mother a
> few months after he arrived] with the Races. The next big
> event is the visit of the Navy. This involves an appalling
> programme of events including reviews and balls and din-
> ner parties and picnics and regattas and what not. Then
> the Opera opens shortly. A full-blown company from
> Paris who play in a perfect period piece eighteenth century
> Opera House. Then we have La Chasse, or the shooting
> season, when we go into the mountains and shoot deer ...
> [A month later he was writing with evident relief that] we
> have come to the end of our naval festivities and now we
> are faced with three dinner parties next week and the
> Opera season. We usually creep away early as I cannot
> stand late nights and have to work next day ... The Gar-
> den Party was very funny. Some 1500 people attended in

Ascot frocks and top hats and morning coat. The Labour
Department was democratic in lounge suits but I see I
will have to invest in morning dress as it is worn quite a
lot here. This really is a ridiculous little colony.

Four years later he still hadn't bought a morning coat.
Clothes, apart from uniforms, were according to his philosophy then a waste of money.

Against this background of *passé* charm, nostalgia and in-
dolence, Twining threw himself into his new duties with
what some people thought unnecessary and rather unbecom-
ing zest. His predecessor had had the appropriately archaic
title of Assistant Protector of Immigrants; he had been a
lowly fellow in the official and the private tables of status
and precedence, and people expected this large, seemingly
ponderous, pop-eyed, ex-military fellow Twining and his
quiet, unsmart wife to be content with their station and to
leave things as they had been before. But within a week or
two of his arrival the new Deputy Head of the Labour Department had started on a systematic programme of visits to
all the sugar estates on the island.

I went out on Thursday and Friday [he wrote] inspecting sugar estates. It was quite interesting but I can see
that I will be sick to death of sugar by the time I have
finished. The labour is very Bolshi and is continually being
stirred up by extreme agitators who you would call Com-
munists. As the French owners are almost feudal in outlook the position is very difficult. Our job is to conciliate,
to make the owners see a little sense, and to wean the
workers away from the agitators. It is a very difficult task
as you can imagine.

Making the owners see sense was something Twining soon
discovered he had a flair for. Most of the sugar estates in
Mauritius were then owned by French families with long histories and aristocratic names. Some of them still had silver
candlesticks and pieces of plate marked with the crest of the
East India Company which their ancestors had acquired from
British merchantmen during the palmy days of the pre-

Napoleonic wars when French privateers operating from a French Mauritius took six million pounds' worth of loot from British ships in three years.

Making people with such antecedents 'see sense' in labour matters was clearly something that was best done over a drink or during a five-course lunch. As the men mostly spoke excellent English it didn't fortunately require any knowledge of French except an occasional 'Oh la la' or 'Bong bong' boomed out in a heavy British accent to amuse some of the older ladies whose English was slight but whose influence behind the scenes was, Twining knew, considerable. The French didn't as a rule have much time for the average British official in Mauritius; they found them honest, lacking in imagination, painstaking, aloof, honourable and very dull. Twining's determined amiability, his easy manners, quick wit, and cheerful volubility eroded their reserve and released the warm-heartedness and the generosity which lay underneath the veneer of formal manners and watchful eyes. 'We found him very jolly,' Sir Philippe Raffray said. 'He was interesting to talk to. He had something to say about everything. He had a sense of humour.' The short precise sentences despite the almost perfect English had a distinctive gallic shape and texture. *Interessant et amusant* were the adjectives Raffray used when he spoke in French, 'but of course he was quite unimportant, you understand, when he arrived, we didn't realise that he would turn out so well...' He sipped at his black coffee, and smiled. He was eighty-one. He had been a leading member of the French Mauritian community for forty years. He had been called to the Bar both in London and in Paris in 1912. His clubs, according to *Who's Who*, were the Curepipe and the Athenaeum.

Weaning labour away from the agitators might seem to have called for different qualities and different tactics. It brought Twining into touch for instance for the first time with trade unions.

We had a large meeting of 450 committee members of the local Trades Unions yesterday which Oswell (the Director of Labour) and I addressed. They were all rather drunk to

start with and Oswell had a difficult time but they had
sobered down by the time my turn came and I think the
meeting did a lot of good. I have 40 more to attend during the next 12 weeks.

In another letter he told his mother how he had had to
deal with some demonstrations by the unemployed.

In one case I dispersed them without much difficulty, and
in the other they were a bit obstinate so I put the leaders
in a taxi cab and sent them for a drive to the other end of
the island and the rest went home.

He and Monsieur Anquetil, the poor, wild-eyed, red-tied
leader of the Mauritius Labour party became good drinking
friends. But behind the shared drinks and the back slapping
and cheerful unorthodoxies Twining's feeling for the under-
dog and his sense of purpose burned, the flames fed by the
'appalling poverty' and the conditions under which most of
the Indians and the creoles worked and lived.

I am very involved [he told his mother in June] in trying to organise a youth movement. The conditions here
are deplorable. The youth of the island—and out of
425,000 people 190,000 are 18 years or under—is deterior-
ating. They are undernourished, stunted in growth, idle,
discontented, undisciplined. The difficulties are enormous.
There is a terribly strict colour bar. The French hold aloof
like the stupid aristocrats before the French Revolution.
The Creoles are the descendants of liberated slaves and
the results of mixed relationships. The Indians are backward ... The conditions are really appalling and more
than confirm the disagreeable doctrine I preach that all is
not well with the British Empire. Here, as in the West
Indies and Palestine, in India, in Kenya and Tanganyika
our standards are lower than those in other colonial
territories administered by French, Belgians, Italians and
even Portuguese and certainly the Germans before the
war. It is the same old tale of a British Government self-
satisfied, complacent, ridden with red tape and bureau-

cratic ideas, content to sit still and do nothing but draw
their pay.

Among the reforms which I hope to introduce is one
which will tackle the problems of Youth in a fair and
square way. My proposal is to organise a League of Youth
on a broad and popular basis with an aim of enrolling
50,000 members. It will have a powerful central body
whose function will be to study the problems of youth and
will cater for them. Boy Scouts and Girl Guides, now
strictly reserved for those of white descent, must expand
to cover all communities. There is real need for boys clubs
in all centres. Playing fields and camping grounds must
be provided and equipped. Football and other sports properly organised. Travelling cinemas with educational films
and libraries are required and so are many other things. I
am meeting with a ready response from all communities and
it is interesting to see that whereas within the local population nobody dare take the lead they do not resent the
initiative being taken by an outsider. It is necessary, of
course, to go slow and I do not anticipate that I will be
able to get my organisation going until September. In the
meantime I am laying good foundations and solid ones I
hope.

It was interesting and challenging work in the Labour
Department or if it wasn't it could be made so by incursions
into other peoples' provinces; but what, he asked himself on
his birthday at the end of June, had he actually achieved
and what was it leading to?

My birthday passed uneventfully apart from a little
stocktaking. It is rather remarkable that I am already 40.
Although I have had a wide and varied experience in one
way and another I don't seem to have achieved much and
in retrospect the ten years in the Army seem to be entirely
wasted years, as, if I had gone into the Colonial Service in
1919, I would have been very well placed now. However I
enjoyed those ten years and they were the link which has
enabled me to get into the Colonial Service...

Nor were his immediate prospects very promising. He had been told that if he made a success of his job as number two in the Labour Department he could expect to succeed Oswell when he left but as the months went by Oswell's reluctance to leave Mauritius became more and more apparent and Twining began to wonder whether he would ever go. He had realised by now that the Labour Department wasn't exactly the classic avenue of approach to the higher administrative and proconsular posts to which he still hopefully aspired. He didn't in any case want to stay in the Labour Department for the rest of his career. He had tried to make a go of it and to interest himself in the work but he often found it discouraging, and he sometimes found it dull. He wanted quite genuinely to improve the lot of the poor in Mauritius, to increase their wages and their opportunities and the standards of their living. It was frustrating to find that not only were their leaders and the politicians who espoused their cause often interested as much in improving their own power and material position as in the betterment and welfare of their supporters, but that the workers themselves were curiously reluctant to do what, in Twining's eyes, was clearly good for them. *Larzent bon mes li trop cer* was a phrase often heard from the creole elements of the population.

'Money's nice but it costs too much' was the sort of hippy philosophy that is apt to dampen the enthusiasm of the most zealous do-gooder in the field of human economics. If Twining urged that the descendants of the slaves freed in 1832 should increase their income by working in the fields the answer was that it was too high a price to pay in dirty work and dignity. Since Emancipation the slaves and their descendants in Mauritius had always refused, out of bitter memory and a sort of inverted pride, to touch the soil; they would cut the sugar cane, and load it and feed it to the mills but they wouldn't plant it or weed it or prepare the ground. It was for this reason of course that Indian labourers had been imported to Mauritius. Their wages were low and their living conditions were bad, but they were so much better than the wages and the caves and hovels that they had left behind in India that, despite contracts that said they had to go back to India and offers of assisted passages, they had stayed and stayed and increased and increased until there were more Indians in Mauritius than all the other races put together. The Indians employed on the sugar estates 'for reasons of health, sloth and habit', only worked twenty-four to thirty hours a week. Suggestions that they should earn more money by working longer hours were not well received; longer hours would mean the end of the labour shortages which their leaders used as a lever against the employers and the government. Twining found these attitudes difficult to stomach.

He was happy in Mauritius. He liked the place and most of the people and nine-twelfths of the climate—'for 3 months of the year the humidity and the temperature made it like living in a greenhouse and going to work in a Turkish Bath.' His wife was working as a doctor and was much involved, with her usual intensity and thoroughness, in the Red Cross and child welfare. Their small son William was doing well in education and in health. But Peter Twining's urge to get on was stronger than his own comfort or his domestic sense, and with the war coming up over the horizon he began to wonder how he could use it to move into fields where the grass was greener and the flowers perhaps were brighter and easier to pick.

I have made up my mind [he told his mother] that in the event of war I shall write in to the Government officially and draw attention to the fact that I am an Officer in the Regular Army Reserve of Officers with special experience in Intelligence work—from being a simple spy to writing the military handbook of a Colony and that my 16 years experience in E. Africa may be an asset: that I am willing to serve either in a military or civil capacity as Government may decide so long as they take into consideration how I may be best employed—considering all things—in the fight to save our so-called civilisation. Should there be no war and Oswell is allowed to come back for a year, which he wants and they don't seem to want, I shall demand the pay I would have got if he did not come back, or a transfer to another Colony to a better

job. I like Oswell very much and would like him to come
back but one must look after one's own interests particularly as I was almost promised the job. But I don't think
he will come back as he gets £500 p.a. more than I will
get even if I am made Director and I can do the job quite
as well at less cost. So there!

The war might, it seems, have other marginal advantages
too.

We are in rather a quandary about returning all the
entertainment we owe. We now have about 120 people to
work off. Neither of us cares for dinner parties (we would
have to have at least 15). The standard of entertainment
is very high and therefore it would be very expensive so I
now am thinking of giving a dance on 3rd November and
a firework display. We could then wipe off the lot at one
swoop, we can get the fireworks from the Chinese Chamber
of Commerce, it will be a farewell to the Oswells and an
introduction to Wilkinson who arrives at the end of the
month and to Evelyn who arrives on 28th October. Our
house lends itself to a dance and perhaps by then we will
have it reasonably well equipped. Should war, unhap-
pily, come, we need do nothing!

Peter Twining himself liked entertaining and did it very
well but only if he could control every aspect of it himself—
the guests, whom he sat next to, the menu, the liquor, and
the party games and last but not least the time his guests
went home to bed. Returning hospitality and formal dinner
parties on orthodox lines were not his cup of tea.

The Governor of Mauritius at the outbreak of war in
September 1939 was Sir Bede Clifford. 'He was the younger
son,' Peter Twining told his mother, 'of the Lord Clifford of
Chudleigh, whoever he might be. His wife is very charming,
though American.' Although Sir Bede Clifford had perhaps
obtained his appointment by patronage rather than by pro-
gression he wasn't lacking in gubernatorial qualities. He soon
saw that there was more to Twining than amiability and a
sense of humour, and he wasn't put off, as some people

were, by the bombast and buffoonery. He noted instead his
energy, his sense of tactics, his enterprise and his unorthodox ability, and he knew of course of his experience and
performance in military intelligence. A few days before
war was declared he sent for Twining and put him in charge
of censorship.

Twining was disappointed at first. He had expected something less civilian, something more glamorous, something to
write home about. 'I am at least glad,' he told his mother,
'to be employed although it can hardly be said to be very
exciting.' Within a few weeks the note of apology and diffi-
dence had disappeared. It was 'war work of the highest importance', it was a show of his own, it was above all
a challenge. He still had his labour duties but he quickly
relegated them, like an unsuccessful football team, to a lower
division. He spent two days a week in his departmental
office; the rest of the time, Saturdays and Sundays included,
he devoted with an invigorating drive and an infectious
enthusiasm, to his new war-time duties. He soon found that
there was more to censorship than opening other people's
letters.

The ramifications of censorship as practised by the British
in the last war were not generally known; but certain
aspects of it were sufficiently obvious and well known for
Peter Twining to be able to mention them even in his
letters to his mother. He was very careful what he said.
He was, as one would expect from his experience, a
security-conscious man. He knew, as well as anyone, that
in war-time letters might be intercepted; he knew too that
his mother had many qualities but that reticence wasn't one
of them.

First of all of course there was the censorship of letters and
telegrams, complicated in Mauritius by the existence of a
polyglot community and added to by the arrival in 1941 of
fifteen hundred Jewish refugees who conducted their correspondence in an additional range of languages. Telegrams
presented special difficulties. There were not only the codes
and jargon of business and of everyday commercial deception to be interpreted and understood in French and Hindi
and Chinese but also the ambiguities of abbreviation. LILY

LOST REPUTATION was easy once you knew that Lily was a brand of soap. Telegrams and letters of special interest or awkwardness were put out for Twining to see in piles marked 'military', 'commercial', 'personal' and 'tripe'. Evelyn Du Buisson, who had come out to join them again and who was as usual soon hard at work, was given some of the awkward ones in French. 'One of the most attractive things about working in Mauritius,' she recalls, 'was that one started, so to speak, from scratch. No one told us how to censor letters or deal with intercepted telegrams...' She took the telegrams home with her and worked them out with the help of tea, cigarettes and a French-English dictionary dating, like her French, from her Godolphin schooldays. It makes a nice picture of British intelligence at work.

Then there was the press, 'the 18 nasty, scurrilous little rags called newspapers'. 'This,' Twining explained, 'was a very delicate task but I put them all on their honour and asked them to seek advice.' There was the cinema and several other things. The border-lines between stopping people doing what they shouldn't and making them do what they should are sometimes indeterminate, particularly in time of war, and as Mauritius was a small place with a limited supply of experienced officials, Twining soon found himself doing a lot of things that weren't normally in the province of a censor.

He took over broadcasting and a local version of the Ministry of Information; and there were 'lectures and many other things to arrange and I have to write some of the Governor's speeches'. Explaining the need for rationing meat and rice and petrol and the other goods that had to be imported, and bringing the war home generally to the people of Mauritius was, it seems, hard work. 'They are prepared to do anything to help win the war except fight, to allow it to cost them anything or to suffer any discomfort.' He found the attitude of the French whom he had liked so much, difficult to understand. They took a very detached view of events in Europe and their somewhat cool estimates of Britain's contributions both to the causes of the war and to its early prosecution came as a surprise to him. He did his best, with his limited resources, to put them right but at official func-

tions and in the cinema one still heard the less than enthusiastic drag of gallic feet as they stood up, and shrugged
'Alors, le God Save...' But Twining was too busy, too much
in love with the figures of flesh and blood and curves that he
had created from the Defence Scheme skeletons of censorship and information, to hear. He had his own kingdom at
last, he was helping to win the war. He blossomed like a
bulb that, after a long winter under the ground, breaks
through to the surface and feels the impact of the sun and
of the air. The war was his opportunity, and he took it with
both hands and both feet.

One of the secrets of Twining's success in war-time
Mauritius was the way he used his staff. By the end of
1939 he had sixteen people working for him in censorship
and information. Two of them, he proudly told his mother,
were 'Doctors of Philosophy'. By 1943 he had several hundred largely made up with what were known in Mauritius,
and even in the cold, but not by any means sexless, corridors
of the Colonial Office, as 'Twining's Twitties'. He may not
have succeeded in making the war effort patriotic for all the
French community in Mauritius but for some of them at least
he made it fashionable. Baudelaire may have made the lan-
guid beauty of Mauritian girls poetic but it was Peter Twining who made them useful. They flocked to his offices to
be enrolled as interpreters, readers, clerks and typists, and
those who couldn't get in or who preferred to be more lady-
like went and rolled bandages for the Red Cross under Mrs.
Twining. Their parents' sympathies were mostly with the
point d'appui of Pétain; but the daughters thought that the
British in general and *les Twinings* in particular were wonderful.

'I worked eighteen hours a day for him,' one of the Ph. D.s
on Twining's staff says, 'and I still wonder why I did.' He
was a bully, a braggart and a showman, some thought, but
there was nothing they wouldn't do for him. He made them
feel as if they belonged to a *corps d'élite*; in the end the
most modest found it difficult not to boast that they worked
for him. He used them, he often took the credit himself for
what they did and for their ideas, but he defended them if
need be with everything he had, and he was always ready to

take the blame if things went wrong. He had the quality too of leaving people to get on with their jobs, to make them feel that he trusted them. 'I'll leave things now,' he would say with a boom and a gesture as he went out for a mid-morning gin, 'in your capable hands.' He told his mother that he had 'a good staff of very keen and willing subordinates. Now that we have got a little better organised I can decentralise, for I am a great believer in distributing work and merely guiding it.' He wasn't lazy. He worked hours as long and as unorthodox as anyone. Many, though not all, of the ideas and the ingenuities were his. He had a fertile rather than a constructive brain, and though several of his ideas were impracticable and some of his ingenuities were expensive follies his inventiveness and his unpredictability kept people on their toes and guessing. They never knew when the ideas would come to him. They would often be rung up in the middle of the night or the early hours of the morning. 'Please get in a taxi-meter cab. I have a matter of the greatest importance to discuss with you.' He could be unreasonable and infuriating; but whatever methods he employed and whatever the results he achieved something was always happening when Twining was about. He reminded one man who worked for him at this time of a Wimshurst machine which, as those who used one in the physics laboratory at school will remember, combined a maximum of dramatic and unpredictable effect with a minimum of preparation and effort.

Oswell went at last on promotion to a better post in Malaya. Although Twining took over his duties then, it was four months before he was officially appointed Director and got the pay. His mother was worried about the delay, 'but one has to be patient,' he explained, 'when dealing with the Colonial Office machine which works slowly'. Now that he had set up his censorship and information arrangements, and the war was in a state of suspended animation as far as Mauritius was concerned, Twining was able to concentrate again, for a time, on his less exciting labour duties.

I am very preoccupied with my social insurance schemes.

It is an intricate subject about which I know nothing but fortunately my committee not only know nothing too but are like a lot of docile sheep. So I am knocking up a couple of practical schemes to cover Old Age Pensions and Health Insurance. But whether the experts will think them workable is quite another matter. I am submitting to Government a tremendous long-range policy to dispose of our surplus population by various means, including land settlement and emigration. Again I start in blissful ignorance but there is so much general apathy that my ideas seem to take on with the powers that be.

It was not only the powers that be who noticed them. Sir Seewoosagur Ramgoolam, the present Prime Minister of Mauritius, remembers that during his term of office as Labour Commissioner, Twining 'initiated many social reforms which helped to improve relations between employers and employees in this country'.

He may not have been a very professional Director of Labour or have understood the complexities of social insurance legislation but there were others who did, just as there were others who could master the sophisticated techniques and languages of censorship and information. What mattered was that Twining was emerging as a sort of directorial Pooh-Bah, a man who could get things done. He was put temporarily in charge of the Red Cross, and in March he was made chairman of a committee of heads of departments, whose task was to draw up an overall development plan for the island under a brave new world concept of colonial policy involving the use of British taxpayers' money for the development and welfare of our hitherto somewhat neglected overseas territories. It was an important and exacting job ('The heads of departments cause me more trouble than the schemes') and, for one who had only just been made a head of a department himself, a considerable feather in his cap. It was not surprising that a year after his arrival in Mauritius he should take stock of his position and come to a not unpromising conclusion.

It has been a very eventful twelve months and a very in-

teresting one. On the whole we like Mauritius. It is pleasant
enough in many ways and there are a lot of nice people.
The work is most interesting. I think the two most trying
things are that it is very remote and that the island is too
small and therefore life is too restricted.

I certainly would not like to be here for long. Of course
owing to the war one cannot make plans. I am ready to go
in a military capacity at any time but they don't seem to
want one or rather they say one's civil work is more important. In many ways I suppose it is. At any rate I am
planning as if the war will not interfere with normal plans.
This year is going to be enormously important for me.
Apart from initiating a very large number of schemes and
reforms, I am on two special jobs which are bound to
attract attention. The first is the social insurance committee and the second is that the Acting Governor has called
me in as a sort of confidential adviser to formulate a policy
of development in connection with the new Colonial Policy
recently announced. This work will take about 18 months
preparation and I then hope to go on leave visiting India
and Malaya en route, and returning via Canada. Once home
I shall move heaven and earth to get a transfer elsewhere.
If I can make a success of these two tasks I think my future
is assured.

Peter Twining was now nearly forty-one. He weighed between fourteen and fifteen stone. He had a full face, a double
chin and a formidable figure. He was a man of considerable
capacity but no one ever saw him the worse for liquor. He
had a deep booming voice, a loud laugh and a disconcerting
sense of humour, disconcerting, and sometimes harsh, because it was often based on the apposition of opposites and
inconsistencies, on laughter and sadness, beer and Bach, sex
and impotence. 'He was a mountebank,' one of his admirers,
a woman, said of him at this time, 'a showman, selling himself, playing to the gallery, if you like, but from centre stage.
He was determined to take centre stage, and worked to that
end beneath all his buffoonery. He had the necessary
eccentricities to become great ... "Let's have a party", he
would say and what a party he gave. Noise was the chief

ingredient and Chicken Feed his favourite game. Two packs
of cards, one scattered over a large table, the others in the
starter's hand. "Ace of spades" shouted the mob and fell
upon the card with fiendish yells. Only one finger was allowed
to pull the card away. It was bedlam and, like a great genie
out of a bottle, Twining rose and roared and pounced on
the card; by sheer weight he forced the other fingers off,
twisted them, squashed them, edging the card towards his
end of the table. Then he would make a grab and put it in his
pocket and refuse to give it up. He would snatch anyone
else's spoil out of their hand or from under their seat or
down the front of their dress, anywhere where they had put
it to be safe. He always won...'
Peter Twining had always since he was a boy been able
to make people like him. In Mauritius they began perhaps
for the first time to respect him, to admire him and to love
him. He wasn't a physically attractive man but there were
many people there of both sexes who worked to the bone for
him and who would have done almost anything to please
him. They liked him as much for his faults as his virtues,
and they readily forgave his imperfections. No one could bear
him malice, 'he was too like a baby'. Under the hard, hearty
exterior, he still had that soft centre, a vulnerability and a
boyishness which appealed to the mothering instinct in most
women, and elicited a similar, more complex response from
many men. His own sensitivity and response to music was
part of this dichotomy in his character. Someone who was
in Mauritius then recalls how 'Twining stood on the steps of
the glassed-in verandah of their little white wooden house in
Phoenix and listened while the Du Buisson flooded him with
glorious symphonies and sonatas from the room behind.'
It was Bach now as well as opera, Beethoven and Brahms,
and requiems by anyone. No one spoke when the gramophone was playing but everyone who was there could see
the range of emotions on Peter Twining's face as the music
touched him or warmed him or hurt him and exposed one
by one the complexities of his feelings and his nature. Cousin
Evelyn was in fact never allowed to work the gramophone.
This was something Twining always did himself but she
was sometimes invited to choose the records. She would try

to meet his mood and taste. She often made mistakes: it wasn't always easy to tell whether those long brooding silences called for Schubert or Sibelius, or when ideas were better brought to quick gestation by Wagner or by Rachmaninov. Much of Twining's thinking was done to music, and it was the food for him not so much of love as of imagination and ambition.

On Saturday mornings before lunch another ritual took place. A servant, summoned in a booming voice, 'entered grinning toothily, dark eyes dancing. "Beer," came the peremptory roar, "large beer, small beer." Back came Mabeeyeh with a bottle of beer and two glass beer-mugs, one large-sized mug and one tiny miniature mug. Twining and his small pink and white son solemnly drank their beer on the sunny verandah and conversed.' So an observer remembers. 'May did not drink with them. She sat and watched her two men with a kind of frustrated, inarticulate affection.'

In August of 1940 Twining went off on a visit to South Africa. The fall of France and the need to choose between the opposite philosophies of de Gaulle and Pétain was a traumatic experience not only for the French in Mauritius but for the people in the French islands and territories in and around the Indian Ocean, Madagascar, Réunion, the enclaves in India and Indo-China. This and Mauritius's geographic situation in the middle of this area presented both problems and opportunities to Twining's censorship and information services. He began again to spend more and more time on this side of his responsibilities and less and less on labour and other matters. His trip to South Africa was the first of several other trips which took him in the course of the next three years to other parts of Africa, to the Middle East, to India, Burma and Singapore, to Madagascar, and to London. He tried several times to get back to the Worcesters or to obtain some other military and uniformed appointment but as his civilian war-time duties in Mauritius became more and more important so his chances of being released from them got less and less.

It seems unlikely [he told his mother at the end of 1940] that I shall go to East Africa [for a possible military intelligence job] because even if I am required it is most unlikely that they would release me here as there is no one to replace me. I would have liked to have gone back to the Army for the war but as I am doing three war jobs here and some of my work may produce results I feel I am doing my bit.

His sense of doing his bit in a place which he was uncomfortably aware had been barely touched by the dangers and discomforts that people in Britain like his mother suffered was temporarily bolstered a little by the hazards of a cyclone.

We have been all hermetically sealed in our rooms with only candles as light, with the hurricane shutters up and the roof leaking like a sieve. It certainly has rained—12 inches in 18 hours—which has quite put the last 3 weeks rain—a mere 42 inches—out of the picture. The wind is terrific, fairly constant at 70 miles an hour and some gusts 100 miles an hour or so. Of course all the trees fell down. The electric cables and telephone wires are down, the trains can't run; in fact everything is at a standstill, and the day has been proclaimed a public holiday or a *dies non*. The wooden houses definitely sway in the wind but I have not seen any of the roofs blowing about yet. Altogether it has been and is still being an interesting experience although not too comfortable. And of course I cannot get into my office today. It is said that it will blow itself off the island by tonight. I certainly hope so for I do not care for the extreme behaviour of the elements such as floods, gales, earthquakes and volcano eruptions. One feels so helpless.

Pearl Harbor and the rapid advance of the Japanese suddenly put Mauritius into an exposed and vulnerable situation which a diminished British Navy based on Ceylon and Mombasa was in no position to protect. In addition to his other duties Twining now found himself involved not only in preparations to defend the island but in making plans to maintain contact and sources of information if the Japanese took and occupied it. He naturally didn't tell his mother about this. Apart from the element of secrecy he didn't want to alarm her; and some of his stratagems which included using the whores of Port Louis for extra curricular intelligence purposes were in any case hardly suitable for an elderly lady now living in a convent. There were indeed many things which Peter Twining didn't tell his mother. He had got himself involved by this time in a number of activities which could also be described as extra curricular. He had dealings with the Ministry of Economic Warfare, and it was contact with the Foreign Office perhaps rather than his continued preoccupation with crown jewels that made some people think that he was getting in looks and style more and more like the late King Carol of Rumania.

With all this activity, and with the island now, in a sense, in the front line of the war, he was irritated at the constant insinuations in letters from people in England that life in Mauritius was soft and easy.

I am very much amused [he told his mother] at the general impression I gather from all our letters from home that we live a peaceful, comfortable life, remote from the war and its worries, untouched in fact by world events, on a romantic island populated by naked savages and that I romp round on luxurious pleasure trips, usually hinted at being entirely unnecessary and at best dealing with labour matters. Actually we have, despite our remoteness, been very closely concerned with the war since 3rd September, 1939 (I since 21st August, 1939). It is true that we have not yet been bombarded from the sea or air or invaded. That may be a treat to come, but from early morning till late at night we are at it and 90% of the work is war work. What do we do?

May is Assistant Island Director of the British Red Cross and an M.O. of one detachment. She organises, inspects, directs, lectures, trains and heavens knows what not. The house is continually full of her cronies making bandages and other such things. She started and runs a naval canteen. She is secretary and M.O. of the Child Welfare Society and in her spare time does various other things.

Self. I have a busy Labour Department but with good

luck and I hope a wise policy we have so far avoided any labour troubles. I have a Poor Law Department with 17,000 paupers. We have recruited thousands of highly skilled artisans and pioneers for Egypt. I am Chief Censor which has its own peculiar problems. I am Information Officer and as such am in charge of press censorship (17 scurrilous newspapers), cinemas (we have 49 on the island) and propaganda generally. I am in charge of broadcasting and our battery of transmitters broadcasts 14 hours of programmes a day and let me tell you some are first class programmes listened to regularly as far afield as Syria. We broadcast in four languages. I am Free French liaison officer, and I do a lot of other things which can only be told after the war but some are of very much wider importance than mere Mauritius. And Evelyn [he added] is a most intelligent hard working and invaluable assistant.

This, as he admitted in a later letter, was an irritable outburst. He didn't always take himself so seriously. He once startled a meeting called to discuss plans to deal with a possible Japanese invasion by opening the proceedings with 'Gentlemen, let us prepare to sell our lives as cheaply as possible'.

Sir Bede Clifford had left Mauritius in 1942 and had been replaced by a more orthodox and less aristocratic governor. Twining was sorry to see him go. It was Clifford who had given him his opportunity, and it was from the patrician, debonair Clifford that he had learnt his first lessons in the mystique of pomp without pomposity. Twining had few of the Hon. Sir Bede Clifford's natural and inherited advantages, but he soon came to realise, by careful observation of his contemporaries, that the lack of these advantages wasn't necessarily a bar to the persistent and the ambitious.

In 1943 Twining was made a C.M.G. for his work in Mauritius and early in 1944 he was appointed Administrator of the West Indian island of St. Lucia. He was nearly forty-five. Before the war it was an appointment which would at that age have consigned him to a pleasant but almost certain obscurity; now, with the British Government stirred by riots in the West Indies into a re-assessment of its responsibilities, it was the threshold to almost certain success. 'It is quite a good job,' he told his mother, 'of the large frog in a small pond variety.' In his next letter he added that 'the Colonial office were very pressing about my accepting and made four references to it being a stepping stone to higher things, so it looks as though for the next sixteen years I may find myself living in Government Houses and sitting on red plush.'

In May of 1944 he left for St. Lucia by air by a very roundabout route. Travelling in war time was difficult, and he had to leave his wife and family, and most of his luggage behind. He set off for his first Government House with two suitcases and a crumpled trilby hat. He had a haircut on the way, somewhere, as one had to say in 1944, in South America.

7

St. Lucia

TO ANYONE ARRIVING for the first time during the war St. Lucia must have looked an enchanting place. A small, unspoilt tropical island with spectacular peaks, lush green hills and valleys rich with sugar cane and breadfruit trees and mangoes: a coastline made up of landlocked bays, of palms and empty yellow beaches washed by seas of every shade of blue. Even the town and the country villages looked picturesque. That at any rate was what the island looked like to the new Administrator when he arrived by air from Trinidad early on a sunny Sunday morning in June of 1944. He was full of expectation and self-confidence. He had an island of his own to administer, and his foot firmly planted at last on the ladder of success. To the people who actually lived on St. Lucia however the island didn't seem quite so enchanting, nor did the prospects look so promising.

Things hadn't gone well for the people of St. Lucia for some time. They had been bad enough before the war with low wages and a lot of unemployment. The war had made things worse. The price of the goods they imported went up and there weren't any ships to spare to take away their sugar. Their port which used to be busy with steamers and schooners carrying cargo or coming in for coal was empty: it hadn't helped its reputation when a German submarine sneaked in in 1942 and sunk two ships alongside in their berths. Even the two American bases in the island, which had been leased out by the British Government in part payment for a consignment of destroyers and which had promised so much at first in the way of employment, had discharged much of their

local labour. There were no tourists or rich visitors. There
had been talk of British money to help with economic development and social services but somehow or other little
appeared to those who lived there to have actually been
done. The island government spent little enough as it was on
roads and houses and schools but even so it spent more than
it had, and the price of the British subsidy which balanced
its budget was the frustrations and indignities of Treasury
control. There was an atmosphere of apathy and depression
and hopelessness on the island. There seemed nothing to
look forward to, not even, it seemed on the 4th of June
1944, to any end to the war.

It was a Sunday though and the people of St. Lucia
thought they might as well go and have a look at the new
gentleman the King had sent to live in Government House.
Nothing much happened on the island and there wasn't anything else to do. They didn't expect much; and their first impression of Mr. Twining matched their lack of expectation.
They saw a large, fat, unprepossessing man step out of the
launch which had brought him across the bay from the air-
strip to the place on the waterfront where governors and
administrators and visiting film stars used to land in peace-
time from their ships. The officials and the local dignitaries
who were there to meet him noted his creased tropical suit
and his rumpled and not particularly new trilby hat. They
themselves were dressed in freshly laundered uniforms or in
their smartest and newest clothes; even the poorest in the
crowd were cleanly dressed for church. They watched in
silence as Mr. Twining started to inspect the usual guards of
honour of police and Boy Scouts and Girl Guides. And in the
silence everybody heard the whispered comment in the patois
which everyone on the island, except the English, spoke
among themselves and understood.

'Qui gros cochon?' The woman who said it was loud and
large and blowsy, and dressed in the sort of clashing colours,
scarlet and magenta and royal blue that only people with
dark skins can wear. She was a well-known character with a
well-known past. Everyone called her Gros Ida. Her whisp-
ers were notoriously audible and her language, even for St.
Lucia which had a rich inheritance from its colourful and

cosmopolitan past of invective and obscenity, noticeably lush.
'Who the hell,' one can roughly translate the meaning of her
words and her inflexion, 'is that fat pig?'

It had seemed quiet, someone who was there told me in
his slow deep West Indian voice, when Twining started to
inspect the guards but it was nothing to the silence which
fell on the crowd when they heard Gros Ida's whispered
words. They watched the new Administrator with even
greater care and even greater expectation. Had he heard the
words, they wondered; and if he had, had he understood
them? And if he had, what would he do?

Twining continued his inspection. He knew about guards
of honour. He hadn't been a Regular soldier for nothing.
He knew what to do, what to look for, what to say and how
much time to take. He finished his inspection with measured
pace and returned without hurry to his saluting base. He
waited there without movement or expression on his face
until the last Present and the last bars of 'God Save the King'.
Then he turned to a corporal of police who was standing
near. In a deep booming voice that everyone could hear he
said, 'Who is that woman?' The corporal said she was just a
woman, no one in particular. Twining said, 'Call her here.'
Gros Ida was called and came. She had in her hand a bunch
of bedraggled flowers which she had picked from someone
else's garden on her way to the ceremony. Twining said,
'Who are you?'

Gros Ida replied, 'I'm Gros Ida.' She spoke in English.
Every St. Lucian spoke English but most spoke it less fluently
than the old French patois. St. Lucia had changed hands
seven times before the British captured it from the French
for the last time in 1803, but most of the villages and the
hills and the coves were still known by their French names
and most of the people still preferred to use the old language
among themselves. It was like the patois they used in French
Martinique, and not unlike, as it happened, the patois they
spoke in Mauritius too. Gros Ida held out her bunch of
flowers and smiled. Twining didn't smile, and gradually fat
Ida's smile disappeared. Twining stared at her for some time
before he spoke. When he spoke the words came out very
slowly partly because he spoke in French, which was always

hard work for him, and partly because he wanted everyone to hear.

'Bon jour,' he said. 'C'est pas un gros cochon, mais...' he paused, '...mais un gros elephant.' He smiled. Gros Ida's smile gradually returned until she was smiling it seemed not only with her mouth and eyes but with her gold earrings and with her fat happy hands and feet. The silence went out of the assembled dignitaries and the crowd like air out of a balloon. Everybody smiled and started to relax. But Twining hadn't finished with them yet. He had been given his opportunity and taken it, and he didn't intend to waste an ounce of it.

'What do you do?' he asked.

Gros Ida said that she sold fruit and vegetables to ships and to sailors in the port.

'Just the person I want. I'm on my own. My wife's not here. I'll have to order things for Government House. Come and see me there. Tomorrow, at ten o'clock.'

Peter Twining bought fruit and vegetables from Gros Ida throughout the time he was in St. Lucia. And every year at the annual flower festival of La Rose, Gros Ida went up to Government House with her chosen band to sing and dance and drink, so long that is to say, as her own special patron was there to sing with her and drink with her and slap her ample bottom. There was nothing she wouldn't do for him after that. And it wasn't only Gros Ida's laughter and affection and admiration that Peter Twining won that day.

The following day he was officially sworn-in as Administrator of St. Lucia. The speeches of welcome were formal and guarded, 'long catalogues', he told his mother in his second letter home 'of their grievances and insoluble problems'. His own reply was short, frank and informal. 'It is my intention,' he told the assemblage of Honourable Members (all members of colonial Legislatures were Honourable), officials, clergy and general public, 'to learn as much about the people as I can, and to study the problems, some of which the honourable member has mentioned, which exist in this colony. I have much to learn and I hope that none of you honourable members will be backward in trying to teach me.

I hope that with the benefit of your advice and stimulus of your criticism I will be guided aright. I will always try and be accessible to honourable members at any time and I hope that by friendly and informal discussions we will be able to get down to the real roots of the problems which require solution. I am not much of a "paper official"—I prefer action, and I hope to get some decisions made so that we can get on with the job; and so honourable members, with the help of Almighty God and your support, I trust that my actions will be for the benefit and prosperity of the people during the coming years. I thank you for your kind welcome.' When the ceremony was over and 'His Honour', to quote the local newspaper, 'had withdrawn', he invited all the elected members up to his house for a drink. 'This,' he told his mother, 'went down very well, particularly,' he added with a pardonable touch of relish, 'as it was something my predecessor didn't seem to have done.'

The date was the 5th of June, 1944. Next day came the news of the Allied landings in Normandy. It was a happy coincidence, and indeed there were some in St. Lucia who, when they saw their new Administrator's enigmatic smile, even wondered if it was entirely accidental. Perhaps, they thought, it was a portent that now at last things would start to happen.

And happen they certainly did. There were about 75,000 people in St. Lucia then, in an island about the size of the Isle of Man. Within a few weeks Twining had visited almost every part of it, and had seen or been seen by a large part of the population. This may not sound very remarkable but in fact it was, both in the fact of his doing it and in the way he did it. Many of the country roads were sketchy and some of them were very steep. No one in St. Lucia could remember any Administrator in St. Lucia going into so many country villages. In one place an old man told Twining that the last His Honour to come there passed through on his way to a picnic and stopped to use the latrine. When his predecessors had travelled they had usually done so in one car with a single aide or an official. Twining went in a cavalcade of cars and he took a host of satellites with him—the Education Officer, the Labour Commissioner, the Colonial

Engineer, the Agricultural Superintendent, the Senior Medical Officer and the Commissioner of Police. Some of them, it
was said, hadn't left their offices in the capital for years.
Twining smiled and shook a lot of hands. He scowled at
people and things he didn't like. He talked a lot, as he usually
did; but he also listened.

The first thing he did when he got back was to sack most

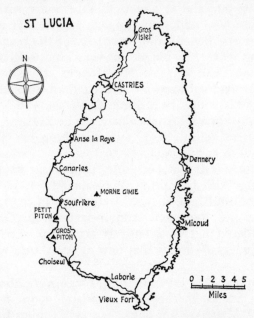

ST LUCIA

of the *maîtres de ville*, the Government-appointed wardens
in charge of the country areas, and replace them with younger
and more active men. Then he summoned all the heads of
the Government departments concerned with economic and
social development and told them to prepare plans to spend
about a million pounds of public money. Some money had
in fact been promised on principle by the British Government for some time and various schemes had been submitted
but Twining somehow managed to produce it as something
new and unexpected like a rabbit out of a hat. As the British
taxpayer was still bearing the burden of the war and the
annual budget of St. Lucia was only about £200,000, a million pounds was a rabbit of some size. He gave the heads of

departments thirty days to prepare their plans. They didn't like it much, and some complained, but on everybody else in the island of St. Lucia both the task and the time limit made a considerable impression.

The island had had a form of democratic government for some years but for various reasons the local elected members had got into the habit of thinking that the only part they had to play in the business of government was to oppose and criticise.

Twining made it clear from the beginning that he expected them to play a more constructive part not only in the central Government but in their own constituencies. They soon found themselves, to their surprise, sitting on Town and Village Improvement Committees which was something few of them had done before. Meetings of councils and committees suddenly started taking place more frequently. It's your own country, he told them in effect, and one day you'll be running it. It's time you started getting used to the idea of doing things on your own and in your own way. He didn't like it much, it's true, if their way turned out to be different from his own. He was sure, sometimes passionately sure, that he knew what was good for them but when things got difficult he usually adjourned the meeting and invited everybody for a drink. He usually got his own way in the end though it sometimes cost him a lot of liquor. There were some elected members in St. Lucia it was rumoured, who were not above opposing him, once they knew his habits, just to get a drink.

As if this wasn't enough he was writing to his mother on the 18th of June, two weeks after his arrival, to say that he

had inspected the excellent hospital, the lunatic asylum, a dispensary, the police and prison, the military garrison and its buildings. I have opened a factory and attended a lecture on education, entertained the Americans and given two 'at homes' to forty and sixty people respectively. I have dissolved the Legislature and ordered a general election . . .

All this instant activity and bonhomie had a traumatic effect on the people of St. Lucia. They had never experienced anything quite like it before. They were themselves for the most part easy-going, amiable, lackadaisical people. They were an amalgam of Carib invaders from South America, West African slaves, Spanish, French and British sailors and soldiers, adventurers and settlers. They had inherited and absorbed something from each of them with the result that they hadn't quite managed to achieve an identity and cohesion of their own. They spoke a kind of French and were passionately addicted to cricket; most of them went to Mass on Sundays in the Catholic churches and also practised forms of ancestral worship which involved blood sacrifices. They kept Empire Day and Boxing Day but it was the ancient flower festivals of La Rose and La Marguerite that they really looked forward to. They didn't know who they were exactly or to what culture they belonged. Martinique was unmistakably French and Barbados was unmistakably British. St. Lucia was neither; it made the people feel less than their neighbours in achievement and prospects, and in self-confidence. Nicholas Taylor, now an amiably self-confident West Indian diplomat in London, was a callow clerk in St. Lucia when Twining arrived and remembers clearly the immediate effect which he had on people there. They suddenly felt that after all things might happen in their poor neglected island, and that they themselves might be given a chance at last to show what they could do.

If Twining made a lively impression on St. Lucia, St. Lucia also made a lively impression on him. His letters to his mother and his wife, who was still in Mauritius waiting for a ship, were full of the island's natural beauty although one suspects from his frequent references to precipices and hairpin bends that when he was being driven along the narrow St. Lucian roads his mind wasn't always on the view. He was also very taken with the people. There was virtually no colour bar in St. Lucia. After the Army and Uganda and Mauritius this was new to him. He found everyone 'friendly and kind' and 'very likeable', although to his mother, brought up as he well knew on somewhat old-fashioned Baker theories about the lesser breeds, he felt it necessary to add the rider that 'the well-to-do coloured people are charming, if handled properly'. He seems to have adjusted himself quickly to this new environment, and soon he was revelling in the colourful mixture of his guests at the noisy and often boisterous dinners, dances, birthday parties and costume balls which he gave at Government House.

It was of course his first Government House. It was not a beautiful building and it was in need of a coat of paint, as Government Houses in small colonial territories often were, but it was his own to survey, to re-arrange, to entertain in and to write home about. It was, he wrote

really very well furnished and equipped. Comfortable beds, good linen and plenty of it, a lot of rather heavy silver, good crockery with the royal crest, good glass, a grand piano, a large frigidaire which makes ice and a radio which doesn't work.

The new occupant made a number of changes not only to the décor but to the routine of the house as well, and someone described it in Twining's time as being half vice-regal lodge and half old English pub. He himself described it in a letter to his mother, whom he not unnaturally wanted to impress, as being 'largish, well-built of stone and really quite commodious'. To his wife, who would of course one day come out and see it for herself, he said it was 'ugly, but solidly built in a Victorian style'. He was however very pleased both with the quantity and, to begin with, the quality of the domestic staff.

For staff [he told his mother] I have an exceedingly competent housekeeper, a coloured lady, Mrs. Perryman by name, the best cook in the island, who has sprained her ankle and is therefore off duty: a female butler whom I propose to replace by a male: an excellent chamber maid who has been here for years: a temporary maid, a washerwoman and a female messenger. Wages are 30/- to 40/- a month without food which is cheaper than Mauritius. Then there are two police orderlies, Joseph who is a Grenada man who is to be my chauffeur when my car comes, and Bruno who is merely decorative. I don't quite know what they do but I suppose they look after the place.

They are quite smart and delightful and put the flag up in the morning and pull it down in the evening with a ceremonious dignity. Then there are two rather elderly gardeners paid for by the Government and six or eight prisoners who come with a warder every day and clean the silver and the brass and the shoes, and chop the firewood and pump the water and sweep the grounds and scrub the back premises and lounge about generally. That I think gives you a brief outline of my household affairs and they are not too bad when one takes everything into consideration.

It wasn't for long that police orderly Bruno remained merely decorative. Bit by bit, he became an important almost an indispensable part of Twining's life. He was always on hand with a smile or a word of advice or a drink to keep master in a good humour or on an even keel. His shining dark face and spotless white uniform followed the new Administrator wherever he went, ready to serve and to respond to his every move and every mood. A special post was created for him on the establishment of Government House and he was made a corporal. Not for the first time, nor the last, Twining showed an unusual capacity for earning the devotion of those who served him well and for not forgetting that they had. Heroes are heroes, they say, to everyone except their valets but in Twining's case they became the most ardent and sincere of his admirers. Some took to the bottle and some it seems grew a little arrogant in their attitude to others but Twining's ability to gain and keep their affection and their loyalty was a talent which many envied and few could equal.

It was not everyone at Government House who served him or pleased him so well. By the end of the year he was writing to his wife (she had managed to get to England by then from Mauritius but there was little prospect apparently of any passage being available to St. Lucia) that he

had no rows with the maids for three weeks which is a pity. I detest them all and Mrs. P. is too weak. She is however doing sterling service in preventing me from

being robbed. The first month we were alleged to have
consumed 27 lbs. of butter, 65 lbs. of salt and 31 lbs. of
bacon. I keep an eagle eye on Mrs. P. and she on the
maids and last month we consumed 1½ lbs. butter, 1 lb.
salt, and 2 lbs. bacon. The cook who weighs 27 stone is
furious that she cannot keep up her weight at my expense
and sulks and I give her hell every time I see her. Nevertheless she is the best cook in the island. It seems to be
the habit for G.H. servants to think they can get away with
it. In Trinidad they told me that the monthly grocery bill
was £180–£200. While in Barbados Lady Bushe could not
understand how she and her husband were eating 65
bunches of bananas a day. When the new Governor of
Jamaica advertised that he would be at home on a certain
day 25,000 people turned up, there were free fights and
everything disappeared, crockery, silver, linen, etc. I do my
stuff with the utmost correctitude and decorum (a trifle
pompous perhaps) and I am glad we are now exerting full
control over the thieving hands of the blowsey servants.
Your ever loving husband, E. F. Peter Twining.

Keeping an eye on expenditure at Government House
was much needed at this time as in the first six months of his
life in St. Lucia Peter Twining did a lot of entertaining.
His first year's entertaining culminated in a costume ball on
St. Lucia's Eve, an old established island event which took
place every year on the 12th of December. He made it an
elaborate and colourful affair. On the first page of the printed programme was a list of the guests. It gives a good picture
of the upper layers of St. Lucia's war-time society. There
were Lieut.-Col. J. P. Shumate and representatives of the
U.S. Army from the American bases, Lt.-Col. K. G. G. Denys
and representatives of the Windward Islands Garrison, and
some British Naval officers to provide a solid base of uniforms;
a sprinkling of clergy and government officials; most of the
local politicians, and a liberal portion of less hierarchical
persons with intriguing St. Lucian names like Bascom, Ber-
gasse, Gaston de Brettes and Lorna Pordage. Among the
dances timed to take place at ten minute intervals was a
waltz called Wine, Women and Song, a beguine called Ti

Chabine Mange Tetine La, (the half-caste baby not so gently sucks), a beer-barrel polka called The New Okey-Dokey Polka, and at twelve-forty a.m. a fox trot called Your Socks don't Match. Fanfare and 'God Save the King' were timed for one in the morning when the guests were firmly told that the party was over and it was time they went home to bed. But the real events of the evening were a grand procession with Twining himself dressed as Le Baron de Laborie, a former French Governor of St. Lucia, and a series of set pieces with mazurkas and quadrilles in eighteenth- and nine-teenth-century costume which had kept the participants busy with dressmaking and rehearsals for weeks. The music played during the grand procession had a distinctly Twining flavour and included Wagner's Grand March from *Tann-hauser* which was at that time one of his favourites. There was however no Berlioz: it was said that Corporal Bruno didn't care for it.

The Ball [he told his wife] was a brilliant success. I had had some misgivings about it (because of the war) but it has done so much good and brought people together in a somewhat divided community that there can be no doubt that it was the right thing to do. The costumes were exquisite and the set pieces perfectly done, especially the quadrilles by the upper sixteen coloured people.

Twining himself led the Sir Roger de Coverley.

In case his mother and his wife, who had in England in 1944 had a less festive and somewhat bleaker Christmas, felt that life was all beer and skittles in the sun in St. Lucia, he added a list of his more dutiful Christmas activities.

There were three do's for the poor, one for the Girl Guides and one for the Boy Scouts. On Christmas Day I went to Church at 7.30 a.m., had breakfast at the Rectory, at 9 the hospital for distribution of presents, then to loony bin ditto, then to the Police and the Prison (we gave our convicts Christmas dinner!), then to Canon Lawrie's dinner for 500 poor, then to the workhouse. Really all quite exhausting. In the evening Col. Denys and I gave a party for 24, several naval and military officers, the Matron and a number of lame ducks. The P.W.D. did a Christmas scene as centre piece, somewhat clumsy but not bad, though not as good as yours. We had an enormous cracker, the Royal Artillery providing the bang. Each group of four had been told to provide one form of entertainment and one game. They had taken great trouble in rehearsing and really were very good. And so to bed.

Despite these obligations Twining enjoyed being a Governor. He was not of course a proper Governor in name or in salary (he got a thousand a year as Administrator) or in constitutional position. St. Lucia was one of four West Indian islands which had for administrative convenience and to save money been lumped together as the Windward Islands under a single Governor. The Governor lived in Grenada but although he naturally visited the other islands from time to time and had the power in theory to control what went on in them, in practice he seems to have left the various Administrators to get on with things more or less in their own way. Some Governors of course visited and exercised control more than others. The Governor in Twining's time was not a very frequent visitor nor apparently did he exercise much control over what went on in St. Lucia. How far this was due to his own wishes and his own assessment of his responsibilities is a matter of conjecture. Twining didn't like having visits from the Governor. Among other disturbances and disadvantages they meant either moving out of Government House or being an awkward sort of guest in it. He didn't like that at all. Nor did he like playing second fiddle in what he quickly came to look on as his own private orchestra.

The Governor of the Windward Islands then was Sir Arthur Grimble, 'a tall, thin man', according to Twining, 'who was rather fond of the ladies'. Grimble was a quiet, sensitive man who felt that he had been given less than his official deserts and who spent a good deal of time and trouble correcting and recorrecting his own and other peoples' prose. The results as we all know were very pleasing but the process of achieving it was apt to exasperate less patient and more actively energetic people. Grimble was charming and lazy and gentle but he wasn't lacking in a sense of his own importance. In both his official and his personal relations with him Twining assumed an attitude of complete equality and independence, 'a state of affairs', according to one local observer, 'which wasn't appreciated by Sir Arthur Grimble'.

Although Peter Twining liked being at Government House when he had it on his own, and thoroughly enjoyed its gubernatorial appurtenances, he never lost sight of two objectives he had set himself when he first arrived. One was to leave St. Lucia a better and happier place than he had found it. The other was to use it as a stepping stone to something better for himself. The first wasn't entirely altruistic, and the second wasn't entirely selfish. Like most men Twining was a mixture of egoist and idealist, of realist and romantic. He wanted to do good but he also wanted to get on. He wanted to help others but also he wanted to help himself. What made him different from the average man was that he felt more strongly about both these things and was prepared to go to greater lengths to get them. It was difficult to say sometimes whether he did something for the benefit of others or of himself. He wasn't a philosophical man, and the odds are that he often didn't know himself. He probably hoped, as most of us do, to kill both birds with one stone. It saved time and energy, and sometimes money; and Twining was interested in most forms of economy.

When he arrived in St. Lucia he straight away, as much perhaps by instinct as calculation, started to look for a suitable instrument for these dual objectives. He found it within a week or two in something called Colonial Development and Welfare. It wasn't new, even in an island as remote and neglected as St. Lucia, but he quickly saw its possibilities both for St. Lucia and himself. He somehow or other managed to make it seem as if it was not only his special interest but almost as if it was his own idea. He plunged into it at once, and for the next twelve months he concentrated with a fierce and possessive enthusiasm on it. He had, as has been explained, called a meeting of the relevant heads of departments soon after he arrived and told them to draw up plans for economic and social development and had given them a month to do it. Meanwhile he studied his subject with care. He wasn't a bookish or an intellectual man; but when he really wanted to understand something he could apply considerable powers of concentration to it, and there were few subjects he couldn't master for his immediate purpose.

He had had a brief experience of the Colonial Development and Welfare idea when he had been put by Sir Bede Clifford to chair an inter-departmental committee on the subject in Mauritius. It had, he knew, stemmed from a Statement of Policy which had been presented to Parliament in London in February of 1940. The history behind the Statement and the reasons why it was made at that time didn't particularly concern him. He was more interested in its present application to the problems of St. Lucia and Peter Twining. He probably didn't read the lengthy report of the West Indies Royal Commission which exposed the mistakes and the attitudes which the Statement of Policy was designed to cure. Although it was prepared and written in 1938 and 1939 it wasn't, for various mainly Machiavellian reasons, published until after the war. What he did read however with great care was the Commission's recommendations which were published at the same time as the Statement of Policy. They were both documents of considerable importance not only for the West Indies but for the whole of what was then known as the British colonial empire.

While the Royal Commission was investigating the situation in the West Indies, the British Government was having a fresh and, many thought, overdue look at its attitude to the colonial empire as a whole. As the Statement of Policy put it:

The primary aim of Colonial policy is to protect and advance the interests of the inhabitants of the Colonies ... Some of the Colonies can make, and have made, great progress in strengthening their economic positions without recourse to outside help; and they are improving, as time goes on, the social services that minister to the well-being of the people as a whole. In some territories larger revenues could be raised without injustice by adjustment of taxation; and considerably heavier local taxation has in fact been accepted in most of the Colonies since the outbreak of war. An improvement of the Government machinery and a reinforcement of the personnel of the development services would in many Colonies result in more successful economic expansion.

Nevertheless, if full and balanced development is to be obtained, and if Colonial Governments are to be placed in a position to maintain administrative, technical and social services at proper standards, some assistance from outside is necessary at this stage. Few of the Colonies have the good fortune to possess substantial mineral wealth, and in comparatively few are there manufacturing industries of any magnitude. The majority are wholly, or almost wholly, dependent on the more limited resources derived from agriculture. The value of agricultural products varies widely from year to year as conditions fluctuate in the world market, with the result that Colonial revenues provide an unreliable basis for a policy of steady development. In some cases the position is aggravated by a heavy burden of indebtedness. However able their Government, however efficient their economic administration, many Colonies cannot finance out of their own resources the research and survey work, the schemes of major capital enterprise, and the expansion of administrative or technical staffs which are necessary for their full and vigorous development. Nor can they always afford, in the absence of such development, an adequate standard of health and education services.

Something indeed had already been done along these lines but the help given by the Colonial Office had in practice been confined to making up deficits of the poorer colonies and to making somewhat limited grants or loans for economic development from a Colonial Development Fund established in 1929. Up to the beginning of the war about seventeen million pounds had been disbursed in this way. The Government now proposed

to invite Parliament to approve an extension of this

policy, and to remove certain limiting and hampering conditions that are attached to expenditure from the existing Fund. The object in view when the Fund was constituted was 'to promote commerce with, or industry in, the United Kingdom', an end which it was hoped to achieve by assisting the development of agriculture and industry in the Colonies. Certain specific objects on which expenditure could be incurred were enumerated. Other objects of no less importance were not included; for example, education (apart from technical education) was outside the scope of the Act. The emphasis was throughout on material development. The intention of the Act was primarily to provide assistance towards capital schemes, though assistance towards recurrent expenditure was not in terms excluded. This intention has been followed, and grants towards recurrent expenditure have not normally been authorised; when occasionally they have been given, they have been made for short periods only. The existence of the Fund has not involved any departure from the old principle that a Colony should have only those services which it can afford to maintain out of its own resources. This principle now calls for revision, and the Government propose that in appropriate cases money from the new sources which they have it in mind to provide should be made available for the maintenance of important works or services over a substantial period of years.

They propose to introduce legislation to replace the Colonial Development Fund, which is limited to a maximum of £1,000,000 a year, by new arrangements providing in a new Vote in the Estimates for assistance to Colonial Governments up to a maximum of £5,000,000 a year for ten years. This assistance will be available not only for schemes involving capital expenditure necessary for Colonial development in the widest sense but also for helping to meet recurrent expenditure in the Colonies on certain services such as agriculture, education, health and housing.

The sums involved and the objectives seem modest and conservative enough by comparison with current standards of overseas aid but at the time they were a radical and imaginative departure from a philosophy which held that colonies should serve the economic and strategic interests of the mother country where they could and, where they couldn't, they should at least be as small a burden on the British taxpayer as Treasury ingenuity and watchfulness could contrive.

Some schemes for assistance from this Fund for St. Lucia had been submitted long before Twining arrived but many of them were still being looked at by experts and economists, and they were for the most part isolated schemes not designedly related to one another. What Twining set out to do was to weld them and a number of new schemes into a comprehensive plan based on an assessment of St. Lucia's long-term needs, and then to use all his energy, persuasion and, if need be, push to get them agreed and put into effect with the greatest possible speed. He bulldozed and charmed his way through the obstacles of conservatism and sectional interests in St. Lucia where the co-operation of the local politicians had to be secured; in Grenada where the Governor's blessing was required; in Barbados where a regional office of the Colonial Development and Welfare organisation had been established; and finally of course in London at the Colonial Office. Each had to be persuaded in turn of the merit, if possible, both of the schemes and of their sponsor. He used different tactics for each obstacle. He had already largely won the trust and indeed the affection of the people of St. Lucia ('I find myself,' he told his mother, 'working in complete sympathy with them, even the politicians') and, with the help of Gordon, later Sir Garnet Gordon whom he thought by far the best of them, he even persuaded the local representatives not only to support his ideas but to bear a substantial share of the cost themselves. Getting the agreement of the Governor of the Windward Islands and of the Comptroller of Development and Welfare in Barbados called for different tactics. Without entirely neglecting the figureheads, he concentrated his persuasion and his infectious enthusiasm on their Chief Secretaries, John Stow and Kenneth Blackburne. He paid frequent visits to Grenada and Barbados and invited them both to stay with him in St. Lucia, where he did his best to undermine their critical faculties by keeping them up to the early hours of the morning with talk and rum. When he had, so to speak, secured his rear and his flanks he sent off his five-year sketch plan for the development of St. Lucia to the Colonial Office, and then followed it up, before any objections had had time to crystallise, with a personal visit. He had in fact been plotting a visit for some time. Apart from his wish to see his wife and younger son whom he hadn't seen since he had left Mauritius, he was starting to feel concerned about his elder son whom he hadn't seen, apart from one very brief visit, since 1939. He wanted very much to see his mother. He also needed treatment for gout, and he hadn't in any case had any home leave for six years. Last, but not perhaps least, he wanted to find out what the Colonial Office had in mind for him. He had calculated that seventeen Governorships would be falling vacant in the next year or two. He had already told his mother in one of his frequent crystal-gazing letters that he could see no reason why he shouldn't get one of them. He went off to London in July of 1945 in a cheerful and optimistic mood.

Twining's sketch plan had created a good impression in the Colonial Office. It wasn't of course the sort of political material that would be seen by Ministers but the officials in the West Indies Department looked at it and thought it was well conceived and well argued. There were however some in the cool corridors of the main office in Downing Street and in the bleak outhouse of Palace Chambers who thought that it had been drawn up without perhaps 'any strict relationship to the money which was likely to be available either in London or St. Lucia'. Another squeak of complaint was that 'lumping lots of things together in one despatch may be very convenient for Mr. Twining but it makes life very difficult for us'. Some found him 'precipitate' and 'unorthodox'. Twining didn't allow this sort of criticism to deflate or discourage him. He paid several visits to the Colonial Office during the three months he was in England. He took several people out to lunch, he wrote a number of personal letters, and he established a good working and drinking relationship with Beckett, the head of the West Indies Department whose wide academic knowledge of his paper province was only equalled by his first-hand knowledge of the public houses in the Lake District.

Twining's St. Lucia development plan was itself on orthodox lines. There were schemes for new roads and improvement to the port, for the resettlement on the land of people who had drifted to the towns, for reclaiming areas that had been unused because of swamps, mosquitoes or the possessiveness of the Lands branch of the War Office, for the introduction of new crops and the prevention of erosion, for building houses and hospitals and schools, and most important perhaps of all, for training local men and women to take the place of expatriate staff. What made the plan distinctive was the way it was related, with broad sweeps of a broad pen, to the inheritance of the island's past and the prospects of its future, and the fact that it included a number of unusual proposals which some thought imaginative and others somewhat eccentric. One was for a nautical training school under a retired naval officer of Twining's acquaintance to 'gather up the waifs and strays and cut off recruits to the wharf rat class'. Another was for a police band which would be 'a much needed source of pride to the island'; yet another was for a director of music. There was a scheme too for importing silk worms and mulberry trees from the Far East. Twining made them all seem very plausible and some, though not all of them, were eventually approved to the surprise and envy of some of his official colleagues in other parts of the West Indies who had thought that it would be more realistic and politic to confine oneself to putting up more orthodox proposals.

It was the practice in the Colonial Office at that time to send draft development schemes round the office, after they had been studied by the geographical department concerned, to be examined by experts in various fields. Many of the experts were knowledgeable and meticulous but some of course were more expert than others, and some were more vocal. There were those, it was said, who knew what they were talking about and couldn't talk, and those who could talk but didn't know what they were talking about. Twining in any case was a match for both. He could not only talk on almost any subject but he also did his homework even if in some cases this involved a further reference to the *Encyclopaedia Britannica*. Before he went back to St. Lucia by air in November he had not only got approval for many of his schemes but he had also persuaded the able but often hard-headed officials concerned in the Treasury and the Colonial Office to agree in principle that St. Lucia should be released from Treasury control. In fact St. Lucia had balanced its budget for the past three years and was about due for this measure of relief but it was Twining who, with his knowledge of money and money talk, welded the facts into a business-like case and was thus able to take back the good news to St. Lucia as one more rabbit out of his seemingly inexhaustible hat.

He was glad to get back to St. Lucia. England in November didn't appeal to him at the best of times, and in 1945 he found it difficult to attune himself to the restrictions and the shortages and the prices of post-war London. He had done what he set out to do, for St. Lucia, for his family and he hoped for himself. His mother was happily settled in a High Church nursing home at Chiswick; his younger son William had been established at a boarding school, and plans were afoot for John, the elder son, to take a term off from Charterhouse and come out with his mother to St. Lucia the following spring. When he got back to St. Lucia there were welcoming smiles and warmth and no shortage of the things that particularly appealed to him. Even his Siamese cat had had 'the sweetest kittens'. He liked travelling and he liked seeing new places but, as he told his mother in a letter, he was 'always very glad to get back to my dear little St. Lucia or Home'. He was possessively attached by now to St. Lucia and its people and soon after he got back he was rushing to their defence when his mother was rash enough to send him a newspaper report of a statement by an Anglican bishop that the Windward Islands was 'the most immoral corner of the world'.

I really cannot answer your letter [he replied] about the wickedness of the world. The world is wicked and always will be but it is probably less so than 30 years ago. From what I have seen and published figures support it, the population of Chiswick is infinitely more wicked than St. Lucia and nobody in their senses would listen to the trickery of those Bishops who try and make old ladies' flesh creep so they can get some money out of them, or to the gossip of mischievous and malicious women who get a sinful delight in spreading imaginative stories about matters on which they cannot have first hand information, and if they have they shouldn't. Apart from original sin with which all mortals seem to be afflicted, these so-called wickednesses are due to a number of social and economic causes which in the colonies we are trying to rectify. If we could get rid of stumbling blocks like Bishop T., who would lose his job if we abolished wickedness, our progress would be faster.

Even the prospect of acting as Governor of the Windward Islands and being called His Excellency while Grimble was away on leave didn't appeal to him.

> I can see neither honour nor glory nor fun nor profit in acting Governor [he told his mother in a somewhat quieter letter] and I have done my best to get out of it.
> You can't do anything and it merely interferes with one's ordinary work. I dislike the prospect intensely.

Acting as Governor meant living in Grenada, and he was very glad when it was over and he could get back to St. Lucia.

This feeling that the place belonged to him was reciprocated by many people in St. Lucia. They came to feel as time went by that Twining also belonged to them. They knew that he worked for them, and argued and fought for them. They knew that he travelled all over the place on their affairs, not only to Grenada and Barbados and to London to get support for his development and welfare schemes, but to Martinique to establish good relations with the French, to Puerto Rico to get some Americans to build a tourist hotel, and to Washington to attend a conference on the use of the runways at the American base for civil aircraft. They felt, what they had not often felt before about transient English officials, that here was a man who really cared. 'One of the reasons why we liked him,' a St. Lucian told me, 'was that he gave us a sense of pride. He made us feel that we were just as good if not better than the people on those other stuck-up islands, that there was nothing, if we helped ourselves and really tried, that we couldn't do.'

It is a reflection of their feeling for him that when St. Lucians reminisce about Twining it is not so much his practical achievements that they talk about as his singularities. They saw him as a man's man who was more at home in the all-male atmosphere of the Castries Club than in mixed gatherings where, as Degazon, a St. Lucian who was his chief assistant, put it, a degree of 'social hypocrisy was often required when women or ladies were present'. His humour was Rabelaisian and his behaviour sometimes reminded them of Charles Laughton in the film of Henry the Eighth, except for the fact that he didn't seem to be particularly interested, as far as they could see, either in women or ladies. They accepted this peculiarity as they accepted his horseplay and his peculiar sense of humour. He was different, he was a man who had to do things in his own way. 'Every day regular as clockwork he left his office in the town and walked to the Castries Club. He left his office at ten to twelve so that he would be there to listen to the B.B.C. news at twelve o'clock. Everybody knew. He had the traffic stopped so that it would not disturb him. He was a big man, the boss, he was entitled to do that. He always sat in the same chair in the Castries Club. No one else sat there. While he listened to the news no one spoke but when it was over they began to talk. He talked to everyone. They talked and talked and they drank gin. In the old days before Mrs. Twining came out he stayed till one o'clock. He had lunch at Government House at one fifteen. But after Mrs. Twining came he left the Club at ten to one. He was driven up to his house on the hill in the car with the flag on it. When he arrived he didn't go into the main part of the house. He went into his office as if he had work to do. Corporal Bruno was there waiting for him with a large glass on a tray. The glass was full of tomato juice. "Give me my blood bath," he used to say. When he had drunk the tomato juice he wiped

his hand across his lips, winked at Bruno and went in to meet
his guests for lunch.'

Almost everyone who was in St. Lucia then has a Twining
story. Some of them are very funny, many perhaps are not
entirely true. True or not, they were told and indeed are
still told with admiration touched with awe. Most of the
stories revolve round Twining's capacity for drinking large
quantities of liquor without it having any apparent effect
on his speech or his behaviour and the stratagems he employed to defeat the surveillance of those who were very
properly concerned with his health and his increasing weight.
One story which is generally believed is that with the help
of the ubiquitous Corporal Bruno caches of bottles were
strategically placed in the bushes and trees in the grounds of
Government House so that His Honour could discreetly refresh himself at times and on occasions when medical or
other restrictions were in force.

There is one thing however which will probably be remembered in St. Lucia long after Twining's other achievements and singularities have been forgotten. At eight-thirty
on the evening of Wednesday the 30th of October, 1946, the
St. Lucia Arts and Crafts Society presented a concert production of Gluck's *Orpheus*. It took place at Clarke's Theatre
in Castries, and it was conducted by Chester Catlow, the
island's Director of Music. It was perhaps of all the things
which Peter Twining sponsored in St. Lucia the one in which
he and the people of St. Lucia took most pride.

In a letter which he wrote to Sir Arthur Grimble before
he went off to London in July 1945 Twining said

the essential needs of economic development and education I have stressed on many occasions but the Colony
needs something more than that; it wants a spiritual renaissance.

The Police Band and the Director of Music were part of
his contribution to this spiritual renaissance. He had the
flair to sense that in St. Lucia it was through such things
rather than good works that such a renaissance could best
be expressed and achieved.

There is a West Indian calypso called 'The Slave'. It is
not an old song but it goes back all the same to the core of
West Indian traditions, and partly explains perhaps why singing is historically and emotionally so important to most West
Indians:

> We had to chant and sing
> To express our feelings
> To that wicked and cruel man.
> That was the only medicine
> To make him listen
> And so Calypso began.

'That wicked and cruel man' was an amalgam of the plan-
tation owner, the Government, the white man generally in
all his parts and offices. 'For various historical reasons,'
Harold Simmons, a St. Lucian scholar, has explained, 'the
West Indian folk tradition is an "underground" tradition.
Its song dances, festivals, beliefs and customs manifest an
attempt to create forms of expression for a way of life which
is at variance with established authority, orthodox religion,
upper class morality, law and other cultural forms having
the sanction of authority. It has nevertheless consistently ap-
propriated to its own use large fragments of the culture of
the world above it. It has been under constant attack from
the pulpit and the law makers, and its language is being
pushed gradually out of existence by educational policy as
well as by social forces not directly subject to control ... The
pattern of St. Lucian folklore falls into the larger mosaic that
may be termed "West Indian culture". Yet the St. Lucia design has distinctive peculiarities, some of them unique and
not found in other islands in the Caribbean. At least three
customs are not known elsewhere in the Antilles. The flower
festivals of La Rose and La Marguerite, the ancestral worship
of Kele, and the A-bwe or drinking songs. The flower festivals
were at one time universally celebrated in the island but
have recently diminished in their appeal...'

The Police Band and Gluck's *Orpheus* were of course alien
ideas but Twining saw that they helped to fill these gaps in
a way which neither the churches nor social welfare schemes

could do. The people of St. Lucia were quick to seize on them and link them to their own languishing traditions and to make them seem in the end as if they were their own. When Twining held a Victory parade at the end of the war and marched round the island at the head of the Police Band it seemed that it was not only their own parade but almost their own victory. There were some people indeed in the crowds which thronged the roads and streets who thought that it was Twining himself, their Twining, resplendent in his uniform and medals, who had won the war. In the same way the story of Orpheus became their own daily mixture of joy and tragedy, the music and the songs and the costumes of ancient Greece became a renaissance of the spirit of La Rose and La Marguerite. The production of *Orpheus* that night was for almost the whole island a source of enormous pride; for Miss Olga Pierre and Mrs. Olga Sweetnam who took the parts of Orpheus and Euridice and for Miss Francis Clauzel who was the God of Love; for the fifty-one sopranos, altos, tenors and basses of the Arts and Crafts chorus—the Adjodhas, Alexanders, Caddles and Calderons, the Lansiquots, the Neales and the Theobalds; for the first violins, the second violins and the piano accompanists: for the stage managers and the carpenters and the hundreds who took part one way or another in the production.

On the night of the performance Twining held a dinner party. He chose his guests with care. He did the same with the food and the drink. He was good at dinner-table talk with people he knew and liked, and that night, it was noticed, he was in particularly good form. Soon after eight o'clock he leant back in his chair and looked at his guests one by one until he had the attention of them all. Then he stood up. 'Ladies and Gentlemen,' he said in his slow booming voice, 'the carriages are ready and it is time ...' he paused and allowed himself a modest smile, '... it is time we went to the opera.' It was as if, one of his guests that night recalls, everything he had done in St. Lucia, his visits, his speeches, his schemes, his parties and his whole impressive array of achievements had been planned and purposed to lead up to this one moment. It was as if, of all the things he had done, to have encouraged and spurred and bullied the people of St. Lucia into producing an opera on their own was the thing of which he was most proud. 'Yes,' he said, 'it's time we went to the opera.'

He had another reason for pride that evening but it was something which for the moment he had to keep to himself. Two weeks later it was publicly announced that he had been appointed Governor of North Borneo. A few days afterwards, on the 17th of November, he left St. Lucia with his wife to take up his new appointment. Mrs. Twining had been less than a year on the island, but in her own quiet, persistent way she too had made her mark with many small acts of thoughtfulness and with the persuasive spur of her zest for medical and social work. Many kind things were said about them in the local newspapers and in farewell speeches, and they both received a great many letters. None touched them more perhaps than one which Peter Twining kept and which was found among his papers. It was from the St. Lucia War Veterans Association and it was addressed in a careful copperplate handwriting to His Honour E. F. Twining C.M.G., M.B.E.

May It Please Your Honour,

It is with feelings of deep concern and mixed emotion that we learn of Your Honour's very soon departure from St. Lucia. We cannot help appreciating the very conspicuous fact that it is during Your Honour's administration the St. Lucian War Veteran ceased to be a nonentity. We will for many, many years to come cherish the memory of Your Honour's able, impartial, democratic and humane administration of our little island, and Your Honour's last benevolent act to us—bestowing the distinguished patronage of Your Honour's presence, and that of Mrs. Twining to our dance on Saturday 9/11/46.

Mrs. Twining like Your Honour leaves St. Lucia carrying with her large slices of the hearts of St. Lucians who have had the privilege of meeting her. After the siege of Calais, the French people said 'Edward has conquered our cities, but Phillipa has conquered our hearts'. Like Queen Phillipa of Hainault Mrs. Helen Mary Twining,

O.B.E. has conquered the hearts of all St. Lucians who have met her.

Good-bye, God Bless you both,
Your Honour's Faithful and sincere well-wishers,
Hubert Montfort. Secretary.

8

North Borneo

IT DIDN'T COME as a surprise to Peter Twining to be made a
governor. He had predicted it for several years, and not only
in letters to his mother. He had felt instinctively that he had
the right sort of personality and the potential of qualities to
enable him to play the part even when he was feeling his
way in Mauritius. His brief experience of the leading role
on the small stage of St. Lucia made him sure of it. He
had tried on the costume there and found that he could wear
it. It was all the same a considerable achievement. He was
forty-seven. Men had been made governors at an earlier age
but few had, in the comparatively recent era of meritocracy
in the colonial service, got to the top in so short a time.
Certainly none had done so after such a slow and unpromising a start. As he told his mother 'there are exceptions to
the proverb that "A rolling stone gathers no moss". They
did not take into account that some stones roll uphill!'

He was not surprised but that did not mean that he wasn't
pleased. He was delighted. He was also determined not only
to make a success of it but to enjoy it too. Within a few
days of his arrival in England he had been to Buckingham
Palace and had kissed hands, as the Court Circular puts it, on
his appointment. He ordered two new tropical uniforms,
complete with plumes, and he started negotiations in the
Edwardian atmosphere of Ede and Ravenscroft, the Court
Tailors and Robemakers in Chancery Lane, for the purchase
second hand of a colonial governor's full dress uniform. It
had belonged to a governor of his shape and size who had
recently retired, and in the end he paid seventy pounds for

it. A colonial governor's full dress uniform was a splendid affair of dark blue broadcloth, cocked hat and silver epaulettes which made the most ordinary of men look like Nelson or Charles Laughton. The only trouble was that it was made of wool and was much too hot to wear with comfort in most places where colonial governors went. The climate in North Borneo was for the most part not only hot but humid but Peter Twining was not the sort of man to allow that sort of point to deter him. He liked uniforms, and he had the figure and the walk to wear them. He went to see his mother and reminded her that she shouldn't address him as 'His Excellency' on her letters until he had actually taken up his appointment. He paid one or two bustling visits to the Colonial Office where, slightly to his surprise, he found everyone friendly and wise and helpful. He paid several visits to the City to see banks and firms interested or likely to be interested in investment and enterprise in North Borneo. He went everywhere by taxi. Buses and the underground were too slow, and a little bit too much cheek by jowl perhaps, for a large-sized personage in a hurry. When the time came for him to go his wife stayed behind again to settle the children into school and make arrangements for their holidays, to let the house at Godalming which they had bought as a family base soon after they were married, and to attend to the business of ordering supplies and equipment for life in Government House in North Borneo.

Twining went off to the Far East to take up his first governorship in a troop-ship. In better times he would have gone by a ship and a route of his own choice with a cabin to himself on the right side for the heat of the Red Sea. But in January of 1947 things still had a long way to go. He had to take what he could get, and that meant sharing a cabin with someone else and sharing the ship, he told his mother, 'with 300 civilians, 300 officers and 3,000 troops'. He fed however 'quite well and quite properly at the Captain's table' and when he telegraphed ahead to the Governors of Aden and Ceylon to tell them he was passing through he was very gratified with the response. The effect was rather spoilt at Aden because the ship arrived after midnight and left before dawn but the acting Governor sent out his A.D.C., who managed, as A.D.C.s do, to give the impression that there was nothing he liked better than to be hauled out of bed in the early hours to say how-do-you-do to fledgling governors trying out their gubernatorial wings. Colombo however was better. He and General Ritchie, who was going out to take up his appointment as C.-in-C. Far East Land Forces, were met and driven to Queen's House in the Governor's car with an escort of outriders from the military police. Best of all however was his reception at Singapore, where, he told his wife in a letter, 'they were fussy about the protocol and order of precedence and nobody was allowed to leave until I had disembarked.' After spending a few days with the Governor and the Governor General 'washing the salt water off' and having his laundry done with impressive speed and efficiency by the Chinese staff, Twining went off on the 14th of February to take up his governorship in a sloop of the Royal Navy.

He set off in good heart and with a robust self-confidence that he could cope, somehow or other, with whatever there was for him to do. He had been chosen for the post by the Colonial Office with care, over the heads of many men with longer service and more orthodox experience. It was barely six months since the British Government had assumed responsibility for North Borneo after sixty years of Chartered Company rule, three and a half years of Japanese occupation and nearly a year of makeshift British military administration. Twining was the first Governor to be appointed by the British Government.

Although much had been done with very little to get things going after the surrender of the Japanese, the problems that faced him when he arrived were still formidable and complex. Not least of the problems was the sheer physical destruction caused by the war. While the Japanese had, in the words of one official report, 'left a trail of death, disease and destruction', a large part of the destruction had in fact been caused by the American and Australian Forces in the process of re-occupation. Whatever the cause the result was that North Borneo was, to quote the same official report, 'probably in a state of devastation unequalled throughout the British Empire'. It was calculated that

out of 840 government buildings 614 were totally destroyed and 226 damaged. Some towns like Sandakan and
Labuan had been burned to the ground, and there wasn't
much left of other towns and villages in the coastal areas.
Road and rail communications were almost unusable; lorries
and cars had been destroyed, ships and fishing boats had
been sunk, and most of the draught animals had been killed
for food. No one knew how many people were killed during
the Japanese occupation, but there were several mass de-
capitations and by the end of the war there were few who
had helped or worked for the British left.

There were of course other problems too, tangible problems of money and supplies and staff, and the less tangible
and less tractable problems of human attitudes and human
frailties in a difficult period of readjustment and transition.
Twining knew from his talks in London and in Singapore
on his way through roughly what to expect, but he was determined to make the best of it.

We arrived [he told his wife] on a perfect day. The
omens were good. Kinabalu the great mountain containing the soul of North Borneo shed her clouds for once and
stood out in all her majesty. In view of the heat in the
cabin I wore white uniform and must have looked a smasher.
The ceremony was simple and dignified in a tumble-down
shack known as the Survey Office. About 150 people. My
Commission was read out clearly by a Secretariat Officer.
The Chief Justice without wig or robes administered the
oaths which had been very badly printed in Kuching on
exceptionally poor quality paper. But I read them in a
resounding voice without blemish. Calder (the Chief Secretary), Bryant a planter, a Native, a Chinese and myself
read out our essays on the same subject and they all sounded exactly the same. Mine was translated into Malay
with some difficulty. Then outside a Guard of Honour of
R.N. and 100 police. Royal Salute. An alleged 17 guns (but
the cardboard charges jammed and they got the wrong
number)...

This was putting on a brave face to what must, for someone who liked his ceremony, have been something of a disappointment. The Chief Justice wasn't the only one who had no wig or robes. No one among those who greeted the new Governor had any uniforms or smart clothes, and their wives, in wives' words, had absolutely nothing to wear. There wasn't any band, and the Survey Office where for want of anything better the ceremony had taken place shook ominously during the seventeen-gun salute. But Twining was determined to take the rough with the smooth, and if need be to extract some smooth from the rough.

For sheer beauty [his letter went on] nothing can touch this place. St. Lucia is ugly by comparison. The climate is the mildest I have met in the tropics. Not too humid and very cool nights and a lovely fresh breeze off the mountain by day. Most pleasant. The town stretches about 4 or 5 miles along a narrow strip of flat land between the sea and the hills. Europeans each have their own little hill. Scarcely a permanent building stands but they have put up most attractive temporary buildings, and the town is spick and span—a mixture between Moyo in style and Kampala in elegance. There are about 70 Europeans, including 20 or more women.

Next week [he ended his letter] I will be able to write a more balanced picture. What I have given you are my first impressions. They have been genuinely looking forward to the arrival of their new Governor. They thank God he was not selected from the Malayan Civil Service and they expect a great deal but within six months we should have got across the worst hurdles.

One wonders who exactly Twining had in mind when he spoke of 'they'. If he was thinking of the various tribes and races that made up the indigenous population of North Borneo, the Dusuns, the Bajans, and the Muruts, or the settled immigrants like the Chinese and the Javanese, he may perhaps have been right. But if, as is more likely, he was thinking of the British officials in North Borneo and the European business community then his certainty was less well based. Behind the polite words of welcome and the assurances of loyal and devoted service and co-operation lay a certain wariness. Twining was careful in his formal reply to the addresses of welcome to pay tribute to the pioneer work done by the Chartered Company in developing the country and to the efforts of the many Chartered Company officers who had returned to serve in North Borneo after the war; but this did not by any means dispel the regret and the apprehension felt by most of them at the change from Chartered Company to Colonial Office rule. They were for the most part conservative people. They were used to the Chartered Company's ways and they didn't want, or see any need, to change them. The new Governor was the epitome of this unwanted and needless change. They would probably have been suspicious of any new Colonial Office governor whoever he was and wherever he came from; what made it worse, much worse, was that to them Twining was an outsider. He had had no previous experience of the Far East, he knew nothing of oriental peoples or oriental ways. They had had governors before from outside the magic eastern circle but they at least had been servants of the Company. They didn't doubt that they would tame Twining, as they believed they had tamed the others, in the end and bring him round to their way of thinking, but they were afraid that under a Colonial Office regime the process might take longer and be more painful. They had other reasons for apprehension too. As ex-Chartered Company men, experienced in the country and its people and their languages, they had been offered re-employment by the new regime but they still didn't know how far their previous service would be allowed to count for pensions and for seniority, and how they would stand in practice when it came to postings and promotion in competition with people with more orthodox colonial service backgrounds. And across all their doubts and anxieties lay a dark shadow which consciously or unconsciously was apt to touch everything they said or felt. Most of them had been interned by the Japanese in the years of defeat and occupation. For some it had been worse than others but it had been a traumatic experience for them all and for their wives. At the end of the war in North Borneo there were in their eyes two sorts of people; those who had been interned, and those who had not. To them Twining was an outsider on every count.

Although the bulk of the British officials in North Borneo when Twining arrived were ex-Chartered Company men there were also two other elements in the official hierarchies. One of these elements, those who had been brought in since the end of the war as reinforcements from colonial territories in Africa and elsewhere, were glad to have a governor who had a similar background to their own; the other element, those who had been seconded from the Malayan Civil Service, were not so sure. They were for the most part regarded by others and often by themselves as rather special people, partly because of their high academic records and partly because of a mandarin tradition which tended to make them feel set apart from those with different backgrounds. Twining was not a mandarin; nor did he have any equivalent to their academic record.

If the men from Malaya and the men from the Chartered Company had made common ground of their doubts and reservations Twining might have found it more difficult to come to terms with them. In fact, as often happens with the forces of opposition, their disregard for one another outweighed what they had in common. To the practical Chartered Company men who really knew the country and the people, the members of the Malayan Civil Service were paper wallahs, the heaven-born who rarely came down to earth. To those from Malaya, 'the Chartered' were better on horseback than on paper, with a past tendency, as the American writer Agnes Newton Keith put it, 'to determine inter-racial relationships more often in bed than in court'. They were in fact as a rule two different sorts of people and it was not surprising that there was sometimes misunderstanding between them and a certain amount of friction. The administrative officers of the Malayan Civil Service had been largely recruited from the older universities by competitive examination or more recently by the exacting selection procedures of the Colonial Office. The Chartered Company had used different methods. The story that the Directors of the Company used to stand outside their offices in the City of London in top hats and Old Etonian ties and hail likely looking young men wearing recognisable but less well-known ties may not be true but they did, it seems, prefer the personal approach; and relations and friends, and friends of friends, turned out sometimes to be as good as those recruited by Whitehall's more impersonal methods.

There were, at first sight, problems more important and more pressing in North Borneo than sorting out differences between different categories of staff and overcoming their prejudices against a newcomer lacking in oriental experience and local savoir faire. But Twining soon saw that this was something that must be tackled first and that neither he nor the country would get anywhere until he got it right. He therefore set out straight away to overcome the prejudices and to try and get everyone to work together. He talked a lot but, as he had done in St. Lucia, he also listened. He sought out grievances and where he could he put them right. He had people who weren't on speaking terms with one another in to meals and drinks and made them play charades and unsophisticated after-dinner games. He looked apprehensive officials, and their wives, in the eye and said 'You know, I think I'm going to like it here'. He invented names for people. They were often silly names like 'Mrs. Blackie-wackie' but they made those on whom they were conferred feel singled out and special. 'He made us feel,' someone said, 'as if our problems were, to him, things we would have a lot of fun solving together and the sooner we jolly well got on with it the better. No time was wasted arguing why or how the problem arose or who was to blame or how difficult it all was. He came at a time when firm direction was needed, when confidence had to be generated, and he saw to it that we got them. His enormous sense of fun and the ridiculous made his company on tour, on launch trips or over a drink, an experience of rare delight.' The man who wrote this was a former Chartered Company man. His only regret in the end was that Twining hadn't come to North Borneo sooner. Twining may not have been brought up in the mandarin tradition or have understood oriental ways but he was a large, self-confident, commanding figure and he looked and acted, even in his eccentricities, like a governor: and that they soon realised was what they really needed.

Twining for his part as soon developed a particular liking

for his British officials in North Borneo. He was struck by the respect and the affection which they had for the gentle, amiable people of the country, feelings which were echoed for the most part at that time by the people of North Borneo themselves. Almost everywhere he went Twining heard stories of the risks which they had taken during the Japanese occupation to help and befriend British officials and their wives who were interned. Few things gave him greater pleasure than to pay tribute to and honour those who had done so and had still managed to survive. If he had in private a number of reservations about some of the Chartered Company officers and those seconded from Malaya, he did not forget that many of them had had a harsh time during their internment and yet had returned to their posts to help get the country back on its feet again after inadequate periods of recuperation and leave. He did not forget this debt, or this excuse, but he was determined all the same to get things right. One small thing for example about the Malayan Civil Service officers which got under his skin was a habit which some of them had of distinguishing themselves by putting the letters M.C.S. after their names. 'Henceforth,' the new Governor is alleged to have directed, 'they should use the letters N.B.G. which also stand for the North Borneo Government.' Although there were some of these officers like Robin Black, later to be Governor of Hong Kong, whom he much admired, and several Chartered Company people whom he particularly liked, he felt that many of them were too much wedded to the past and to their own somewhat parochial traditions to be able to adjust themselves to new concepts and new conditions, and he soon made up his mind that the right answer was to bring in men and women with fresh ideas and fresh enthusiasms. One of the first things which he did when he arrived was to set this process in motion. He asked the Colonial Office for a mixture of experienced staff from other colonial territories, and of the new recruits of exceptionally good quality who were coming into the colonial service after being in the Armed Forces during the war. In this way he laid the foundations of an expatriate civil service which had a fair balance of local knowledge and accumulated love of the country and its people on the one hand, and of new blood and outside experience on the other. Despite this more practical and long-sighted achievement, Twining is chiefly remembered in the nostalgic memories of those who served with him in North Borneo as the man who got them to forget their retrospective grievances and small internal feuds, and work happily together.

Although the new Governor busied himself in his first few months with the psychological complexities and practical problems of his officials, his letters home to his mother and his wife were mainly filled with more domestic matters.

Government House [he wrote) is well situated on a hill top and has one-sixteenth of an acre of garden with no soil. There is downstairs a long but useless verandah, a small drawing room which I hope to have enlarged as eight people fill it. A more spacious dining room. Upstairs a dark bedroom with bath and our room larger and more airy than St. Lucia but not so nice. It is all very crude with unfinished planks. But it gets the breeze without the rain and is really good enough. We have a nice verandah and a bathroom but no wash basin or hot water. The furniture is simple, heavy, ugly, badly made and very uncomfortable, especially the beds. In the middle of the bedroom is a most effectively mosquito-proofed cage in which one sleeps. There are a few bits of broken crockery, some stolen glass and half a dozen old rusty army knives and forks. The servants are nice but the most incompetent I have ever employed. No. 1 is Mejun, who speaks 23 words of English which absorbs all his energy. No. 2 is Liman, a nice chap who speaks no English which absorbs all my energy. No. 1 cook is excellent, clean and has worked for years in G. H. He speaks English and is Chinese (the others are Malays, Dusuns and Bajans). No. 2 cook is a nonentity. There are two water carriers who of course do not carry water and there is an amah who does the washing but refuses to see me. Ali is the chauffeur and he drives well but does not understand how it works. There is rather a dignified messenger. We are looking for a personal boy but as all the experienced ones were killed off it is difficult. Government pays all the staff.

The supply situation is very tricky. Apart from a small hoard the Calders accumulated for me there appears to be no tea, no sugar, no milk, no butter, no jam, no marmalade, no toilet paper and no tinned food. Buffalo meat of the most astonishing toughness is plentiful, vegetables and fruit are all right, ditto eggs. Poultry is dear. We have too much flour and not enough rice. Fish is scarce as all the fishermen were killed by the Japanese. One fishing village is inhabited now by 79 women (all of whom are having babies), no adult men at all, and the village headman is a boy of 14. Nobody has any clothes. The G.H. boys have one suit each which they wear on very special occasions. Mine is the only dinner jacket in the Colony. Very few Europeans possess collars or ties and the parson has no sock suspenders. Textiles are in very short supply and cloth is strictly rationed to half a yard per head per month. There is no whisky left though they were on a ration of half a bottle per month per family up to last November. There is no stationery and no envelopes. Little soap. Plenty of matches and salt. The water supply is all right but electricity is difficult, only on from 6.30 to 11 p.m. and as it is dark until 6.30 a.m. and I wake up at 4.30 a.m. it is rather tiresome. There is no soda water and no ice though G.H. has two large refrigerators which sometimes function. There is an atmosphere of laissez faire and I have already gingered them up and ordered toilet paper, stationery, whisky, soda water, electric plants, etc., etc., etc. The place is very nice withal and in a very interesting stage. We have a Ford V 8 car and a radio set which only works when the electricity is on and I'm in bed.

This and later letters seem to have caused some concern to his medically minded wife.

You need not worry unduly [he assured her] there is neither cholera nor typhoid here though a little gonorrhoea passed on by the Australians. I don't eat uncooked food and water and such fresh milk as we get is boiled.

There had also it seems been a lot of wifely questions

about rationing and the cost of living about which he had added some alarming sounding footnotes which he now proceeded to revoke.

Why you should still consider we are starving or need anything I can't think. The rationing was a simple way of dividing out what the Army had left behind and most people did not take it as they could get all they wanted from the shops, although the latter were more expensive, e.g. Eno's is 8/- a bottle (so I am buying a supply from the Navy) and chickens 15/- each, eggs 6d. So I am getting supplies down from up country at half the price. We also get over from Singapore the things we can't get here and they come over in the aeroplane—asparagus, pâté de foie gras and aspic.

This was later to evoke some caustic comment from his wife in exiguous post-war England but meanwhile his earlier statements about the lack of equipment in Government House had not surprisingly sent his wife off to shop.

In re. Hamptons [he blandly went on] I was unaware that we needed any Pyrex. We seem to have plenty for my supper for 100 tomorrow. The china and glass will be useful as I can hand back what we have to the Custodian of Enemy Property for issue to someone else. The linen will be nice. We don't use mosquito nets as we sleep in mosquito-proof cages, and I hope shortly the R.A.F. will send their special Dakota over to spray the whole town with DDT. It's difficult to advise about cretonnes. They are going to pull down the drawing room and rebuild it some time and they have not yet got the plans out. In any case there won't be any windows and the wind which blows everything in the room down would make curtains a damned nuisance. The bedroom is not suited to curtains either as the openings are large, more like a verandah. The chairs are either cane or simple wood with two blue cushions. There are no sofas. We have enough cutlery of a sort for a dinner or lunch party for 40. I certainly shouldn't buy any. It's no good bringing bedsprings because the beds

wouldn't take them. They are locally made with cane bottoms and kapok mattresses and pillows—quite comfy.

This change of tune naturally led his long suffering wife
to cancel some of her orders. Realising that he had now gone
too far the other way Peter Twining sent his wife a list of
the things on the Government House inventory.

To this [he noted] must be added two fixed basins, two
large mirrors and a towel rail I have had put in the bathroom and an asbestos wall I have had put up between the
two bedrooms as my guests' snores keep me awake. Everything else is on loan from the Custodian and varies from
day to day as guests recognise their property and go off
with it.

After the war the Army had appointed a Custodian of
Enemy Property who had collected together all the furniture
and household equipment he could find and had issued it out
to the British officers and officials on a rough and ready military scale. As the Chartered Company men came back they
and especially their wives started to see things that had belonged to them before the war and to claim them back. Some
people argued the toss but the new Governor, wifeless, let
things go. It was not surprising that Mrs. Twining found it
difficult to know what exactly her husband and Government
House really lacked. When she arrived and saw things for
herself she had several surprises.

Despite all this exchange of questions and answers and
misconceptions about the house he lived in, the new Governor didn't stay in it for long. He wanted to go everywhere
and talk to everyone, and he was soon on the move. North
Borneo was a country of 30,000 square miles and 300,000
people and there was a lot for him to see. One of the first
places he went to was Sandakan in the eastern part of the
territory. It had been the capital for a time in the good old
days before the war and the Colonial Office, and there were
many people in Sandakan who still thought the decision to
transfer the capital to Jesselton was a mistake. And the
decision, they knew, was Twining's. It was therefore an im-

portant visit and he organised it with considerable care. He
wanted to make an impression—on the British officials and
the European business community, on the Chinese and on
what were then without embarrassment to anybody still
known with exactitude as the native races. Different people,
he knew, were impressed by different things but one thing
he was sure would impress everyone was a ship of the Royal
Navy. It would make the point which he very much wanted
to make that however impressive governors had been under
the Chartered Company he was something they had never
been. He was the representative of the King. It may have
been partly vanity but it was also in 1947 good public relations, and public relations was a subject that he knew. So he
used his charm and persuasion on the Admiral at Singapore,
whom he had met there on his way through, and in the end
the Admiral came up not with one ship but with three. The
new Governor set out on the 18th of March in H.M.S.
Adamant, a submarine depot ship of about 13,000 tons, with
a destroyer and a submarine in attendance. This might have
been enough in weight and style for most newly appointed
governors on their first official tour, but Twining had firm
views on how a governor should travel. His party for the
voyage consisted of the Chief Justice, the Attorney General,
the Financial Secretary, the Director of Agriculture, the
Director of Public Works, the Harbour Master, the Commandant of the North Borneo Constabulary, the Commissioner of
Customs, and Professor Benham, the economic adviser to
the Governor General. This was in addition to his personal
staff of aides, secretaries, orderlies and servants. This may
not sound particularly impressive to those who are not
familiar with official hierarchies in the colonial territories
but to those who are it will be recognised as a considerable
array of local talent for a governor to take away with him.
He also took his full dress uniform. He would have taken a
band too if he had had one but there was no band when
Twining arrived in North Borneo and it took even Peter
Twining a certain amount of time to achieve one.

'The sun was shining,' he told his mother, 'the breeze was
cool and everything was auspicious.' He had entertained the
Navy well when they had arrived at Jesselton the previous

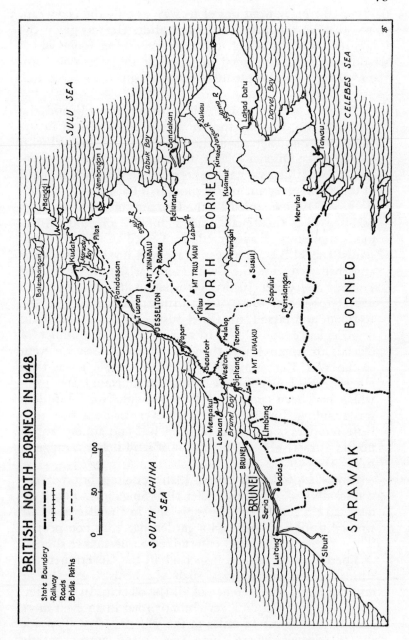

BRITISH NORTH BORNEO IN 1948

State Boundary
Railway
Roads
Bridle Paths

0   50   100

day, and the Navy went out of its way, as only the Navy can, to see that he was properly looked after. He was given the Captain's quarters 'a big day cabin, a dining room which would seat 24, a very good night cabin and a private bathroom'. There was also plenty of duty-free gin.

We soon settled down [his letter continued] and the next day was Monday and we arrived at Sandakan in the early morning. Robertson, the Resident, came aboard with Wookey, the District Officer, to meet us and having attended to everything we went ashore, where there was a guard of the Royal Navy and one of the North Borneo Armed Constabulary. Accompanied by the Captains of the three ships and the Flag Lieutenant and a number of other distinguished visitors, I inspected the Guard of Honour, presented the M.B.E. to a very brave and loyal native officer and then went into the Court House where we found His Honour the Chief Justice very hot in his newly arrived scarlet robes and wig. After a little speech-making by the Resident and myself, the Chief Justice delivered the Oaths of Allegiance and the Oaths of Office to a number of officials to whom I was then introduced. Then we went to the War Memorial where I laid a wreath. I was then allowed to change before being taken round the town which had been completely flattened out. Not a building was standing, but they have, however, made a very nice little temporary town out of palm leaf and timber and it nestles attractively on the flat bit of land below a range of hills.

It was a good deal hotter than Jesselton but not uncomfortably so, certainly cooler than Singapore. The Resident gave a lunch for 36 people and in the afternoon we worked until 4.30 and had a garden party for 200 people. Then I re-embarked and entertained 24 persons to dinner.

The following day we inspected all the Government institutions and installations, such as schools, hospitals etc. and then held a conference of all the officials. In the afternoon we drove out on a very bumpy road in an even more bumpy jeep about 15 miles to the war cemetery alongside the aerodrome, where there were 2,500 graves, mostly

British and Australian prisoners of war. They are still
bringing in bodies for burial and they expect to get up to
about 3,000. They seemed to be a bit off-hand with the
parcels of war bones which came in wrapped in newspaper,
but these were then given, very properly, with decent
ceremony a Christian burial. 800 of the soldiers buried
there were too sick to march across country to Jesselton,
so the Japs simply murdered them. Of the 2,800 who did
start on the march there were only four survivors and two
of those died.

We then took tea with the Officer in charge of the Australian detachment who looks after the cemetery and we
drove back another way and thereafter went to a party
given by the non-official Europeans. After that we re-embarked although they wanted me to go to a dance but I
declined.

It wasn't only his dislike of dances, that is to say, other
peoples' dances that made him decline. The sort of programme that was laid on for him at Sandakan and the concentration of nervous and physical energy that he devoted to
every part of it made him tired by the end of the day and he
was impatient with anything that kept him from an early
bed. And there was always tomorrow to be coped with, and
the day after that; new places to see, Lahad Datu, Tawau,
Kudat and Labuan, new people to meet and to talk to,
lunches to give, dinners to attend, speeches to make, rubber
estates, tobacco farms, coal mines to be visited. There were
schools to be inspected, and hospitals and public lavatories,
and all the ceremonies and the functions which distinguished
visitors are expected to enjoy, native dances, football matches,
pony races, physical training displays by nervous children.
There were some things however Peter Twining really did
enjoy. A Chinese banquet 'which consisted of (1) the most
delicious shark-fin soup, (2) the most excellent fried chicken,
(3) bird's-nest soup—which is really rather uninteresting, (4)
octopuses' air bladder, (5) very finely minced chicken, (6)
some special fish, (7) pork and prawn rissoles.' He also liked
the ceremonies on board ship at the end of the voyage.

In the morning we had a great ceremony on board the

ship at which I addressed the ship's company and presented them with three head-hunters' swords, one for each of the ships, and to Captain Bryant in command of the flotilla, a Brunei silver cigarette box. In return they presented me with a photograph of *Adamant* and my flag which they had concocted by putting the lion of Borneo in the middle of a Union Jack with a laurel wreath round it, which was flown from the mainmast during our voyage.

On the Friday evening we all dined in the Ward Room and had to make speeches and they presented us with a gavel, a polished wooden hammer on a stand which you bang on a block of wood to keep people in order at meetings, in a beautifully made oak casket.

If he was bored by some of the events, as he often was, he was careful not to let it show. He knew the time and the care that had gone into the preparations and the rehearsals. He had prepared and rehearsed events for visiting governors himself, and he had the knack, which many hadn't, of being able to give the impression that each visit and each event was as important to him as it was to those who had prepared it. And he expected others to do the same. Some of the heads of departments who accompanied him on his voyage on H.M.S. *Adamant* had thought, as they settled into their quarters and started to drink the Governor's gin, that it would be an escape from effort and concentration. They were soon disillusioned. 'What,' Twining would ask them when they arrived at each new place, 'have you planned to do today? And what,' they were asked each evening, 'did you actually do, whom did you see, what did you promise to do and not to do?' He listened carefully to their answers, and made it clear if he was or wasn't pleased. He went off in the submarine early one morning when most of his party on *Adamant* were still in bed. They submerged and carried out an exercise which included a mock torpedoing of the depot ship. The exercise gave him great satisfaction.

There were other journeys too.

I had a very pleasant little tour last week [he wrote].

We left early one morning in the Royal Train (a bare coach with open sides and very hard seats which rocks a lot) for Beaufort. Lots of people seemed to get on and off. I don't know what they all do. Beaufort is a pleasant little station of the usual pattern. Three or four European officials, a large green open space around which are the Government offices and police barracks. About 100 Chinese shops. We had the usual programme, with a garden party and an evening party for the 20–30 Europeans from the nearby estates. Next day we crossed the river and set out on the other railway—the Great Southern through many rubber estates to Weston, the terminus, which is a fishing village built on stilts. By the smell fish is the main industry. We did not dally but boarded the Royal Yacht—the *Rajah Gaya*. Gaya is a big island at the entrance to Jesselton harbour and the Governor bears the title of Maharajah of Gaya. The 'yacht' is a launch of about 30 tons which can do 16 knots but only does 12 as a rule. Forrard is a spacious deck where you sit comfortably under an awning. Behind the bridge are two minute cabins, each with two bunks and behind that the galley and saloon. The latter is like a large packing case with a tiny table which might seat two, possibly three at a pinch. Aft are the quarters of the crew of 9. I did not dare go below. She is alright up rivers and where there is no sea but if it is at all rough she is said to roll beautifully and as she ships water forrard you are driven to the cabins where ample arrangements have been provided for you to be sick in comfort and privacy. On that day the sea was calm and we had a nice little run of $1\frac{1}{2}$ hours to Sipitang, a delightful little Lotus Eating station. There we slept in a spacious rest house and I presented the M.B.E. to a chief who had cut off 144 Japanese heads during the occupation. The following day we went to another Lotus Eating place for an hour—Mempakul—the centre of the sago industry. The people prefer sago (which incidentally is made from a palm) to other food. They must have poor taste as my recollection of it is that it is only just a little less nasty than tapioca or semolina. So on to Labuan...

Peter Twining loved this sort of travelling. He liked going to new places and meeting new people, and he had a special fondness for small stations off the beaten track with neat, well laid-out buildings and lawns and gardens and District Officers with young wives and small children, men with affection for their people and knowledge of their ways, and pride in their virtues and their vices, men bursting with ideas for doing this and developing that, for growing two blades of grass where one grew before. 'If I were 17 years younger,' he told his mother, 'I would like to have been a District Officer in North Borneo...'

On the 14th of August he wrote

Tomorrow I shall have been here 6 months and I have been taking stock to see if anything has really been achieved. Certainly there are many changes but not many can be claimed as due to me. When I arrived the shops were empty and they are now full. Most of the staff were sick and all were disgruntled and quarrelling ... All the ailing ones are on leave, we have borrowed a lot from Malaya and have many new officers. They are quite a good lot on the whole and show great devotion to duty and work hard and don't complain about the rather uncomfortable circumstances in which they live. The economic life of the Colony has recovered well and the developments that are taking place augur well for the future. The finances are getting into good shape. Instead of having to call on the poor British taxpayer this year for half a million pounds it won't be for more than 50 thousand. Buildings are popping up everywhere, only temporary ones as we can't build permanent ones until we get a Town Planner and the C.O. cannot find one. I doubt if they are trying. Jesselton is now the capital and is becoming quite a big place. Sandakan has recovered remarkably but at Labuan the scars of war are very noticeable and have not been helped by a recent fire which burnt down all the shops. The railway is working. Quite a lot of cars are on the roads which are gradually being repaired and extended. The regular shipping service is regular. The R.A.F. weekly air service should soon be replaced by a bi-weekly one by Malayan

Airways. I have submitted my recommendations to the Secretary of State for a Constitution and a reform of local government. The laws are being revised and the judiciary reorganised. The Advisory Council have agreed to a complete revision of our taxation policy and to pay more taxes. The cost of living is too high still but under control. And so it goes on. One can hardly call life dull.

Six months later in another stock-taking letter he admitted that his first year as a Governor had been a very happy and a very busy one.

He had indeed been busy. Although he himself had concentrated on making his presence felt in all parts of the territory and in dealing with the doubts and the apathies and the inadequacies of some of his European and Asian officials, he had set his staff to work on three problems which needed particular attention. One was to work out a settlement with the home government about the financial consequences of the war and the Japanese occupation, and about buying out the Chartered Company's shareholders. Another was to prepare a statement of North Borneo's long-term economic needs and a plan to meet them. The third was to work out proposals for the evolution and if need be the creation of democratic institutions which would lead to the people of North Borneo having at first more say and eventually all the say in the management of their own affairs.

'For some time past,' the Governor said in a public speech in 1948, 'it has been clear that if this Colony is to progress in the way it should, it was necessary to place its finances on a firm basis. The position was complicated by such fundamental changes as the Japanese occupation, the period of the British Military Administration and the taking over of the sovereign rights by the Crown. Large sums were required for reconstruction and development. Increased revenue was needed for the expansion of Government services. But so long as the Colony was dependent on Grants-in-aid from His Majesty's Exchequer, so long was it necessary for the Colony's finances to be under close Treasury control. It is, of course, the first principle in political progress to be able to run your affairs, particularly your financial affairs, and it has been the aim of Government with, I am glad to say, the full support of Honourable Members of Advisory Council, for the Colony to exert every effort to help itself to balance its budget and only to go to His Majesty's Government for assistance which was essentially beyond our means. As a result of this policy the Colony has, since civil government took over, been able to meet all its recurrent expenditure and to contribute approximately $3,000,000 towards reconstruction. It was clear however that if we were to execute our programme of reconstruction and development with a flow of continuity and on a sufficiently large scale, it was necessary for us to be sure of having sufficient funds available during the next few years to finance such a programme. With this in view Government submitted its case to the Secretary of State for the Colonies with a request that the Colony should come to a final financial settlement with His Majesty's Government.'

The settlement which was made in the end was generous to North Borneo. Although the case was of course prepared and to some extent argued by his staff there is little doubt that Twining had a hand in shaping the policy and in presenting it both on paper and in person in a palatable and persuasive form. Even the Treasury in Whitehall, which did not as a rule have a high opinion of colonial governors' grasp of the principles and the intricacies of public finance, were impressed with Twining in this respect. And the North Borneo settlement bristled with intricacies as well as principles. Briefly it provided that H.M.G. would meet the full cost of acquiring the sovereign rights and assets of the British North Borneo (Chartered) Company. This went eventually to arbitration and cost the British taxpayer one million four hundred pounds. It was a sizeable millstone for Twining to have offloaded from North Borneo's neck. In addition the settlement accepted the continuation for the next four years of Grants-in-Aid from Britain amounting to a million and three quarter pounds. Twining tried as hard as he could to pull or wriggle himself off the hook of Treasury control, which he had found so irksome in St. Lucia, but his attempts to get the financial help he needed in a form which avoided such control did not noticeably move the polite but experienced officials at the Treasury. Twining did however get a promise

of a grant and loans from Colonial Development and Welfare
funds of two and a half million pounds towards the cost of
his five-year development plan against an undertaking on his
part to provide contributions of a hundred and fifty thous-
and a year through increased taxation from the Colony's own
resources. Nor was this the end of the help which he obtained. He persuaded the Treasury to redeem the currency
issued by the Chartered Company by a grant of half a million
pounds instead of by a loan as had originally been intended;
to waive any claim on the Colony for the cost of the British
military administration; and to provide loans and grants of
eleven million Malayan dollars to meet war damage claims.

North Borneo had certainly suffered from the war but it
was by any standard a handsome recompense, and Twining
was not afraid to say so or to remind those who didn't think
it was enough that it was made when Britain was facing one
of its periodic post-war economic crises and when the British
taxpayer was 'taxed to a degree which would have seemed
fantastic a few years ago'. 'I have always taken the view,' he
went on in his speech, 'that we would not be deserving of
this generous consideration if we did not play our part in
helping ourselves to the maximum.' The part they were to
play, it later transpired, was the introduction for the first
time in North Borneo of income tax.

Nor was this the end of his financial problems. He found
himself responsible too for the liquidation of the affairs of
the State Bank which had operated under Chartered Company rule and which had been taken over by the Japanese
and some of the accounts transferred without the customers'
consent to the Yokohama Specie Bank. Another complicated
problem was the registration and settlement of claims against
the Japanese authorities for goods and services rendered willingly or unwillingly by commercial firms and private individuals in North Borneo during the war. There were fortunately men in the Secretariat and the Attorney General's
office, and on the staff of the Chartered Bank of India, Australia and China, who understood these things and did all the
work but it was useful sometimes in such matters if the Governor knew more or less what was going on. Twining not only
made a point of knowing what was going on in all financial

matters but he often surprised and sometimes alarmed the experts with his knowledge. He could at least talk their language and understood it which was something that by no means all governors could do.

Twining himself thought that his greatest achievement in North Borneo was his Development Plan. This plan, which appeared early in 1948 as a 'Reconstruction and Development Plan for North Borneo 1948–55' came out under the signature of E. W. Ellison, an official who had been especially assigned to this task with the title of Development Secretary. The Introduction ends with an acknowledgment 'of the invaluable assistance rendered to me by His Excellency the Governor who gave advice and made suggestions at every stage of this report'. Others who were concerned with the preparation of the report may have used different words to describe the extent of the Governor's participation but everyone seems to be agreed that Twining did indeed have a great deal to do with it 'at every stage'.

The original idea, following no doubt on the success of the St. Lucia development plan, was his; the aims—eliminating the need for financial help from the British taxpayer and avoiding Treasury control, fulfilling an administering power's obligation to develop the resources of its dependent territories, and providing a sound economic basis for eventual political independence—these too were Twining's or, if not precisely his, part at least of the philosophy of colonial administration in the Twining period. Some of the detailed proposals bear the Twining mark as well, whether they were grandiose schemes for putting large areas of North Borneo under irrigated rice cultivation with the use of mechanical methods employed in the United States and Australia, or small specialised items like producing orchids for export to America or 'a gelatinous substance produced from the saliva of a swift which lives in limestone caves' for bird's-nest soup in Hong Kong and Singapore.

The report ran to 128 pages. One section dealt with the need, as the framework for all economic development, of improved communications, ports, roads, railways, air services, posts and telegraphs. Another section was devoted to the development of the Colony's natural resources, of its soil for growing food, and crops for export, of its livestock and fish, its minerals and its timber and other forest products, of its water supplies for irrigation and for power, and of the local materials and skills which could form the basis of secondary industries. A final section set out North Borneo's needs in the way of social services, schools and hospitals and houses.

Parts of the report read, as they were meant to read, like a business prospectus. Twining wanted to attract new capital. Apart from the material damage of the war, North Borneo had suffered during the sixty years of Chartered Company rule from a lack of capital investment. The Company had limited resources of its own, and when it made a profit there were always the claims of its shareholders to be set against the claims of the men in the field who wanted the money spent on roads and machinery and schools. The Company was chary of allowing others to invest in their own province and when it did allow them to come in it did so usually by granting monopolies which brought in royalties and excluded competition. One result of this, as the report was quick to point out, was that North Borneo was a comparatively undeveloped country and offered more in the way of prospects and challenges to investors who were prepared to spend money and take a chance than other places whose resources had already been more extensively chartered and exploited. Another reason why North Borneo was attractive was that it was, as a special correspondent of *The Economist* put it, 'in an early stage of political evolution, and large concerns are bound to be interested in a part of Asia that is still free from nationalism, political discontents and labour troubles'. This particularly applied to British firms in other parts of the Far East whose interests had suffered from the changes and the disturbances which were taking place in Burma, Indo-China, Indonesia and Malaya in the years after the war. Business men who had thought of North Borneo before as the exclusive domain of headhunters and of Harrison and Crosfield began to take a fresh interest and to send out emissaries. They found a governor overflowing with enthusiasm and ideas, a man who could talk their language and who could, if need be, out-drink most of them without losing either his acumen or his dignity. If they were concerned, as they mostly were, at the lack or the disinterest of local labour, they found that the Government of North Borneo was already working on plans to bring men in from Java, the Philippines, Timor and even from Iraq where, his mother had told him, there were thousands of poor Assyrian refugees who wanted nothing more than to live under the British flag and join the Church of England. The inhabitants of North Borneo were amiable and graceful people but, apart from the Chinese, who were bursting with initiative and dynamic energy, they were not the human material with which to work an economic miracle. 'The natives,' one writer on North Borneo said, 'always win because they have more lethargy than we have energy.'

Not all the ideas and schemes which the Development Plan plotted bore fruit, or bore fruit that could be eaten or exported, and not all the schemes which Twining himself propounded got off the ground. Jesselton was already establishing itself as a home of economic pipe-dreams and there were some critics who felt that Twining's large visions and wide horizons would have been better suited to North Borneo in the established and prosperous fifties than in the exiguous years immediately after the end of the war. He acted all the same as a catalyst, and a catalyst too early was better than no catalyst at all.

One of the first things Twining found waiting for him when he arrived in North Borneo was a despatch from the Colonial Office asking him to start making plans 'for associating the inhabitants with its government and administration on a basis as broadly representative as conditions permit'. In the light of later developments this may sound a somewhat cautious approach but it came from a Labour Government and it was an approach which if only for that reason some people in North Borneo found distinctly radical. At that time the only representative body in North Borneo was an Advisory Council which consisted of the three senior officials, the Chief Secretary, the Attorney General and the Financial Secretary ('that admirable triumvirate,' as one writer on colonial constitutions described them, 'who figure in so many constitutional documents'), and eighteen other persons nominated by the Governor, of whom six were Malays or representatives of the indigenous races, four Chinese, and three Europeans acting on behalf of the expatriate settler and business communities. The other five were government officials. Twining did not, it seems, take the Advisory Council very seriously, though it was useful, when he wanted to get agreement from the Colonial Office, to be able to say that he had consulted the council and that what he wanted to do had their unanimous approval; and it was something too to be able to show off to visitors, particularly itinerant Ministers and Members of Parliament. The Native representatives at any rate looked impressive in their traditional costumes and ceremonial robes.

People in North Borneo and particularly the old stagers were afraid that the new Governor would use the Colonial Office despatch as an opportunity to try and impose ideas of representative government and indirect rule based on his African experience, as Sir Douglas Jardine, an earlier Governor, had done under Chartered Company rule. Jardine had been dismayed and his local advisers delighted when the first recommendation of his Native Chiefs Advisory Council had been to revive stoning to death as the punishment for incest instead of imprisonment. Twining did not make the same mistake. He took local advice and he didn't try to go too fast. The proposals which he eventually put up offered enough conformity with current trends and enough promise of future flexibility to satisfy the Colonial Office and not enough actual departure from existing practices to disturb the more conservative elements in North Borneo. 'I have been at pains,' he explained, 'to build from existing foundations rather than impose an alien structure.'

The main factor which Twining and his advisers had to take into account was that the indigenous inhabitants who made up two-thirds of the population were for the most part unsophisticated people. The Muslims, who lived on the coast and along the lower reaches of the rivers, had had some contact with the outside world, but the pagan tribes who lived in the not easily accessible interior of the country had the material disadvantages as well as the less tangible blessings of having kept their way of living more or less intact. Of the two main divisions of these races the Dusuns were a gentle, peace-loving people, the mild men of Borneo. The Muruts were the wild men, the headhunters that everyone has heard about. Hugh Clifford, one of the first Europeans to have contact with them, thought them to be 'one of the lowest and most debased races of the human stock. They were lazy, improvident and abominable in their habits. They converted their annual crop of rice into atrocious native liquor wherewith they achieved a condition of chronic intoxication punctuated by periodical drunken orgies. In these men, women and children took part, for these drinking bouts had a deep religious significance and sanction. At such times all the members of the tribe absorbed incredible quantities of the poisonous stuff which they sucked up from jars in which it was stored by the aid of long bamboo tubes.' Twining liked them very much, and was much concerned about their dwindling numbers; he had a fondness for the unsophisticated and those who declined to alter their ways when they came in contact with the West. Perhaps he was partly attracted too by their appearance. Agnes Newton Keith described one Murut as 'dressed simply and solely in his cardinal red loincloth, his teeth filed to the gums for beautification, his incisors knocked out to admit his poison-dart blowpipe, his gums dripping red saliva from the juice of the betel nut he chews, his long, lank black hair hanging down to his small-buttocked behind...' It was not surprising therefore that the indigenous people of North Borneo lacked the dialectical skills to play an active part in a Whitehall and Westminster type of representative government, or the resources and the cohesion to hold their own with settlers of more vigour like the Chinese, and with the Malays. They weren't pressing for self-government or even greater representation. What they wanted then was not power but protection. Twining calculated that 'it would take 15 or 20 years before a generation of fairly educated natives has grown up'. Similar arguments were no doubt used in other places as a negative excuse for preserving a convenient status quo but in North Borneo they also provided the reason for a positive process of very gradual change. This positive process of very gradual political change in the interests of the majority of the inhabitants was as much part of the philosophy of the Twining period as the belief that a country must have a viable economy before it could prudently be left to run its own affairs.

What Twining's constitutional proposals amounted to in practice was the establishment of an executive council or embryo cabinet whose agreement the Governor had to get as a general rule before he did anything of importance. The fact that there were to be more Government officials on it than local representatives did not mean that the Governor would always get his own way. The officials were free to speak their own minds and often did, particularly in defence of what they thought were Native interests, and the Governor rarely acted against the advice of the local minority if they felt strongly about something and put up a united front. It was to operate in practice much more democratically than it looked on paper. There was also to be a legislative council or parliament. There had been legislative councils before in Chartered Company days but the minority of four members who were not officials only represented the Europeans and the Chinese, though Native interests were represented, and ably represented, by Chartered Company officials who knew them well. The new Council would still have an official majority but the local representatives were increased to nine persons chosen by the Governor to represent all sections of the people of North Borneo. The main part of the proposals however were concerned with building up a hierarchy of local authorities and giving those that already existed wider powers; and providing for a gradual process of change from a system of direct rule by British Residents and District Officers and Native chiefs and headmen appointed by them, to one of indirect administration through local leaders chosen by more traditional or more democratic methods. It was hoped that from this system would come elected representatives of the native peoples who would first advise, then share, and eventually control the central government.

Governors, according to the Concise Oxford Dictionary, are in their mechanical sense 'automatic regulators of gas, steam, water etc. to machines, to ensure even motion'. Twining's constitutional proposals had several governors as well as brakes and other safety devices designed to avoid excessive speeds or cutting corners but they were nevertheless a start on what then seemed the long slow road to self-government and independence. The Colonial Office accepted them on principle, but in the course of correspondence and drafting a number of changes were made to the original proposals and the new constitution didn't in the end come into force until 1950, when Twining had already left. He thus had the benefit of acquiring a reputation as an architect of constitutional reform without actually suffering any increase in democratic limitations on his powers. For a man who was chiefly interested in economic development this was a convenient coincidence; and there were inevitably some who suggested that it wasn't entirely accidental. Whatever the cause, R. H. Hickling in his admirable chapter on the Borneo territories in *The British Commonwealth—the Development of its Laws and Constitution*, was able to say in 1961 that 'North Borneo has, possibly for historical reasons, been somewhat less precipitate than Brunei and Sarawak in its constitutional advances to that admirable virgin, national independence.'

All this political and economic activity kept the Governor busy and his staff hard at work. Some of them indeed were relieved when in the middle of 1948 he went back to England for a few months leave. Mrs. Twining had come out to join her husband towards the end of 1947, and with her driving enthusiasm for child welfare and the Red Cross and with what her husband once described as 'poking her nose generally into the affairs of the Medical department', there were also others who were relieved for the sake of apathy and peace, when they heard that she was going on leave too. Those who were genuinely concerned with these problems were as sorry to see her go. They may have been disturbed by her persistence but they recognised her ability to get things done.

Peter Twining went home to England by sea. This time he was able to choose his ship and his cabin, if not his route. He had hoped to touch new ground by going across the Pacific to Canada but in the end it had to be the Red Sea again and the Suez Canal. His wife went home by air. Twining had intended to spend part of his leave badgering the Colonial Office and the City of London about North Borneo affairs, and as much of the remainder as he could wandering about Europe in pursuit of crown jewels. The war had interrupted his pursuit and his wanderings, and he wanted to make up for lost time. He arrived at Southampton on the 11th of June, but his return was not what he had so long planned and hoped for. He was carried ashore on a stretcher and taken straight home in a taxi by his wife. The trouble was partly a pain in his knee and partly a recurrence of his gout.

We saw Copeman yesterday [he told his mother in a letter on the 25th of June] and he was charming, efficient and gave one confidence. I am to go into hospital for 2 or 3 weeks where I am to stay in bed, have further tests, a special diet (rather more generous than what I have been having) and special treatment under his supervision. He has no doubt my trouble can be cured and future attacks anticipated or at least the chances of such severe ones reduced.

I am a little tired of all these medical tests. The blood doctor fortunately was stone deaf as he thought I was a doctor and prattled away about all the latest methods and my somewhat unscientific replies would no doubt have surprised if not shocked him. The results were quite satisfactory, perhaps he forgot to do the most important test. The radiologist heaved me about the table and took X-Ray photos of various members. As I expected the photos showed nothing to do with my present complaint but revealed a foreign body the size of a walnut in my left knee joint. May thought this would necessitate my being thrown to the butchers to have it cut out, a course of action to which I would never agree. Copeman said it was due to the injury I suffered when I fell over at the Mount in 1905 ... There is some difficulty in getting a bed in a hospital but we think there may be a vacancy at St. John's and St. Elizabeth's at St. John's Wood which is R.C. and run by nuns! While I am resigned to all this nonsense and buffoonery it is most exasperating. May has been marvellous here and considering all she has to do in the house, at the Colonial Office and working for the Surrey County Council it is very hard on her to do all this heavy nursing and as I cannot put foot to the ground it is heavy. She is a wonderful nurse and a devoted wife.

Two weeks later he was writing to say that the surgeon had confirmed that

> the Foreign Body must have been there a long time and is probably connected with my 1905 fall. He might be able to wrench it by manipulation but there would be a danger of it popping back. He therefore advised having it removed. I agreed and he will do so on Sat ...

The growth which was indeed the size of a walnut apparently had a certain technical interest and eventually found its way, to Peter Twining's delight, into the museum of the Royal College of Surgeons. It is still there labelled 'Small Cartilaginous loose body of traumatic origin and encrusted with Sodium biurate crystals to a large size— Removed from kneejoint of gouty male subject'.

Meanwhile he was having treatment for his gout which involved restrictions on his diet and consumption of liquor which he didn't care for.

> As to the gout Copeman has considered this (he suffers from gout himself) and while there is undoubtedly a gouty element there is probably something else as well. He was careful to explain that the old idea that gout was due to over-indulgence was a complete myth, although a drinking bout of several bottles of port and overweight might aggravate the condition. I dislike port but am slightly overweight. It is he says an inherent constitutional weakness very often hereditary. I have been closely examined as to whether you or any other of my forebears have suffered from gout. To which I have replied that as far as I know you were gout free and if what I have is gout I hope you always will be. In any case it is supposed to skip a generation.

When his mother told him that the Bakers had all had gout he answered that 'as I am pronouncedly Baker I must have

inherited that tendency too'. In the same letter he had to
tell his mother that Copeman was 'not an R.C., but a Rheu-
matism Consultant'. The late Dr. W. S. C. Copeman, a most
distinguished rheumatologist, had been at Lancing with Peter
Twining and they were old friends.

By the beginning of August Twining was out of hospital,
to his great relief. He was not the only one to be relieved.
He had been an impatient patient, easily depressed and often
irascible. Walking was still painful but he was soon busy
making plans.

I am definitely coming up to London [he told his
mother] but I shall be pretty busy. I have sent the Colonial
Office an agenda of over 30 important subjects to discuss
and I have 17 engagements with Big Business and similar
sort of people as well. It seems unlikely that I shall be
able to walk very much the first week. But I will keep the
afternoon of Sunday 22nd free and try and get down and
see you between 2.30 and 3 p.m. and stay until 5 p.m. if it
is not too tiring for you ... I have written to my Private
Secretary and told him to send you one or more parcels—
3 tins tea, 3 tins cheese, 6 tins boned turkey, 3 tins marmalade, 6 tablets toilet soap and 3 packets Sunlight. They
will take about 2 months to reach you but should keep
you going until I get back. I also said that if there was no
shortage of sugar there they are to pop a few pounds in.

He had been sending parcels to his mother since the beginning of the war. He was busy but he was never too busy
to be thoughtful about his mother. He also saw something
of his sons. The elder was doing his National Service in the
army before going up to Oxford, and the younger was at
home for the holidays from Charterhouse where, despite his
father's misgivings, he had in the end followed his brother.
Peter Twining also went up to Hereford to see some aunts.
He had, one way and another, a lot of things to do before he
went back to North Borneo but he managed all the same to
find time to get away to Paris and the continent for a week of
opera and good food and searching for crown jewels.

During the time he was Governor of North Borneo

Twining began to meet at close quarters a sort of people whom before he had as a rule only seen as a spectator—the sort of people who had succeeded and got to the top, admirals, ambassadors, bishops, business men, generals, other governors, politicians, scholars, as well as various visitors of a quality and interest that he hadn't really come across before. It was particularly interesting and important for him to meet them at this time because Twining used his period in North Borneo not only to confirm his reputation as a man who could get things done but also to evolve his own distinctive mystique of governorship and the exercise of power. He studied his successful visitors and acquaintances therefore with particular care. He was interested in how they had got to the top and how they behaved once they had got there: he was interested too in the advantages with which people had started and in the obstacles which those who had also been born without silver spoons had overcome. If there were many among those who came to North Borneo who interested and impressed Twining, there were also several who were equally fascinated and impressed by him. As they listened to him talking when he took them out for evening walks along the beach, or watched his style of governing events and men when they accompanied him on his official tours or his impromptu visits, his visitors were not necessarily struck by the same things. Some, like Lord Milverton, were struck by Twining's ability to combine the dignity and lonely authority of his official parts with a warm and very personal informality, which was something which he, having been a colonial governor for nearly twenty years, knew was not easy to accomplish. Sir Owen Morshead, one time librarian at Windsor Castle, was intrigued by the range and the diversity of Twining's talents, 'at once administrator, martinet, scholar and droll'. He remembers him as a remarkably good host, 'his talk always interesting, often recklessly amusing'. The two men had corresponded for many years about crown jewels but it was the first time they had met. From the sophisticated knowledge which Twining's letters had disclosed Morshead had formed an image of a man 'of finely drawn features and quiet dignity giving utterance in terms of measured precision': in the flesh there were moments when he was reminded of the comedian Harry Tate. Among the visitors to North Borneo in Twining's time were two particularly perceptive women. One also noted his 'quick way with words and his appetite for the gay and the ridiculous'. She remembers him, as many of his visitors do, with real affection, and forgave the showmanship and the occasional boasting because she sensed that they stemmed from 'a deep-down feeling of insecurity, a need to be noticed all the time and to be assured of unquestioning appreciation'. The other thought that of all the governors she met in her travels, he was undoubtedly the greatest. 'I first knew this in Borneo when I found myself with him in a small launch on the way to somewhere and for three hours he talked to me of North Borneo, the people and their difficulties, his problems and hopes. Only someone with an immense and effervescent interest in what he was doing would have bothered to do that with so insignificant a listener. And surely no Governor was ever better fun or less pompous. I have so many memories, one of the best being the splendid occasion when he stepped off the train at the end of that mini-railway line in N.B. and began shaking hands with all the "notables". Up rushed the A.D.C. saying "Sir, Stop, Stop, these are the porters, the notables are over there"—but quite unperturbed he went on down the line of porters and only when he had greeted the last one turned to the others...'

One of the reasons why Twining met more people of quality or of hierarchical importance than a colonial governor in a small colony would normally have done was that south-east Asia was at that time an area of considerable interest to the British Government. It was in a state of ferment. Just as the British, like the French and the Dutch and the Americans, wanted to re-establish their positions in their dependant territories after their initial defeat and humiliation by the Japanese, so were there elements both inside those territories and outside as determined for various reasons that they should not do so. In order to cope with this situation all the British territories in this area were put under the overall authority of a Governor General. All the British armed forces were similarly put under the control of overall commanders, and a Special Commissioner was also appointed to co-ordinate relations with foreign and Commonwealth governments in this part of the world. A considerable amount of establishment talent was deployed to fill these positions. Mr. Malcolm MacDonald was the Governor General, and Lord Killearn the Special Commissioner. They, and the Service commanders, all lived with their staffs and satellites in Singapore. It was there that regional meetings usually took place. When this happened the lesser fry, the ambassadors, the governors and the rest converged on Singapore, and met their overlords, and one another. Field-Marshal Montgomery came to one meeting too.

I go to Singapore [Twining told his mother] to participate in a Defence Committee meeting. Montgomery is going to preside. There will be 3 Admirals, Palliser, Boyd and Egerton. Two Generals—Ritchie and Cox. One Air Marshal, Pirie. One Special Commissioner for S.E. Asia Lord Killearn. One Governor-General—Macdonald. Four Governors, of Singapore, Malayan Union, Sarawak and North Borneo. All with Chiefs of Staff, Secretaries-General and what not. They are finding it so difficult to arrange the protocol for the order of precedence that they are giving it up. The real reason I have decided to go is to do some shopping...

From Singapore he later gave her his impressions.

We arrived here on Thursday. Having left Jesselton at 7 a.m. we put down at Labuan half an hour later, at Kuching 3 hours later where we picked up the Governor —Arden-Clarke and so three hours to Singapore. An uncomfortable journey but reasonably short. We are staying with the MacDonalds who are charming as usual. They occupy the Sultan of Johore's Singapore house—rather like an Italian Villa with spacious rooms downstairs but only two bedrooms occupied by the MacDonalds and her very charming children. Arden-Clarke and I are in a comfortable cottage in the garden.

On Friday we had a prolonged conference on Borneo

and South East Asia affairs which Arden-Clarke and I
thought was a complete waste of time. On Saturday we
had the big conference with Admirals, Generals, Air
Marshals and Governors two a penny. I never think Very
Important Personages look up to much en masse. Monty
seemed to possess few of the human qualities but he did
not swashbuckle as I had expected and when he spoke
impromptu for 2 hours he was quite brilliant, incisive,
clear. It was all very interesting.

Lord Killearn I like. He is two or three times my size,
very ugly but charming with a great sense of fun, rather
like a schoolboy. He is coming over to stay with me. The
Admirals were typical. Fresh, manly, the salt of the earth
(and sea). The Air Vice Marshals were quiet, serious, modest. The Governors were a rum looking lot ... Yesterday
evening we had a very grand dinner party—superbly well
done—for 74 of whom half were Malays and Chinese including several Johore Royalties. It was rather hard work
coping with them. Monty looked thoroughly bored. Tomorrow I dine with General Ritchie who is as nice as ever.
On Tuesday we fly back to Jesselton. Everyone is very
friendly but how I prefer the simple life of Borneo to the
life of a great and cosmopolitan city.

Someone once said that to start with Agatha Twining,
remembering her Peter as a boy, watched her son's rise in
the world with amused disbelief. By the time he was made
a governor however she was watching it with unconcealed
pride. She seemed to flourish on the evidence he gave her of
his consorting with persons of rank and title, and of his own
insouciant response. He had his own methods of showing his
apparent disdain for people in Singapore who might have
looked on him as a country boy. He dined once at the house
of a man who had been at Oxford in the twenties with the
Prince of Wales and kept reminding his guests of the fact as
one exquisite dish after another was exquisitely served by
his impeccable Chinese staff. 'Thank you for my excellent
dinner,' Twining said when he left. 'You must come and
have some curried buffalo bum with us in Jesselton one day.'

The meetings didn't only take place in Singapore. Mr.

MacDonald was a keen traveller himself and he had a particular liking for Sarawak. He went there frequently not only to hold meetings with the administrators of the British Borneo territories in order to discuss common problems and to keep the three places in step against the possibility of an eventual federation, but also to disappear into the interior parts to gather photographs and other material for a book he was writing on the birds and the people of Borneo. Twining was a great admirer of Malcolm MacDonald. He admired his easy informality of manner, his quick brain and quick wit, and his ability to get the best out of other people. Mr. MacDonald had however some talents and tastes which Twining didn't share, and which therefore he less admired. He told his mother for example that he was not surprised when MacDonald got typhoid as 'he will go off on his own to remote parts of Sarawak and sleep in Dyak long huts and eat their food which is silly'. Twining believed that governors and governors general should always travel in style. Whether he was visiting the interior of Borneo in a train or going in a hired car to a City lunch he liked to travel, as someone said of Curzon, as if accompanied by elephants.

Although Twining met many people of distinction and success during the time he was in North Borneo and went out of his way not only to study them but also to make his own impression, he didn't let this diminish one of his most engaging characteristics, that of taking trouble over people, as a junior member of his staff once said, who didn't matter. When A.D.C.s or typists or cypher clerks or the ladies who emptied the sanitary buckets looked tired or sad at the end of a long day he always seemed to find the time and the care to make them laugh or to infuse them with fresh spirit. He had always remembered and helped those who served him well; now more and more as his self-confidence and his means of helping others increased he went out of his way to do kindnesses to those to whom he owed no debt.

Twining had always had a flair for the cultivated eccentricity. It may perhaps have started when he was a boy and hadn't shone at anything as a means of drawing attention to himself, but as a governor in North Borneo one might have expected the eccentricities to lessen. This however doesn't

seem to have been the case. One Borneo official's wife found
herself sitting one evening at dinner, by the exactitudes of
protocol in distant places, on the Governor's left. She hadn't
met Mr. Twining before but she had met other governors in
the Chartered Company days and she was on her best behaviour. She tried not to look surprised when, bending down
to pick up her napkin, she saw the whiteness of naked thighs
and sock-suspendered legs. The Governor had pulled his
trousers up to well above the knees. 'Pardon my shorts,' he
said, 'but it's cooler that way.'

Another Twining eccentricity in his Borneo days was Tilly
stories. The principle of Tilly stories was very simple once
one knew what it was; but for those who didn't and hadn't
got the sort of eleven-plus mind that quickly sees the common factor, Tilly stories could both perplex and irritate.
Which does Tilly like, the questions went, tea or coffee? To
start things off Twining himself would provide the answer
which was coffee. Which does Tilly like, cotton or silk? A
guest would be chosen to answer. Some would shrug or shake
their head, or answer and say silk and get it wrong. It was
the sort of game which went on and on. Which does Tilly
like, red or yellow, pinching arms or pinching bottoms, eating bread or butter? Some people got it straight away, but
others, and Sir Charles Arden-Clarke the very able Governor
of Sarawak was one of them, couldn't see that Tilly liked
things with double letters. Tilly stories could have been a
harmless, even an amiable piece of after-dinner nonsense,
but it wasn't always played to please or put the awkward
at their ease.

'We have sent to Bangkok,' he told his mother, 'for a pair
of Royal Siamese cats.' Ever since he first went to Africa
Peter Twining's letters to his mother had been full of the
animals which he, like Sir Samuel Baker, had kept and carried
about with him. Loneliness and a sense of isolation are not
of course the only reasons why people keep pets but being
a subaltern in the K.A.R. or an assistant district officer in
the northern parts of Uganda were isolated occupations, particularly if one didn't play games or go to dances or spend
the evening at the club. And being a governor, he discovered,
could be lonely too. One's house was always full of guests,

one rarely had a meal alone, even the shop window in which one lived had its passers-by and its shop assistants. Governors must be approachable but they cannot afford the seeming partiality of having friends or having whom they would choose themselves for company. Twining had learnt about this sort of loneliness in Government House at St. Lucia but in North Borneo he tried to cushion it by making a sort of extended family of his personal staff, his Private Secretaries and his A.D.C.s. He thought too that he could escape with impunity from his official isolation into the private company of a few chosen people in whose company he felt at ease— people who could talk and drink with him and play charades and make him laugh, and yet knew instinctively or from experience to what lengths of informality they could and could not go with him. He may not have found North Borneo as lonely as St. Lucia but he paid a certain price for it: he got a reputation for having a favourite inner circle of associates and of listening overmuch sometimes to their advice.

It was however only the perceptive who saw such faults. To most people Twining in North Borneo was a gay and persuasive extrovert, a man who talked well and had a good head for liquor, a man whom people liked to work for, a man who got things done, a man who couldn't stand red tape, pretension or small officialdom. He pricked the balloons of conceit and pretence in other people but he had a strong sense of occasion and style and dignity for himself. And he could hold his own now in any company. He found himself in November 1948 at a conference in Singapore. Present, according to *The Times*, were the Ambassadors to Siam, Burma and China; the consuls-general at Saigon and Batavia; the Governors of Hong-Kong, Sarawak, North Borneo and Singapore, and a representative of the High Commissioner for the Federation of Malaya. Mr. Malcolm MacDonald was in the chair. At a dinner party Malcolm MacDonald, who tended to take the formalities of ranks and style with a pinch of salt, asked someone to propose a collective term suitable for such an impressive gathering. There were several clever suggestions in light, Foreign Office voices but there was also one in a deep slow voice from the lower reaches of the table.

'An excess,' Twining suggested, 'an excess of Excellencies.'
Mr. MacDonald smiled. He liked Twining and he liked men
with a wit as quick and as sharp as his own. 'Just the sort of
answer,' he replied, 'that I would have expected from an
Excellency of such excess.'

It wasn't only in Singapore that Twining was appreciated.
He had been made Governor of North Borneo early in 1947
for a term of five years. In April of 1949 he was appointed
Governor of Tanganyika. Tanganyika was one of the largest
of the colonial territories ('4th,' he informed his mother after
looking down the list of governors' salaries, 'in order of importance'), and the size and the speed of his promotion came
as a surprise even to him. It was by any standard a considerable compliment and an achievement of which anyone could
be proud. News of this sort however presented Peter Twining
with something of a problem as far as his mother was concerned. His mother, as he well knew, wasn't good at keeping
things to herself; but for her to learn of such things from the
papers or even worse from her relations or friends would, he
also knew, upset her very much. He dealt with the dilemma
with a characteristic mixture of bluntness and diplomatic
skill.

My darling Mother, [he wrote] I have a nice surprise
for you. May and I are to fly home next month! Unfortunately we are not to return here which is in many ways a
grievous blow as we have been so happy and our task is
yet uncompleted. But I have always gone on the principle
that one must go to where one is sent although it is emotionally upsetting to be uprooted every two years or so.
This is of course all most secret and should not be mentioned to anyone except Stephen—no gossip with the maids
or the Nuns or in letters to your sisters. I have asked for
the announcement to be made as soon as possible as it is
absurd and very trying leading a double life. When one
starts to pack one can fob people off by saying one is going
for a prolonged stay up country. But when one takes the
pictures off the walls they begin to smell a rat.

A few months earlier he had had to deal with a similar

problem when he knew about a month in advance that his name would appear in the New Year's Honours list as a K.C.M.G. Cautiously he kept this news to himself until the last moment.

I expect [he told her on the 30th of December] you will see something in the New Year's Honours but we do not take any prefix until we get the warrant. There must have been a very cold winter or an epidemic or something which killed off a lot and left a number of vacancies in the establishment. It is rather like waiting in a fish queue except however bad you are you may be sure of getting your reward which is not so in a fish queue.

I do not seem [he added in a later letter] to have had much choice in what I propose to call myself as everyone has addressed me as 'Sir Edward'. May who is very happy about it cannot get accustomed to being called Lady Twining and answers the phone with 'Dr. Twining speaking'. I have had to issue the sternest instructions that it is most improper for either of us to be addressed with these titles until I receive the accolade or the Royal Warrant dispensing with it. The correct form of address is E. F. T. Esq., K.C.M.G. ... So much for all that except to say that it is unlikely to make any difference except to put an extra 10% on our bills.

Many letters were written to the Twinings when they left North Borneo; polite formal letters and small private notes and printed addresses on parchment and paper heavily embossed. One has seen such letters before to other people and other governors on their departure; but it is difficult not to be moved by the mixture of pride and of sadness in these letters written in April 1949 to Peter and May Twining. A long beautifully flowery letter from the Representatives of the Native Community of North Borneo was the most impressive but a shorter letter from the Chinese consul makes perhaps a better epilogue.

Although you have been here only for two years, you

are a success. What by your rare democratic modesty, and what by your deep interest in the welfare and happiness of the people, you have made a complete conquest of their hearts. As to Lady Twining, I think she is wonderful. So much has she done for the sick and needy that she has won the universal affection and respect of all women and men. Your Excellency and Lady Twining will be remembered with gratitude and admiration by the people long after you have left the colony.

In view of your approaching departure from Jesselton I would like to be favoured with the pleasure of your company at a Chinese dinner. Any evening next week would suit me.

> With warmest admiration and kindest regards,
> Respectfully yours,
> Pei Chun Yu.

When the time came for Peter Twining and his wife to go, he wept. He may have been ambitious but North Borneo and its people had come to mean a great deal to him, and there were several moments as he said his goodbyes at the public ceremonies and at the smaller more private valedictory occasions when he wished that the spur of fame was not so compulsive or so burdensome, and that he could stay in this pleasant and happy country which he and his wife had somehow made their own and which, they sensed, could and would never be replaced in their affections. A cartoonist caught the mood exactly with a drawing of a large, boyish Twining handing over a balloon to a thin successor. The balloon, proudly full and riding high, was marked North Borneo. The caption said 'Take good care of it. I blew it up myself.'

9

Tanganyika : the beginning

TWINING HAD BEEN offered the governorship of Tanganyika
by telegram. 'The Secretary of State,' it said, 'would not in
the ordinary way have proposed moving you after just over
two years' service in a post which he knows had many attractions for you but he feels that you have all the qualities
specially needed now in Tanganyika from Governorship of
which Sir William Battershill has had to tender his resignation on grounds of ill health. It is essential, as the territory
has been without a substantive Governor since June last, that
the post should be filled with the minimum delay and if you
accept please say earliest date you could arrive here for discussions before taking up appointment.' The telegram was
sent on the 6th of April, 1949. By the middle of June Twining had arrived in Tanganyika and been sworn in as Governor. During that time he had wound up his affairs in North
Borneo, said his goodbyes there and in Singapore, flown to
London, kissed hands on his new appointment and been
formally knighted at Buckingham Palace, had his discussions
at the Colonial Office with Creech-Jones the Colonial Secretary
in Mr. Attlee's post-war Labour Government, flown to Nairobi for talks with Sir Philip Mitchell the Governor of Kenya,
and finished the journey in a specially chartered plane to Dar
es Salaam.

It was no coincidence that, just as Twining had been sent
to St. Lucia when it was in the doldrums and to North Borneo when it needed a fresh start, so he was despatched to
Tanganyika when that country wanted not so much an infusion of new spirit as an electric spark to ignite it. The

new spirit was in some measure already there. After the economic stringencies of the early thirties and the political uncertainties of the later thirties caused by persistent German claims to recover the colonies it had lost in 1918, there came with the end of the war a renewed sense of purpose and a clearer idea than most people had had before either in London or in Tanganyika of what ought to be done both in the way of economic and of political development. The ideas were there, and so for a change was the money to pay for them and enough staff to carry them out. The only thing that was lacking was, so to speak, someone to press the buttons on the spot. For various reasons, some of which like ill health could perhaps be attributed to bad luck, the Governors appointed to Tanganyika after the war had not managed to press the right buttons with sufficient force or dexterity to ignite the mixtures of potential and good intentions.

There were some, no doubt, among the Government officials and the representatives of the African, Asian and European communities who waited on that hot Saturday morning for the new Governor to arrive who hoped for a man who would be content to leave things as they were. Inertia has its attractions, even in temperate climates, for those to whom change means not only effort but a disturbance of positions and interests carefully acquired. There may have been some who felt like that but it is unlikely that there were many in Tanganyika in 1949. People of all races were for the most part more than ready for a change both in the tempo and the style of governing. So it was that those assembled at the airport and in the streets and in front of Government House watched and listened with particular interest for indications of the character and the nature of the man who had come out this time to govern them.

The ceremonies and the procedures of arrival and inauguration were, they noted, more elaborate than usual, more elaborate and more colourful. There were fanfares of trumpets from the roof of Government House and speeches from the balcony: two guards of honour each, as Peter Twining told his mother, 'of 3 officers and 100 men of the King's African Rifles with the King's Colour': and there was a drive round the town in an open car with the Lord Mayor. People

nodded their heads in approval, things they realised had become a little drab. 'And at least,' they thought in English
and Swahili and Arabic and Gujerati, 'he looks the part, with
that girth and that resplendent uniform, at least for a change
he looks like a governor.' They listened to his speech and
felt that it was refreshingly short and to the point. 'In the
past the development of this great Territory has been retar-
ded by the uncertainty of its future status and by lack of
financial resources. I do not consider that there is any need
for anxiety on the grounds of uncertainty and if anyone still
has doubts on this point I do not share them. With regard
to finance, very large sums of money are now available for
expenditure in the Territory and we must make sure the
best use is made of these funds. Tanganyika has embarked
upon a great programme of development which is likely to
gain momentum in the next two or three years. The effects
of this programme are likely to be far reaching and should
bring benefits to all who live in or have interests in the
Territory. The new problems which will arise will call for a
strong Government on the one hand and a high degree of
statesmanship from the unofficial representatives on the other.
As a newcomer I have tried to look at the picture of Tanganyika today objectively and in the right perspective. What I
see—whether it is the great strides the Africans are making
in their own advancement; or the splendid work of the
Missions; or the bold enterprise in agriculture, industry and
commerce; or the selfless devotion of Government officials
and others—I find it heartening and stimulating.

'To the Civil Service,' he went on, 'I wish to say this. You
have a fine tradition behind you. You have a reputation of
which any Service might be proud. But you are called upon
to adapt yourselves to rapidly changing situations and new
ideas. The standards which I shall expect from you will be
high. The pace at times is likely to be fast...'

If some of the more conservative or lethargic stirred un-
easily inside their ceremonial uniforms and robes at this early
talk of adjustment and speed it was what Twining intended.
He meant to start pressing the buttons and sparking off the
dormant mixtures right from the start. For the same reason
he was by no means sorry if the conventional and the ortho-

dox were upset by his singularities of behaviour, 'at my drinking in the bar and eating at the Club and doing my own shopping', at his going off for walks alone in the early morning and in the evenings and talking to everyone he met, and at his habit of sending his guests firmly off at half past nine so that he could go to bed. 'My broader jokes,' he added in a postscript to Evelyn Du Buisson, 'are not understood.' A Greek was surprised and enchanted to find the new Governor browsing in his shop and laughing aloud over one of his more earthy books. 'What-a-fun!' his comment was when he told his other English customers what he had seen. Many other observers thought the same but some of Twining's advisers were not so much amused when he called a meeting for early on the morning of the day after he arrived. It was a Sunday.

Twining was a showman who took a lot of trouble over his entrances and his first performances. It was not by accident or natural aptitude alone that he created a good impression and stamped his personality on his audiences in a way they would not forget. He was by now experienced in such matters and knew what sort of effect he wanted to produce and how to achieve it. He was not of course alone among public figures in this respect but with his military background he appreciated more perhaps than most civilians in shop-window positions that successful performances in public depended largely on meticulous attention in private to their details. It was originally planned that he would arrive in Dar es Salaam by sea from Mombasa and an 'unexpurgated version' of the notes which he himself dictated on the 'arrangements and ceremonial to be observed on the arrival of the Governor' show how carefully and exactly he arranged the smallest items. '... On arrival at Dar es Salaam someone, possibly the Commissioner of Police, should come forward prepared to escort me off. I shall meet him on board and then will go and change into uniform which will take me 15 minutes. I will then disembark immediately. (N.B. I had an operation on my knee last year. As a result it is inclined to creak like an old motor lorry when I go downstairs. I am also apt to trip up over my spurs, and my sword invariably but inexplicably finds its way between my legs especially

going downstairs, so I may need a discreet helping hand.)
As you suggest, I shall disembark at the Governor's pier
where you and the other notables you have mentioned will
meet me. We will then proceed to the place of the ceremony.
On arrival we take our places, the Clerk of the Council reads
the Royal Commission, which I understand is being sent to
you by airmail. I shall bring my own copy in case of acci-
dents. The Chief Justice will administer the oath. I shall
prefer to sign them subsequently as the pen provided invariably is unsuitable and the ink gets over my expensive
gloves.'

A few days after he arrived at Dar es Salaam Twining, who
knew his Gibbon, wrote 'The preliminary impression one
gets in Tanganyika Territory is the immensity of the problems rather than their nature. The areas and distances are
vast; the development schemes that are going on are huge;
the population is enormous; the volume of government business tremendous and the over-centralisation stupendous.' It
was not surprising, after the small islands and segments of
islands in which Twining had spent the previous ten years,
that it was the sheer size of the country which made the
greatest impact. Indeed there were times in the first few
weeks, as he thought of the areas he had to cover and the
number of people he had to get to know and understand
and meet, that he looked back with nostalgia at the happily
familiar, cosy nature of the country and the people he had
just left. But the challenges that now faced him quickly forced
him to submerge any regrets he may have had, and soon he
was immersed and totally absorbed in the problems of Tanganyika.

From all the other places he had served in Peter Twining
had early on sent his mother a description of the country
together with details and statistics of its people, its principal
products and its offensive insects. He had sent her maps so
that she could follow him on his travels with the fingers of
her mind, and he had provided her as a rule with lively and
sometimes uncomplimentary thumb nail sketches of the
officials and other persons with whom he had to deal. In the
case of Tanganyika he did not send her so much background information and one is tempted to wonder why. He

told his mother that Dar es Salaam was 'like an adolescent boy who has outgrown his suit' and that Government House was 'exactly like a wedding cake' but there is little about the country and its people as a whole. His mother, it is true, was now nearly eighty but there were no indications that she had aged in mind or that she had become less receptive or less interested in her son's activities. Indeed she seemed, as he told his wife in a letter, 'to have taken on a new lease of life, sacked the maid, given notice to the nuns and arranged to go to a R.C. place in Harrow'. A more likely reason perhaps is that Mrs. Twining already knew a certain amount about Tanganyika and that there was less need for the usual historical and statistical information. From those who went to visit her at the Little Sisters of Mary's Nursing Home at Harrow at this time one gets a picture of a dowager of distinctive views and lively mind who spent most of her time in bed and yet contrived to make her invalid state more a source of strength and advantage than of weakness. She was still a handsome woman and always carefully groomed and dressed as if ready to hold audience at any time; and she was very well informed about both her family's affairs and about the country with which her younger son was now concerned. She talked to everyone she met, and she wrote and received a large number of letters. She read *The Times* every day and she was a regular reader too of the publications of missionary societies like the Universities Mission to Central Africa. The simplest and most probable explanation however is that Tanganyika was so large, so varied and so complex that it was more than even such a good son as Peter Twining had time to summarise and commit to paper in his weekly letters.

Tanganyika when Sir Edward Twining went there in 1949 was a country of 362,688 square miles and about seven and a half million people. It was more or less square, about 600 miles across in each direction. Although it was four times larger than Great Britain or a little less than the combined areas of France and Spain, much of it consisted of what its earlier maps described as 'featureless, waterless, uninhabited bush'. This did not however make it a natural entity. While its southern and western limits had originally followed the lines of rivers and a chain of lakes, its northern boundary had been drawn with rulers in the Foreign Offices of various Western capitals by men who were more concerned with the balance of power in Europe than with the natural features and the human needs of eastern Africa. A kink in what otherwise might have been a straight line was due, it was said, to Queen Victoria's request that Mount Kilimanjaro should be put on the German rather than the British side of the line because her grandson little Willie wanted it so much. Even Tanganyika's western boundary was altered in 1918 by the excision of Ruanda-Urundi, an area of three million people, as compensation for a Belgian contribution to the Allied war effort in East Africa which many thought at the time deserved something less substantial.

If the area for which Twining found himself responsible in 1949 was not an entity by geography, it was even less of one by history or by race. Up to the time that the European powers created Tanganyika on the map as an area of German interest in the eighteen-eighties, it had never been a single country or a nation. It had merely been a slice of Africa inhabited by people who differed considerably from one another in colour, language, religious belief and social organisation. The majority, it is true, had a remote common external origin and spoke dialects classed as Bantu which were linguistically related but they had for the most part lost any sense they may once have had of unity or affinity. Interspersed with them were people of more recent arrival, Hamitic speaking races who had come in as conquerors from Arabia and the north about a thousand years before the birth of Christ: and mainly on the coast the residues of Asian peoples like the Arabs and the Persians, and of Europeans like the ubiquitous Portuguese.

In the sixty years or so of German, and after 1918 of British rule, some things were done which had the effect of giving the country an incipient sense of uniformity—the introduction of common systems of law and administration, the spread of Swahili as a rough and ready lingua franca, the building of roads, of a sort, and railways. Tanganyika was therefore more of a country in 1949 than it had been when the Germans arrived in 1884 but it was still a long way from being a nation. It was in many respects still an artificial European unit peopled by about 120 African tribes. The influx of traders and artisans from India after the British occupation had indeed added a fresh element of racial difference and complexity. There were about 70,000 Asians and 14,000 Europeans in Tanganyika in 1949, and just over seven and a half million Africans.

The fact that Tanganyika had such a small number of people in such a large area of land, an average of not much over twenty to each square mile, was an indication of its poverty and backwardness. It is fashionable nowadays to attribute such things to the shortcomings of the administering powers but in the case of Tanganyika it was at least as likely to have been partly due to other causes. Some of them were physical: poor rainfall, lack of natural resources and the presence of insects and diseases which limited the areas where man could multiply and flourish. Another cause was the Afro-Asian trade which in the nineteenth century alone probably took over a million men, women and children from Tanganyika to the Middle East for purposes of slavery. Whatever the cause, the fact remained that in 1949 Tanganyika was some way behind its neighbours in Kenya and Uganda in most fields of economic and social development, and a very long way behind other British territories in West Africa and the Far East.

One other thing the new Governor had to take into account was that Tanganyika had a special status. When the 1914–18 war came to an end it was agreed, largely in order to meet American prejudices against colonies on the one hand and a desire not to be excluded from their economic benefits on the other, that the German and other enemy colonial territories should be administered as Mandates by their new Allied owners in accordance with certain principles and subject to a certain degree of international supervision. In practice this did not mean that the Mandated territories were run very differently from other less circumscribed colonies, and it is unlikely that many of the people who actually lived in them were even aware that they had the benefit of any special status; but the idea had taken root in international diplomatic circles and at the end of the

Second World War the administering powers were induced to accept as Trustees further principles and a more extensive form of international supervision. Again in practice the principles—respect for human rights, paramountcy of native interests and an obligation to lead the country to self-government—did not materially differ from those which Britain generally adopted for its other overseas dependencies. The element of supervision however was real and quite distinctive. It meant that a report had to be sent to the Trusteeship Council of the United Nations in New York every year; that the Council was entitled to send representatives to visit each territory every three years; and that the inhabitants could send petitions to the Trusteeship Council or appear before it in person if they had any complaints or pleas. It was the first time Twining had had experience of international supervision though some of its manifestations reminded him sometimes of his experience of American interest in the politics of Ireland.

Twining's reaction to the immense size of the country for which he was responsible was to go and look at it at once. Apart from his liking for seeing new places and meeting new people, he was not the sort of man who cared for dealing with things on paper unless he had himself seen the places and the people concerned on the spot. He was not a natural bureaucrat. He liked to be personally, even emotionally, involved in every situation that came to him whether they were problems of people or of fact. Within a few weeks of his arrival therefore he had made plans to visit each of the eight provinces into which Tanganyika was divided. Each of the provinces, he told his wife, was larger than the whole of North Borneo except for the smallest one and even that had more people. As he feared that the country taken as a whole might be too large for the personal touches which he and his wife had so successfully applied in small places in the past, 'I shall,' he added, 'regard the 8 Provinces as 8 Borneos.' He set off on his first trip on the 16th of July, less than a month after taking up his post. By the middle of September he had visited all the eight provinces and a third of the fifty-seven districts into which they were sub-divided. He travelled by

rail and by road and by air, and he did part of the journey
by lake steamer.

Everything [he told his mother as he started on the last
lap] is going well. I still continue to have a good press and
my safari has been triumphantly acclaimed by everyone.
The ingredients are quite simple—Plumes, Band, For-
mality on Parade, Informality and personal touch off parade. At any rate I am very gratified because I did put a
lot into it and it is very often exacting, exhausting and
very boring.

A record which Twining kept of his first safari, as almost
any kind of journey in East Africa was called, gave his mother
a vivid picture of what these visits involved.

E.F.T.'s Safari 16 July—1st August 1949.
The Train

The train consisted of the best engine and tender; a post
office van; two luggage vans; a third-class van for the band; a
mixed 2nd and 1st class coach; the Governor's two coaches;
two bogie coaches for the train staff and two trucks for the
motor cars. The railway were very pleased with the Governor's coaches which I found disappointing. One consisted of
two bedrooms with real beds and Dunlopillo mattresses, a
bath room with a long bath, a small drawing room and an
observation car. The other of a dining room for eight, two
bedrooms and bathroom for Priv. Sec. and Housekeeper,
kitchen and pantry.

Dramatis Personae

The party consisted of the Provincial Commissioner of the
Province in which we travelled; the Priv. Sec., the housekeeper, the Public Relations Officer, the official photo-
grapher, the Editor of the *Tanganyika Standard*, and two
directors of the Colonial Development Corporation with
£105,000,000 to invest. There were two cheerful if hard-
bitten Scotch business men whom we nicknamed Laurel and
Hardy. There were also the European Rly Officials. The Band
consisted of a Sikh Bandmaster who was riddled with gout

and with his beard tucked up in a lady's hair-net. There was also a police guard of 7, my boy Ali, an Orderly Rashid, the cook, the dhobi, two boys and 2 drivers and a number of others. Nearly 100 souls all told.

16th July.

We went to the station at 7.30 p.m. and found a large reception committee. We settled in to the train, had dinner and the train left at 9 p.m. It rocked merrily as though on square wheels and with the Dunlopillo mattress one bounced about and had great difficulty in not hitting the ceiling. We arrived at Morogoro at 3.30 a.m.

17th July.

I got up at 6 a.m. and went and explored Morogoro incognito. It was very cold. It is rather a nice place, very spread out with the houses on hills behind the town. There are nearly 200 Europeans with more in the neighbourhood on sisal estates. At 8 a.m. we had a guard of honour on the station and all the people were presented. Only the élite were meant to be, but the ceremony got out of hand and hundreds filed past to shake hands including the train sweepers. As soon as we had changed from uniform we started on an exciting programme. First we paid a visit to the Tanganyika Cotton Company's office, then to the District Office, the Court House, the Native treasury, the Police station and lines, the Prison, the P.W.D. Yard, the Agricultural Dept. and Entomological Laboratory, the Social Welfare Centre and the British Legion, the Indian Association with a thimbleful of sweet champagne and speeches, the Labour Office, the Game Dept., Sir Alexander Gibb and Co., Consulting Engineers, schools, hospitals and I then struck and would do no more. After a dull lunch with a loquacious Bishop and a planter we retired to bed. At 3.30 a garden party in the sun. At 6.30 p.m. a party at the Club. At 8 p.m. a dinner party on the train enlivened by the lights fusing. At 11 p.m. the train left. The Band played ceaselessly all day long.

18th July.

Arrived Kilosa 3 a.m. Escaped at 6 a.m. for my incognito

walk. At 8 a.m. guard of honour outside the railway station
and presentations. Drive round town and Govt. offices. At
11.30 a reception on the train. At 1 p.m. train left. The
Band played ceaselessly all morning. At 8 p.m. arrive Kongwa
the great groundnut place. Transfer to the District Commissioner's house. He is a first-class chap. A veritable ball of
fire and a very nice Old Etonian A.D.O. A quiet dinner and
bed.

19th July.
I went for a long walk before breakfast. On returning I
was overtaken by a black man in boots. He introduced himself as a Mauritian. He thought the new Governor was arriving the following day and as he had served in Mauritius he
might know him. Did I? I said I had just met him—a short,
thin little man and I thought he was arriving that day. We
then parted!
We had a big parade, hundreds of Europeans, thousands
of natives. A baraza under the trees. I made a speech in
Swahili and was given two sheep which I did not know how
to dispose of. Then various meetings, lunch with some
groundnutters. A party for 100 in the D.C.'s house followed
by dinner for 12. The Band played ceaselessly all day.

20th July.
Up bright and early for a walk. Then an exciting day
driving round a corner of the groundnut area. We covered
over 100 miles and saw only a fraction of the area. It is really
most impressive, a vast scheme but there has been much
bungling and waste of money. We had lunch in a tent in
the middle of a field. Very good chaps, as keen as mustard
but rather critical of Government. After tea I went and addressed the Mauritians, 100 of whom are rather unhappy.
I don't know what my friend thought. Then a vast cocktail
party followed by a dinner from which I escaped at 9.30,
boarded my train which promptly left. The band played
ceaselessly all day.

July 22nd and 23rd. Dodoma.
We arrived before dawn and I went for my usual walk,

unrecognised and inspected the elaborate arrangements made in front of the massive old German fort. It looked as though there was going to be a public execution but it turned out to be the site for the ceremonial. At the baraza I addressed the Chiefs in Swahili. The Priv. Sec. was very disapproving of my grammar, especially as he had typed out a master speech which I ignored. Dodoma is a funny little town, an important junction of communications, with a most excellent hotel, 200 Europeans, the HQ of the Geological Dept, a nice prison and two Bishops. I unexpectedly found myself attending a service in Swahili at 7.30 a.m. in the very improbable C.M.S. Byzantine-style cathedral built by Wills' Cigarettes. There were only 8 Africans and no Europeans in the congregation and I was told that was very good. The Church plate was quite magnificent. The Bishop, Wynn Jones and his wife were most charming. He conducted the band at the evening party and I subsequently entertained them to dinner at the hotel. She took home half the chocolate souffle in two butter dishes for her daughter who had mumps . . .

24th and 25th July.

We got down nice and early to the airfield. But nobody could make the aircraft start. I said we had better motor to Mbeya but was told that it would take two days as it was 420 miles away. Finally the editor took off his coat, turned the handle and it started. Two hours later we landed at Mbeya. This is a most lovely place, 6500 ft high, cold, English flowers and fruit. Several hundred Europeans, a large European primary boarding school and much else to recommend it. Oldaker, the P.C. was at Lancing with me. We had a very nice quiet time and everything done very well.

26th—28th July.

We flew to Tabora in 2 hours. A large, untidy, sprawling place, very dry. In fact there was only 15 days water supply left and until next Feb they will have to bring it in by train at the cost of £250 a day. A very big baraza with some 7000 or more people. Boys and girls secondary schools (half holidays). Two very nice and one nasty prisons. An appalling

approved school. One good and one bad hotel. Lots of Arabs
from Muscat. We lived on the train and worked quite hard
as there are a lot of problems there.

29th July.
   We arrived at Shinyanga early. This is one of the H.Q.s
of the huge Sukumaland populated by the Wasukuma, the
most numerous tribe in Tanganyika. We had a great baraza
with all the Chiefs in their ceremonial robes and lion skin
headdresses. The Royal Drums, each of which is kept in a
separate hut were brought out and beaten for the occasion.
Chief Kidaha who is going to Oxford in October spoke in an
Eton accent but danced according to native custom. I was
wearing my white uniform with the trousers so strapped
down that one can't bend one's knee. As I got into the car
there was a rending crash and the seam of my left leg was
rent in twain from ankle to fork and all my left leg fell out
of it. No one saw unfortunately. It would certainly have
added to the gaiety of the baraza if it had happened in the
middle. I would have sent for a blanket and wrapped it
round me, saying that was the ceremonial custom of Governors. Having changed we went and watched the dances. One
was somewhat unexpectedly a snake dance. Having got into
the middle of a circle of natives I found myself confronted
by three dancing cobras. The native keepers then brought
forth several boxes of treasure, some tied up, some not. Out
of the first they brought an enormous python, 24 feet long,
which they hung round their necks. From the next box a
puff adder and from the next a horrid mamba which kept
on coming for us. I beat a dignified retreat. Then on to
Malya where a great experiment is being undertaken. The
band played ceaselessly at both places.

30th July. Mwanza
   The sight of Lake Victoria made me feel quite homesick.
It is a beautiful place, a little warm perhaps, but attractive
in every way. We stayed in the P.C.'s charming house on a
splendid position. We had the usual programme for two days
and at 6 p.m. on 31st July we embarked on the good old
S.S. *Usoga*. The band, which had played ceaselessly through-

out the two days, was of course playing on the wharf and played 'Auld Lang Syne' as we left. Then they packed up their instruments, embarked on a train and went off to Dar es Salaam and 14 days very well deserved leave.

This at least is how such journeys seemed as far as the Governor himself was concerned. They didn't always seem the same to his staff or to the officials stationed in the places he visited, or to the Africans and other people whom he met. Some of them not surprisingly found them hard work, and some were less than enthusiastic about the new Governor's occasional eccentricities. Twining developed, or perhaps re-acquired a taste for guinea fowl and venison on his travels, and some senior officials found themselves shooting for the Governor's pot for weeks on end to keep Government House supplied with the quantities required; and Bishop Wynn-Jones for example didn't care at all for the idea of conduct-ing the band in front of his flock and had to be persuaded by a suggestion which wasn't entirely humorous that 'a serious breach in relations between Church and State may result, my Lord Bishop, if you do not oblige'. The com-plaints and irritations were small however in comparison with the general effect. There was hardly anyone who met or even merely saw the new Governor on those first presenta-tional and exploratory tours who was not moved by some quality of his personality or style. Different people were of course moved by different things but Twining seemed to have something in his range and repertoire for everyone. The effect in any case tended to be positive and lasting. Every-one was stirred into action or reaction of some kind, no one was left to stand aside, as many had done before, in the comfortable margins of apathy or indifference. Thousands and sometimes tens of thousands of Africans saw him at the barazas, the public gatherings that were laid on for him, or at the traditional tribal ceremonies of dramatically over or under-dressed masculine or feminine display. They were im-pressed too by his own display of uniform and band and retinue and pageantry, by his large, self-confident, command-ing presence and, when he relaxed and joined in with the sweat and dust and noise of the tribal dances, by his in-

fectious sense of fun and gaiety. Those who met him at closer
quarters, at his visits to schools and hospitals, when he walked
with a chief or headman down a village street or wandered
on his own in the early mornings and talked to people about
their crops and their cattle and their women and their beer,
were struck by the way he listened to their problems and
their hopes and their grievances. They were made to feel that
he was really interested and that he really cared. Most of
them had never met a governor before or, if they had, one
who had talked to them in this easy way. They may not all
have been able to communicate with him directly because of
his limited Swahili but at least he tried to speak to them,
and his eyes were alive when he listened to what they had
to say. It was this approachability and informality which impressed Dunstan Omari, later to be Tanzania's first High
Commissioner in London, when as a young and unknown
teacher he first met the new Governor at Tanga in 1949.
Another young and unknown teacher called Julius Nyerere
was then just about to start on the first of his three years at
Edinburgh University.

They were not the only people to be impressed. Missionaries were surprised and pleased by his high regard for the
work which they were doing in schools and hospitals, and
Roman Catholics in particular noted his lack of sectarian bias.
Europeans and Indians engaged in trade and industry and
agriculture were struck with his grasp of their needs and his
appreciation of their contributions to the economy; and professional and technical officials who had often felt left out in
the cold on Governors' visits were flattered and sometimes
disconcerted by his knowledge of their subjects. The greatest impact however which Sir Edward Twining made was
on the African tribal rulers and on the field officers of the
Colonial Administrative Service. This was by no means
accidental. Twining remembered from his earlier Uganda
days enough of the realities of East Africa to gauge that for
the vast majority of the people who lived there it was still
not the politicians or the officials in Dar es Salaam and
London and New York but these tribal authorities and
administrative officers on the spot who really counted and
were effectively and tangibly the government. They were the

people who settled disputes and collected taxes, and who protected the ordinary African from lion and locusts and his
neighbours, and from careless or avaricious European and
Asian employers and traders. It was they who apprehended,
judged and sentenced people for acts of assault and theft and
witchcraft, and who in practice ran and even built most of
the schools and roads and markets and dispensaries; the men
who for good or ill were still spoken of as the mothers and
fathers of their people. It was, Twining believed, these African rulers and British officers who really knew the people
and were known by them, and who could best judge what
could and should be done and equally what could and should
not be attempted. He reckoned that if he were to achieve
anything at all in Tanganyika he had to win their respect and
trust, and harness their enthusiasm. It was in 1949 and the
early fifties a fair and accurate assessment.

The hereditary tribal chiefs were in Tanganyika for the
most part persons of real importance. Some were corrupt,
some idle and some harsh, but they were almost all people
of power and authority. Under a system of what was called
Indirect Rule initiated in Tanganyika by the drive and imagination of Sir Donald Cameron in the twenties, they had been
recognised and in some cases sought out from hiding and re-
established by the British administration between the two
world wars as integral parts of the government machine. The
system may have been started, when the country could only
afford a limited number of expatriate officers, as one of those
convenient marriages of principle and public parsimony to
which the British seem particularly addicted, but it had developed through the years into an arrangement which provided the people of Tanganyika with considerable experience
in managing their own affairs. Many of these chiefs were
men and women of colourful and distinctive personality.
Some also had real administrative ability, and there were
several like Kidaha Makwaia, Fundikira, Adam Sapi and,
later, Thomas Mchitwapya who felt an affinity with the new
Governor in style and office, and became his close friends.
Twining went to great lengths on several occasions to help
them and advance them, and to do small acts of kindness

and thoughtfulness which went beyond any interpretation of the needs of policy or duty.

The administrative officers who ran the provinces and districts into which Tanganyika was divided were for the most part Pooh-Bahs of considerable quality and ability. They were used to acting on their own but many had become dispirited by what seemed, in the mental and physical isolation of what were often remote and lonely stations, as a lack of interest and direction and support in higher places. As soon as they met the new Governor these feelings seem to have disappeared. One said, 'When Twining arrived in full dress uniform at my small, isolated, apparently forgotten District in two aeroplanes with a large staff and a host of senior officials I felt as if he had brought the whole resources of the central government to listen to my ideas and deal with my problems.' They were made to feel, as a Service, that they were the people who really mattered, and as individuals that each was the Governor's particular and especially chosen lieutenant. Soon after he arrived Twining had attended a meeting of Provincial Commissioners. They were depressed. They had submitted a memorandum saying that the vital part which administrative officers played in all political and economic development was not being reflected in recent actions and attitudes of the central government. They had been given a dusty answer. The first words Twining said were, 'Gentlemen, I've read your memorandum. It's interesting but it has one great fault.' Twining paused and looked at them over his glasses. They expected to hear the same evasive platitudes as they had heard before, the same suggestion that they had perhaps slightly overstated their own importance. 'Yes,' Twining went on, 'it has one great fault. You have been much too modest.' All those who were at the meeting became and remained firm Twining men. It was not only on senior officers that he had this effect. The most junior administrative officer was made to feel special and important. Remembering now how they felt twenty years ago, some use different words but the sense is strikingly the same. 'He made me feel good.' 'He had an extraordinary ability for getting the best out of me.' 'He seemed really interested in all I did, in all the schemes and ideas I had for the development of my District and the welfare of the people.' 'He did good every time he came and we were really sorry when it was time for him to go.' There was of course another side of the picture too. 'It was exhilarating but exhausting,' one of his more regular hosts remembers, 'and I sometimes wondered if I could keep pace with it...'

When he had finished with the first of his travels Twining went up to the Governor's Lodge at Lushoto to sort out his thoughts and set down his first impressions. He had had a look at the Lodge on his first journey and had liked it very much.

> Lushoto [he had told his mother] is very beautifully situated at 5500 feet above sea level in the Usambara mountains. The Govt bought a small estate in 1937 and built a lodge on it. It is more like a shooting box built in the Dutch Colonial style. It is most comfortable. Downstairs is a sizeable drawing room and a panelled dining room, a large study and an office ... There is a lovely garden with running water and English flowers (even daffodils and narcissus) and peaches and pears and of course strawberries.

After the heat and the dust and the bustle of his travels, and the hot-house atmosphere of Dar es Salaam in September, it was a good place for sorting out one's thoughts. The results headed 'Notes by His Excellency the Governor after his first safari through the eight provinces of the Tanganyika Territory' give an uninhibited picture of what Twining really thought at that time about the people and the problems with which he had to deal.

He started off by summarising his feelings about the different races. Of the Europeans permanently settled in the country 'not more than half are British subjects, a large number being Greeks. Of those who are British subjects a substantial proportion are retired people who are making the Usambaras and the Southern Highlands into a tropical Cheltenham and add little or nothing to the agricultural wealth of the country. This very fact makes them somewhat apathetic to local politics and the only two areas where an active interest is taken in politics are Arusha and Moshi. Here politics seem to be a profitable outlet for bad farmers who however receive only nominal support from the good ones. In the Northern Province the settlers have formed an organisation called the Northern Province Council ... I arranged for a small deputation of the Council to meet me at my house at 10 a.m. on the Sunday (the bars don't open until 11 a.m. on Sundays). A formidable deputation of twelve people came, who started to read at me long, closely-typed sheaves of foolscap. It was a very unimpressive display and it would have been difficult for them to have made a worse presentation of such case as they had. They claimed that they were the only democratically constituted body in Tanganyika (by which they meant that they had cajoled some 700 European men and women to join their Council), and that they were therefore the standard-bearers of European civilisation and should be given control of the Legislative Council so that they could achieve what was their right i.e., to govern Tanganyika. This theme became inextricably mixed up with other little themes, such as potholes in access roads, the desirability of teaching Afrikaans and the need for Greek schools. At 11 a.m. only half the delegation had read their homework and I had to tell them to go as I had another engagement at 11 a.m. which was entertaining a number of Africans at my house ... The truth about political development, particularly among Europeans,' he concluded, 'is that there is a general apathy towards politics amounting to indifference; and moreover there are few individuals who have the means or the leisure to take an active part in politics.'

Twining's attitude to the Indian communities was more sympathetic. 'The Indian community seems to present such difficult problems that, while one is constantly warned in confidential terms that it is the biggest problem affecting Tanganyika, no positive action seems to have been taken to find a solution. In approaching the problem, one must note the following facts. The Indian community is long established in Tanganyika and a second, third and even fourth generation of locally-born Indians is growing up. It is of course not one community but several; each however is compact and displays a commendable unity. The Khoja Ismailias, followers of the Aga Khan, are the most numerous, the most wealthy and the most important. They also appear to be highly disciplined. There can be no doubt that the Indians have played a very great part in the development of Tanganyika, a part which could not have been played by any one else. They now find themselves cut off from their links with India, increasing in numbers through a high birth rate and, owing to their prosperity, a relatively low death rate, while at the same time there is increasing pressure from the more forward African tribes to enter into the fields such as retail trading and transport where in the past the Indians have had it nearly all their own way. It is quite clear that this problem must be very closely examined and plans drawn up to ensure that the Indians can continue to play their part in the development of Tanganyika and be treated with due fairness in getting their share of the public services.'

When he came to write about the African people of Tanganyika it was at this stage their human rather than their political problems which seem to have touched him most. 'A problem which has caused me some concern is the great gulf there is between the highly educated Africans and the rest of the people. They must be the loneliest people in Tanganyika. They often feel that they no longer belong to their tribe. The non-natives deal with them all right during office hours but completely neglect them afterwards. They have no means of using their superior education except in the narrow limits of their office work...' Later on he noted that 'we are making African life very dull. Authority— usually the Missions—frown on their dancing; Government has restricted their hunting; everyone disapproves of their drinking, and so on. In return we give them a smattering of education; we have given them a thin veneer of Christianity, and we have taught an even smaller number to play football. The African has much latent creative genius and this we must mobilise, and two powerful means to do this are broadcasting and the cinema. I do not think that the African Film unit has the slightest hope of providing what is required. They are making documentary films with the highest technical proficiency and I imagine at great expense. The African does not want to see films on the sexual life of mosquitoes. He wants to be amused. He likes to see his own comedians and actors, to hear them laugh, chat and sing, and to act everyday little comedies and tragedies.'

Many pages of these notes are concerned with the possibilities of economic development. Twining still believed very sincerely and very strongly that political progress could and should only be made on the basis of a viable and expanding economy, and that a country could not be left to stand on its own feet politically until it was in a position to pay its own way. He believed that this could only be done in Tanganyika, where the Europeans and the Indians possessed so many of the skills of industry and commerce and played such a large part in the production of its wealth, by the combined efforts of all the races in the territory. His conclusion reflected this philosophy.

'Tanganyika is at present at a very interesting stage of its history, and the progress that is likely to be made within the next five or ten years should be very great. In fact I predict that within five years it will be taking the lead in East Africa economically and within ten politically ... There is a very good spirit abroad and there seems a real possibility of the three races co-operating economically and politically and on the success of their co-operation depends the future of Tanganyika.'

When he had finished his private summary of his first impressions, the Governor went back to his headquarters at Dar es Salaam to work out with his officials what he would say publicly at the opening of the Legislative Council at the end of November. It would be his first major speech since he had taken up his appointment and he and his advisers devoted much time and thought to it. The speech which he eventually delivered was a long one. 'It was,' a local paper reported, 'filled with infectious optimism and energy, an energy typified by his personal endurance, for he spoke for over an hour and a half in that crowded hall, dressed in full ceremonial dress and disdaining the glass of water which even his listeners longed for in that November heat.' The speeches of public men are not as a rule good evidence for biographies as they are more often than not written and thought out for them by anonymous public servants, but there was one paragraph which was certainly Twining's own both in the wording and the thinking. He had been talking about the progress made in injecting a democratic element into the somewhat feudal structure of tribal government, and about the establishment of District and Provincial Councils on which all races were represented.

I should like to state emphatically that I believe that this development, which has as its two main features inter-racial co-operation and building from the bottom instead of from the top, is of the greatest importance to Tanganyika. If we can make the Provincial Councils efficient and responsible bodies, they may become the foundation on which to base the future political life of the Territory. It is important that, at an early date, we should ensure that the unofficial representatives on these Councils should sit with some form of popular support. If these Councils can be properly established, then they may become the electoral colleges for unofficial representation on the Central Government.

Twining did not think that at that time there was any general desire or need for any change in the constitutional arrangements at the centre. A majority of officials sat on both the Executive and the Legislative Councils together with a number of local representatives of all three races who had been carefully chosen for their sense of responsibility and their knowledge of English in which the business of the central government was then conducted. It was in practice a benevolent bureaucracy tempered by critical and effective if undemocratic popular representation, and Twining was not the only one who thought that it met the needs and the realities of the Territory at that time. Most of his experienced officials thought so too, and so apparently did the four Africans, three Asians and seven Europeans who had been selected to represent the interests of their communities in the Legislature. The right way to make a start with democracy, they believed, in a backward country which had not yet achieved any real sense of unity, was in the tribal areas and in the districts and the provinces. In deference however to the Colonial Office which was anxious, among other reasons, to have something to show to the United Nations Trusteeship

Council, Twining appointed an inter-racial Select Committee of the Legislature 'to review the present constitutional structure of the Territory, both local and territorial, and to make recommendations for future constitutional development in the Territory.' When its chairman Charles Mathew, Tanganyika's able and pragmatic Attorney General, submitted its report in 1951, another Committee was set up under the chairmanship of W. J. M. Mackenzie, Professor of Government at Manchester University, to examine a number of consequential problems including the question of holding elections at some unspecified date in the future.

With, so to speak, his political rear secured by the existence of these two committees Twining was able to concentrate his attention on what he regarded as the more urgent and important matter of economic development. The knowledge that the outcome of the reports of these constitutional committees was likely to be a slow and gradual approach to questions of popular representation enabled him to persuade those who were thinking of investing large sums of money in the country or of extending their existing operations that Tanganyika, at any rate, was politically stable and likely to remain so for many years. Independence was not regarded then as a practical possibility for at least another generation.

10

Tanganyika : the middle years

THE NEXT FEW years were good years for Tanganyika. Its main exports, crops like sisal and coffee and cotton, and minerals like diamonds and gold, were stimulated by the high prices resulting from the Korean war, and provided increasing wealth to the country as a whole through wages and contributions to the revenue. Although these activities were well established and flourishing when Twining arrived, he took a lively and active interest in them and in the problems which prosperity, no less, he noted, than depression, seemed to produce. Bird and Company made a profit of over a million pounds from sisal in two successive years. Its local manager Eldred Hitchcock, who might well have served as a model for a character in a novel by Graham Greene, had proved a thorn in the thin flesh of some earlier Governors, but Twining was more than a match for his barbed tongue and his somewhat caustic approach to relations with the Government. Although they both had in private reservations about one another, they got on well together on the surface and each persuaded the other to do things for the benefit of the industry and of Tanganyika which more orthodox men might have found difficult to achieve. What Twining could not achieve with Hitchcock he accomplished through his friendship with Sir Charles Ponsonby who looked after the London end of the business, and with Abdulla Karimjee whose quick brain and quiet charm often produced better results and bigger profits than the sharpness of Hitchcock's cutting edges. Twining for his part made the annual dinner of the Sisal Growers Association one of his most regular and colourful engagements. His after dinner speeches came to be regarded as an event of some importance in the calendar of public entertainments especially when, as once happened, he dramatically tore up the speech which had been prepared for him by his officials and delivered in its place a seemingly extempore economic analysis of considerable wit and brilliance.

With Williamson, a Canadian geologist who after many lean years had found diamonds in the north-west of Tanganyika estimated in 1952 to be worth twenty-two million pounds, Twining's relations were, because of Williamson's solitary and suspicious nature, less frequent and less informal, but this did not stop him involving himself in a disagreement between Williamson and De Beers Diamond Corporation over price and marketing which held up the sale of Tanganyika diamonds for two years. Eventually an agreement was reached in 1952 which guaranteed Williamson, and Tanganyika, ten per cent of world sales of gem and industrial diamonds and a minimum income of a million pounds a year. Although Twining may perhaps have scorched his fingers by his involvement in this complicated and ruthless dispute he thoroughly enjoyed his excursion into the world of millionaires and high living, and extracted large sums from both parties in the process for various projects of his own in Tanganyika for African advancement.

While none of his other excursions into the world of business were on quite this scale, Twining devoted much time and travelling to bringing new money, new industry and new trade to Tanganyika. By March 1951, he calculated with his penchant for statistics, he had travelled 50,000 miles since he had first arrived. Much of that mileage was taken up with visits to neighbouring countries in eastern and southern Africa and with two trips to London during one of which he escaped for another quick tour of Europe. Most of his time was devoted to some aspect of Tanganyika's interests. He found time however to do some crown jewelling in Italy and paid several visits to the opera, and he stayed with the Aga Khan whose son Aly and his wife, the former Rita Hayworth, had been his guests at Dar es Salaam. A

typical week in London at this time was described in a letter
to his mother.

On Tuesday a hard fibre magnate came to see me for
lunch and to talk business, and in the afternoon I had
meetings at the Colonial Office. Oliver Woods the *Times*
African correspondent came to dinner. On Wednesday I
went to the East African Office and dictated some letters
and interviewed the Chairman of the New Consolidated
Gold Fields. Jim and Bill Du Buisson came to lunch as
their firm is thinking of growing sugar in Tanganyika. In
the afternoon I had a conference on our diamond troubles
at the Colonial Office. In the evening Cohen the head of
the African Department came to dinner. On Thursday I
visited the legal adviser to our diamond king and gave
him a little advice. I then had an hour's meeting with
Lord Reith, the Chairman of the Colonial Development Corporation, which was not so acrimonious as last time and
had lunch with Lord Milverton who is always interesting.
Then after a meeting with a couple of Governors at the
Colonial Office I went to the E.A. Office and had $2\frac{1}{2}$ hours
with representatives of English Electric...

His life in Tanganyika was no less busy.

We are thankful [he wrote in June 1950] that the last
fortnight is over. Everything went very well but we hardly
had a moment to ourselves. We had 17 people in the house
off and on, a State dinner party for 40, a frightful Garden
Party for 500 at which I wore a top hat, another given by
the Aga Khan's community for 1500; the King's Birthday
parade, a grand presentation of Orders, decorations and
medals, a Tattoo and a fireworks display; 3 receptions, 2
meetings of Legislative Council and 1 of Executive Council besides our ordinary work. On 3rd we go to Bagamoyo.
On 6th I fly to Mombasa to open the E. African Navy as
Chairman of the High Commission ... Then on 12th July
I fly to Johannesburg to see Mining Magnates and others.
On 17th I go to Salisbury for 2 nights and then to Zomba
for 3 ... On 1st August some of us set out on safari to

Mahenge; Sumbawanga; Ukerewe Island; the opening of
the new railway to the Mpanda mine; to Kigoma for the
consecration of an R.C. Cathedral. Then back here for a
visit of 16 from the Imperial Defence College; then the
week's visit of the flagship H.M.S. *Mauritius*. On 5th Sept
to Tanga, on the 9th to Lushoto for the consecration of the
new Anglican Church, then to Arusha, Masailand and the
Serengeti Plains ... Then we go down to Mbeya and drive
thence to Nairobi for a meeting of the E. African High
Commission. In the last week of Oct we pay a State visit
to Madagascar ...

He spent most of his time in South Africa with his millionaires. One was John Schlessinger.

We are arranging for him to start an African film industry in Tanganyika under Government control. The filthy
muck which is now shown is quite unsuitable for Africans
and does immense harm. Schlessinger is to make films,
process them and distribute them while Government will
provide the stories and African performers. We hope to
turn what is now a weapon of evil into a weapon for good.

The other millionaire was Sir Ernest Oppenheimer of
De Beers, some of whose family jewelry he saw and described in knowledgeable detail to his mother who had an
appetite for the rich as well as for royalty and aristocracy
which her son always did his best to satisfy. He didn't however care for much else in South Africa.

I must say I neither like Johannesburg, Pretoria or
South Africa. The first is a soulless city of Mammon, the
second is a sprawling symbol of hatred of everything British and the third is an arid inhospitable land inhabited
by people whose outlook is foreign to ours and who dislike
or despise everything we prize ... Though I am enjoying
the change and meeting interesting people I shall be glad
to get back to my own stamping ground where our standards are so much more simple.

In his own stamping ground Twining had by this time

worked out a routine both for his working and his leisure hours. Some of the basic elements of this routine went back many years but it was in Tanganyika that the finishing touches were applied and the routines acquired some of the qualities of ritual. He described the framework in one of his letters.

Ali [a Comorian personal servant from his early Uganda days] brings me tea at 5 a.m. I get up at 5.15 and write letters or work on the files. 7.15 shave, bath, dress and have breakfast. 8 a.m. to office and dictate minutes, letters despatches and memoranda which have formed in my mind. 9 a.m. The Chief Secretary comes in for his daily hour. 10–12.15 interviews. 12.30 lunch and forty winks. 2–4.15 meetings. 4.15 tea. 5–6 walk or deck tennis. 6–8 files. 8 dinner. 9.30 bed. One gets [he concluded] into a pretty cast-iron routine which is the secret of good health.

Those who knew Twining well or worked closely with him during this period will remember other details, like his complete unapproachability at breakfast, the 'ideas from my bath' which successive Chief Secretaries had to absorb or discard at those early morning meetings, the somewhat longer periods usually allowed for drinks before lunch and for the forty winks afterwards, and the stratagems and devices employed before dinner to absorb more whisky than those concerned with his health thought advisable. Nor was '5–6 walk or deck tennis, 6–8 files' a fair summary of what he actually did on most evenings. Much of Sir Edward Twining's most effective work as Governor was done during these periods when friends or critics or government officials would be invited or summoned to come for a walk to be pumped or primed or persuaded to some new idea, and visitors who had dutifully or hopefully signed the book at Government House would be asked in to drinks and, particularly if they were men of business potential or journalists and writers, filled up with facts and figures and points of view. He took a great deal of trouble over his relations with the press and with those who used their pens or typewriters as instruments of power, and he was on particularly friendly and mutually admiring terms with Oliver Woods of *The Times* and Colin

Legum of the *Observer,* and with John Gunter whose 'Inside' books were then widely read and quoted. Twining was by no means as bad at paper work, at files and minutes, letters and despatches, as he often pretended to be, but he was at his best with people. When he really set out to charm and interest and persuade, or to dissuade, there were not many people who could resist him. He respected those who did, and although he used intimidation and abuse and a show of temper sometimes in order to get his own way he was usually disarmingly generous with his apologies if he thought he had gone too far. When he had people in to dinner, as he often did, he had his own methods too of passing and hastening the awkward hours between the end of dinner and the time his guests departed. Sometimes it was charades or a rough and tumble form of billiard fives for which he sometimes changed into shorts to give himself a winning advantage over his less easily dressed guests. On more formal occasions when a police or military band was brought in to play he would conduct the band himself partly for fun and partly, it was said, so that he could himself choose the time to play 'God Save the King' and send his guests firmly off to bed.

There was another long established detail of his routine which was not mentioned in his letter. On Sunday morning at half past ten he would shut himself away with his records and his gramophone. He was usually alone, and not to be disturbed but he would sometimes ask special persons in to share this ritual. Verdi's *Requiem* and Berlioz's *Grand Messe des Morts* were among his favourites at this time but he had also developed a taste for Russian music which, however, stopped strictly short of Shostakovich. Sometimes he paced up and down while he listened, and sometimes he stood quite still. Sometimes he smiled, and sometimes he was moved by more complex emotions. His need of music, and his dependence on it to stimulate his thought and his imagination seemed to increase rather than diminish with the years.

Twining had always been a man of habit. He had a sense of waste over time that was unoccupied. Routine filled the hours and gave them purpose. He urged the virtues of routine on others and imposed them on himself. They were particularly important, he found, when he became a governor. A colonial governor's job, it could be argued, was to direct and control and inspire, and to perform a number of royal and presidential duties. It was for his staff and his officials to do the work. When Sir Andrew Cohen was subtracted from the Colonial Office and made Governor of Uganda in 1953, Twining, who had a great respect for Cohen's mental ability and energy, told him that it was a bad appointment because he wouldn't have enough to do. He was wrong in this particular case as it happened but he knew from his own experience that as a general rule it was as well for men in representational positions to have regular habits and plenty of hobbies. Otherwise they were apt to get bored or restless or what was worse, they tried, as they say of brigadiers and generals, to run the platoon. Twining had both his routines and his hobbies, and much of those early hours between 5.15 and 7.15 were in fact spent on his crown jewels and his collection of stamps. He was rarely idle and he was rarely bored; and he didn't often interfere with other people's detail.

He followed the same sort of routine at Lushoto where he usually had his base during the hot humid months between December and April. He liked however to play the squire in the small local community, and was often to be found keeping himself up to date with the gossip of his African neighbours or sharing the supper of the children of the District Officer. And instead of his daily talks with his Chief Secretaries in his office at nine o'clock he would get them on the telephone and discuss the ideas that had come to him before he went to sleep or while he had his bath. This sometimes took a long time, and as the line went across 400 miles of Africa nailed to crooked poles or trees, which didn't improve audition, most of his Chief Secretaries developed what one of them described as telephone ear. Twining's four successive Chief Secretaries, Surridge, Bruce Hutt, Stapledon and Grattan-Bellew were men of different temperaments and talents but they all, one feels, for one reason or another deserved the honours and promotions which eventually came their way.

Although the Governor used Lushoto to some extent as a

retreat and a place in which to think he invited a large number of people to stay with him. He was a good host anywhere but visitors remember him as being particularly thoughtful and entertaining when he was at home at Lushoto. He was good too to his relations and his family. He had a wide and generous sense of genealogy. Both his sons came out several times to stay with him and accompany him on his travels, and so did Evelyn Du Buisson though she was soon put willingly to work translating and transcribing French and German books and documents on European crown jewels. His wife's able and amiable brother William Du Buisson came out more than once. His own brother Stephen and his wife were also invited to stay, and some of the younger members of the family circle were employed as A.D.C.s. Twining liked to surround himself with his relations and to involve himself in their affairs, and as in North Borneo he tended to treat all his personal staff, his private secretaries, his A.D.C.s, his confidential stenographers, even his special African servants like Ali and his driver Salehe as if they were members of the family. His guests too sometimes received similar treatment. When Colin Legum brought out his very young son to stay at Government House at Dar es Salaam the boy was taken by Twining to sit in the Governor's chair. 'You are the Governor now. What would you like to do?' After a pause the boy said that he'd like to go for a swim. 'See those buttons there? Press that one and see what happens.' The button was pressed and the A.D.C. appeared. 'You are the Governor,' Twining said. 'Tell him what you want to do.' The boy smiled and said he wanted to swim. 'Don't tell him with a smile. Tell him with a growl and a horrible scowl like this.' The boy did his best and the A.D.C. clicked his heels and went to get a towel and a bathing dress and the official car. A few minutes later the boy went off to the beach in state. It was something he did not forget.

While Twining liked Lushoto, and still had his official duties and his many official visitors to attend to in Dar es Salaam, he did not by any means neglect the objective he had set himself of seeing as much of the country and its people as he could. He bought a Rolls-Royce, second hand, for dignity and comfort, if not speed, and he persuaded the Colonial

Office to sanction the purchase of a new and larger private plane by the simple expedient, it is said, of sending them a photograph of himself emerging bottom first from the old one in the presence of a large crowd and a guard of honour. His wife was a conscientious and persistent traveller too, and the schedules and the details of their joint and their separate journeys make impressive reading. Between them they enveloped a lot of ground and a lot of subjects and a lot of people. Lady Twining was especially interested in health and medicine, in Red Cross work and in children's and women's welfare. Twining himself was still more concerned with economic development—with making the country self-supporting and self-sufficient, with improving its communications and with harnessing and controlling its limited and uneven supplies of water. He visited, with one small exception, all the administrative divisions in the territory so that he could see things on the spot, meet the officials and the inhabitants of all races who were concerned with these activities, and find out what he could do to help. Although he was not perhaps unmindful of the credit which could be extracted from these projects for himself and his administration, he often became deeply and very personally involved in some of the schemes which he learnt of and took under his own wing. Typical of these schemes was the Sukumaland Development Scheme on which about two million pounds was spent between 1948 and 1955 in a concerted effort to improve the crops and the livestock of one of the largest tribal groups in the country. There were several other such regional development schemes in Tanganyika during this period. They all had the same basic objective but the emphasis was on different things. In some it was the prevention of soil erosion or the improvement of grazing; in others on culling or the introduction of new crops. In one area the main problem was supplies of water, in another the elimination of human or animal diseases. In all there was a need for education. The administrative and professional officers who thought out these schemes and fought for them and saw them through with the help of the African tribal authorities were dedicated and often passionately enthusiastic men and women, and they and their schemes appealed both to Twining's hard-headed sense of economics and to his less hard-headed emotions. He cajoled and bullied to get money for them, and he paid frequent visits to see for himself how they were getting on and to give the people working on them the benefits of his encouragement and his criticism. Although he had not been concerned with the planning and the initial spectacular disappointments of the scheme to grow groundnuts in Tanganyika, he was attracted by the grand design of the scheme and by the idea of large-scale mechanised agriculture as a means of enabling Africans to grow enough food to meet their own needs. He was therefore more interested in salvaging a residue of its good elements, in using the ports, railways and roads which had been built hopefully to carry groundnuts and sunflower seeds, for more practical and comprehensive purposes, than in the then very popular game of trumpeting its failures. Many estimates of cost and forecasts of achievements were made for the Groundnut Scheme but when it was clear at last that a total of about thirty-five million pounds had been spent and that it had cost an average of more than fifty pounds an acre to clear the land for planting instead of the estimated three pounds seventeen shillings and fourpence, there were many who wanted to close the scheme down altogether. It was partly due to Twining's efforts that it was agreed, as a compromise, that it should continue on a reduced and more realistic scale, and that when a local body took over responsibility from the London based Overseas Food Corporation in 1953 it only did so on condition that it inherited the assets without the liabilities. Twining could fairly claim therefore some of the credit for ensuring that part at least of the Groundnut Scheme survived to make a contribution in the end to the economy of Tanganyika.

Seeing that a country grew enough food to meet its own requirements and improving communications were problems which Twining had dealt with before. The problems of water development however were largely new to him. Mauritius, St. Lucia and North Borneo were mainly countries of good rainfall, and he hadn't really come across things like drought and thirst and huge areas of useless arid soil. Soon after his arrival he paid a visit to an out-of-the-way place called Newala. In sole charge there of an area the size of an English county was a young District Commissioner of twenty-seven. John Chant had been a major in the Black Watch during the war and had then gone back to Balliol to take a First in History. He had come into the Colonial Service after the war, like others of his generation, because it seemed to present challenges and opportunities which no other job could offer. The Governor looked at him and his young wife, sized them up and liked them. He said, 'I'll give you quarter of an hour to tell me about your District.' He was told that it consisted of about 1750 square miles most of which was an almost waterless plateau. At the bottom of a thousand-foot escarpment there was a river called the Rovuma which was the border between Tanganyika and Portuguese East Africa. Very few people lived by the river. Almost all the population of 175,000 Africans, 400 Asians and a dozen Europeans lived on the plateau. The Africans were Makonde, who years before had been driven from their homes on the other side of the river by a warlike southern African tribe called the Ngoni. They found the plateau empty and settled there. Experience had taught them that it was better and safer to be thirsty and unwashed than to live near water. They were hardworking and resourceful people and they had adapted themselves to a situation in which they were walking during the dry seasons up to twenty miles a day to draw water from wells at the foot of an escarpment which was so steep in places that they had to use bamboo ladders to climb up it with their heavily laden containers of water. It was the women and children in practice, though not in theory, who did most of the carrying. Up on the plateau the Makonde grew crops of cassava, millets and pulses. Because of the nature of the soil they only cultivated their fields for three years and then let them lie fallow for nine. It was a good way of keeping up the fertility of the soil but it used up a great deal of land. They had spare land but the area they could use for cultivation was limited by their need to live within reach of water. As the population grew the pressure on the land had increased and the Makonde were having to plant fields again after they had lain fallow for only two or three years.

The Governor looked at his watch. He wasn't in a hurry

but he liked people to be concise. 'What then is your main problem?'

The main problem, he was told, was how to produce water all the year round on top of the plateau.

'Has any thought been given to solving it? How would you do it? How long would it take? How much would it cost?'

Several plans and several attempts had been made in the past but none of them had come to anything because of technical difficulties or for lack of money. The present plan was to pump water up the escarpment to the town of Newala and then, if that worked and it was economic, to pipe it from there to different parts of the plateau. An enthusiastic engineer named Mitchell had worked out the details and the cost.

Twining said, 'Sell me the idea in five minutes.'

There were, it was explained, three advantages. The drudgery and the hardship and the waste of time involved in all that walking and carrying would be ended. Twining nodded. With water available on the plateau unused land could be brought into cultivation, existing crops could be increased, new crops like cashew nuts could be introduced and there would be a surplus of food for export. With the extra money they earned from this surplus the people could repay the cost of pumping up the water and piping it to the places where it was needed. Twining nodded again. The third advantage was that at Newala there was a hospital run by the Universities Mission to Central Africa. A Sister Edith was brought in at this stage to explain in pathetic and gruesome detail what it meant to run a hospital for Africans on a few gallons of water a day. It took rather longer than ten minutes but Sister Edith made her point. Twining stood up and turned to the District Commissioner. 'I'll get the money for the first stage of your scheme, for pumping the water up to the town. I'll come back in a year and see how things are going. If it's a success we'll talk about the other stages. And if it's a success, young man, if it's a success, we'll talk about your future too.'

When the Governor got back to his headquarters his enthusiasm was met with some rather dry civil service reservations. There were those concerned with the territory's finances who doubted if the project would pay its way; and there were the experienced and the cynical who doubted whether the habits of generations of Makonde would be changed in a day. It was not the first time, or the last, that his enthusiasms evoked such reactions. 'The dead hand of Dar es Salaam,' he called it. For Twining however the scheme was the sort of mixture of the romantic and the practical which he found difficult to resist. It would not only relieve the burdens of women and children and help a deserving Mission, but it would eventually produce dividends in the form of more home-grown food and some exportable crops. It would not only pay for itself but it might also make a profit which could be ploughed back in the form of hospitals and schools. He used all his powers of persuasion and push, and in the end he got his way.

Three years later in October 1952 Twining formally opened the Newala water supply.

I promised them water [he told his mother] and this is the first instalment which will reach 50,000 people ... The opening of the water supply was quite dramatic. I pulled a cord and the Union Jack fell away whereupon a man in a kiosk turned on a tap and the water spouted out of two pipes. The crowd of several thousand let out a deep and spontaneous Oooooooh! Then 20 water maidens came up with water pots and filled them and everyone was overjoyed.

That wasn't the end of the Makonde water scheme by any means but it was a good start. The news of the scheme and of the Governor's part in it spread. By the end of 1952 there was hardly a place in Tanganyika where it wasn't said that Twining had, if not a magic wand, at least a warm heart and a conjuror's skill.

On the 1st of January, 1953 Sir Edward Twining, whose knighthood was in the Order of Saint Michael and Saint George, was promoted to be a Knight Grand Cross. It was a considerable compliment and a comparatively rare distinction in the hierarchies of ambassadors and governors. It carried with it the right to wear a 'beautiful saxe blue silk mantle lined with scarlet silk with the great star of the Order in gold on the right breast'. Twining liked it very much, and wore it sometimes in temperatures and on occasions for which it was perhaps not designed or intended. He told his mother about the award with his usual discretion and insouciance.

By the time you open this [he wrote on the 27th of December] you will probably have seen in the New Year Honours' List that I have been elevated to G.C.M.G. While it is highly gratifying to receive so high an honour one must keep a sense of proportion about it. There are a limited number of 'G's' and when there are vacancies they are first given to those who have completed 10 years service as a Governor and then they turn to those in 1st. Class Governships in order of appointment ... I have of course, [he continued] been very lucky as in St. Lucia, North Borneo and here I arrived when things were at their lowest ebb and it was difficult to do anything wrong. Moreover we have a superlatively good staff in Tanganyika and the team spirit is excellent so given a little leadership they immediately respond. The result is that we live in a happy country and although we have one or two tender spots we do have an understanding and sympathy between people which is unique and is remarked on by all visitors. Long may it last. My part in all this is not really very great. One gets a good deal of undeserved credit but it is a thing of long standing and there are thousands of nameless people who selflessly work away at it without recognition. All one has to do is to apply the principles on which one has been brought up; think quickly and keep a step or two in front of events; and be accessible and friendly.

1952 had also been a good year for Twining in other ways. His elder son John had been accepted for the Colonial Administrative Service in Uganda, and the younger William had won a State scholarship to Brasenose College, Oxford. Their father was very pleased and proud. If he gave some an impression also of surprise, that may perhaps have been due to modesty. He had also managed to combine a trip to London with some pleasant travelling in France and

Switzerland and Italy, and to pay a quick satisfying visit to New York. His visits as usual were purposeful as well as pleasant. Apart from his continued pursuit of crown jewels and opera, he went when he was in Geneva and Rome to see people in various United Nations agencies like UNESCO and W.H.O. and F.A.O. and 'put up about a dozen schemes ranging from the training of midwives; the preservation of rock paintings; the establishment of a public library; a hydro-electric survey; geological surveys; training of staff for a T.B. hospital; and so on.' In New York he lectured the Trustee-ship Council of the United Nations on the virtues of his administration in Tanganyika.

It all passed off [he told his wife] quite nicely. I spoke for 50 minutes and was listened to with respect. The pass-age about the status of women which I put in to please you was enthusiastically received.

Afterwards he 'had a couple of friendly talks with the Russians'. According to Sir Alan Burns, who was Britain's permanent representative on the Trusteeship Council, Twining made more of an impression on the Russians out-side than inside the Council chamber. When he talked to them in the corridors and at parties, the warmth of his per-sonality and his frank, undiplomatic language seemed to move them appreciably more than the reasoned arguments and cool defences of his formal oration. They were also im-pressed by his ability to match them in drinking without any loss of guile or clarity of thought and speech. Twining was not an eloquent or compelling public speaker but in the cut and thrust of liquid conversation he was very good indeed.

Another success for him in 1952 was that Batsford, the pub-lishers, to whom Twining had been introduced by Sir Wil-liam Teeling, M.P., started to show an interest in publishing a book on the crown jewels of Europe on which he had been for so many years at work. Even the illness he had earlier in the year had its compensations.

It has [he told his mother] been a very convenient ill-ness which I have much enjoyed. It came at a most suitable

time and has afforded me a splendid rest and enabled me
to cancel all my engagements until the end of May. It has
completely foxed the doctors which is splendid ... All
they have succeeded in doing is to prove that it is not para-
typhoid, that it is not glandular fever, that it is not any of
the ordinary things they thought it might be, so to fox the
public they called it bacteriaemia which means that a dear
naughty little bug is floating around having the time of its
life giving me a temperature. However it is remarkable
that as soon as I stopped taking the doctor's pills at 5/-
a time, I started to recover and I have not looked back
since. At any rate they say that it is a warning not to try
and do too much and that it has been a gentle warning, so
this gives me a very good excuse for leading an easier life
in future.

Twining was fifty-three. His mother was eighty-one. She
must have smiled. She had been using her health as an instrument of policy for many years.

It had been a good year on the whole both for Twining
and for Tanganyika. It had been a year of peace and progress
and increasing prosperity for most people of all races there.
The previous year, and the year before that had been the
same. There had however been 'one or two tender spots', as
Peter Twining had told his mother, and one of these in particular had given him considerable trouble.

Between the two mountains of Kilimanjaro and Meru in
the north of Tanganyika there was a saddle-shaped plain in
which during the years of German and British administration the competing interests and claims of its various occu-
pants and users had led to considerable disharmony and friction. It was used for grazing by the nomadic Masai, for
mixed farming by a number of European settlers, and as an
area of expansion by the rapidly increasing African peoples,
the Chagga, the Meru and the Arusha who lived on the
fertile and overcrowded slopes of the two mountains. In an
attempt to remove the sources of friction and to provide
for the future needs of the African peoples concerned a special
Commission was appointed. The Commissioner was an Irish
judge named Mark Wilson. He was a particularly able and

fair-minded man. He made his report in 1947, and after much thought and discussion his recommendations were generally accepted by the Tanganyika authorities and the Labour Government in Britain a few months before Sir Edward Twining took up his governorship in 1949. The recommendations involved the transfer of large areas of European-held land to the Chagga and the Meru, and of some smaller areas of African land to the Europeans. This was advocated partly for the sake of harmonious homogeneity and partly to facilitate the control of cattle diseases. Between 1949 and 1951 some changes in these arrangements were made in attempts to secure the agreement of all the people concerned. These did not however succeed in meeting all the objections and it was during this period, according to a White Paper issued by the Tanganyika Government in 1952, that

> the European-owned farms which Judge Wilson had recommended should be made available for African use were acquired, some of them compulsorily under the Land Acquisition Ordinance, owing to the refusal of the owners to sell voluntarily or to exchange. When the time came to move the Meru similar opposition was encountered, neither the Europeans nor Africans wishing in the event to give up their holdings to further a scheme which, although designed for the benefit of the community as a whole, nevertheless adversely affected them individually.

The Meru were offered a larger and better area of land ten miles away. They were offered generous compensation in cash and kind. They still refused to move from land with which they were or had become very emotionally involved. In the end the Government moved them by force. Although the move was carried out with humanity and care it was eviction none the less, and eviction is not an easy or a pleasant operation either for those evicted or for those whose job it is to evict them. Inevitably some things happened on both sides which led to bitterness and misunderstanding. There were indeed many among the British officials who were directly concerned with the matter at the time who thought that, however good the motives, the decision to evict the Meru was a mistake. Although Twining defended the action taken against criticism in East Africa and in Britain and when he appeared before the Trusteeship Council in New York, he admitted some time later that he too thought it was a mistake. It is difficult to say when he came to that conclusion but it is perhaps significant that soon after the evictions took place Twining picked out one of his ablest administrative officers and sent him to live for five years with the Meru to try and re-establish their confidence in the Government. Twining said, 'I'll give you anything you want. I'll back whatever you think it right and necessary to do, but get it right.' When eventually Michael Davies and his team of social development officers and anthropologists succeeded in overcoming most of the Meru's suspicions and bitterness, Twining was unusually profuse in his thanks and generous with his response.

Twining may in the end have got things right as far as the Meru were concerned but the evictions also had far-reaching and longer-lasting consequences. Judith Listwel in her book *The Making of Tanganyika* says that 'the Meru affair served as a catalyst in the early 1950s providing a rallying point for forces which were in existence but had hitherto lacked cohesion and purpose.' How far Africans in other parts of Tanganyika were in fact deeply stirred at the time by what was happening to the distant and somewhat separate Meru is a matter of opinion, but there were certainly some among those who later became associated with nationalist forces who noted two things. One was that the Trusteeship Council seemed more than ready to give a sympathetic hearing to a representative of the Meru who went to New York to plead their case. The other was the support given to the Meru point of view by a number of influential people both in Britain and America. It was a coincidence that Julius Nyerere finished his studies at Edinburgh University in 1952 and returned to Tanganyika to start work as a teacher in a Roman Catholic school; but he of course noted these things too, and he did not forget them.

Speaking in Legislative Council on the 17th of November, 1953 Sir Edward Twining said, 'When the history of this Territory comes to be written I feel that the end of 1953 is likely to mark the close of the first chapter of post-war Tanganyika. It will record how we changed over from war-time conditions to what there was every reason to expect would be a new era for the territory ... When we turn over the page to the new chapter we can only speculate what it is likely to contain. I like to think that its sub-title should be "Stability and Confidence", and that it will cover a period of a decade or longer'.

One of Twining's first contributions to this new era was to show that he had the will and the means to deal with violent threats to law and order. He was not a man who used force lightly or with satisfaction. He knew from his experience in Ireland that it often caused more problems than it solved. He didn't however lack the courage to act quickly and firmly, particularly if he was convinced that inaction would breed a chain reaction of events which would mean the use of greater force in the end. He had felt strongly about Britain's failure to act quickly and firmly in Abyssinia in 1935 and in Czechoslovakia in 1938, and he had not forgotten the lessons he had then learnt. When the Mau Mau rising started among certain sections of the Kikuyu in Kenya in 1952 there were about 16,000 Kikuyu living or working in the northern part of Tanganyika. As a precaution a small number of active supporters were immediately arrested and sent back to Kenya. When a year later information reached Twining that others were planning acts of sabotage and murder, an operation was launched on Christmas Eve to arrest two hundred of them. The forces kept to maintain law and order in Tanganyika were very small, about 3000 police and 2000 soldiers in a country of eight million people, but Twining knew, again from his own experience, that if one has to use force one must use enough and have enough on the spot in reserve to achieve one's object quickly. He therefore concentrated 800 police and 1000 soldiers for this operation. When the Mau Mau elements responded by killing one of their own tribe whom they believed to have given information to the Government, another 450 were arrested, and in due course all the remaining Kikuyu were removed from the border area, some for their own safety and some for the safety of others. When, a few months later, a band of Mau Mau Kikuyu

came in from Kenya to try and steal arms and ammunition
they were dealt with with equal speed and decision. All these
operations were carried out by African police and soldiers
led by a handful of European officers, and one of the reasons
why they were so successful was that they had the support,
and sometimes the very brave and resourceful support, of
the Tanganyika Africans who lived in the area and who didn't
particularly care for the alien Kikuyu. The Governor played
a large part in the planning and direction of these operations,
and made a point of visiting outposts in advanced and vulnerable positions to commend and exhort those who were
concerned in carrying them out in his execrable but effective
Swahili. He was proud of his military background and played
the part of a general *manqué* with a full command of the
rituals and the vocabulary. It was not only those in possession
—the Europeans and Asians and the established African
tribal authorities—who were impressed by the Governor's
determination that no one should upset the peaceful conditions which were necessary for his era of stability and confidence to flourish. Twining's stock in 1953 and 1954 was
high in all parts and among all races in Tanganyika. This
was partly due to the way in which he dealt with the exotic
menace of Mau Mau but it was also for another and quite
different reason.

In the summer of 1953 Twining wrote a letter to his
mother from Germany. It was the summer of the Coronation,
and when other Governors were at their posts attending parades and banquets and sorting out the jealousies of protocol
at local celebrations of this event, Peter Twining was in London. His story, when people asked him how he had managed
to depart from precedent and practice in matters of this
kind, was that he had successfully pleaded that his interest
in crown jewels and regalia made him a special case. When
he had finished with the Coronation he went off to Germany.
It was not, this time, crown jewels that he was after. He was
looking for a skull.

My darling mother, [he wrote] Sultan Mkwawa of the
Hehe tribe was a great character and a man of courage
and resource. He trained up his young men as warriors

and inflicted on the Masai the only defeat they have ever suffered. On two occasions he ambushed and annihilated German columns and it took the Germans three years of persistent campaigning to run him to earth. He shot himself rather than surrender and the Germans put a bullet in his head to make sure and cut off the head as a trophy. The Hehe were very upset that they had to bury their great Chief without his head. In the 1914–18 war the Hehe were very helpful to us and as a result specific provision was made in clause 236 of the Treaty of Versailles for the return of the skull which had been sent to Germany. The London authorities however were not very interested and the Tanganyika ones did not persist. Finally a man named Winston Churchill who was Secretary of State wrote and said that the matter had better be dropped.

The whole affair has become something of a legend and the modern Hehe Homers invented, spun and embroidered the old story of Sultan Mkwawa until truth and fiction are inextricably mixed and intertwined to the glorification of his memory and the vast entertainment of those who like to hear the twilight stories round the fires of Uhehe.

I heard about this in 1950 and as the young Chief Adam Sapi—a fine, polished specimen of modern Africa—is rather a friend of mine I agreed to take it up again . . .

The rest of the letter explains in somewhat racy and abbreviated terms how after a protracted and persistent correspondence it eventually emerged that the skull might be in a museum in Bremen, and how to avoid any possibility of a mistake he decided to go and look for it himself. To help with identification he had the heads of Chief Adam Sapi and his sister scientifically measured as old men remembered that their famous grandfather had had a head of the same distinctive shape. He also knew the calibre of the rifle with which Mkwawa had been shot in 1889 by a German sergeant-major, the trajectory of the bullet, and the fact that after the head had been severed it had been dried. After a long search, in which he was much helped by the Director of the Museum, he found what he was looking for in a store cupboard. Photo-

graphs were taken and carefully examined by Chief Adam
Sapi who in the end, to quote the official record, 'considered
that the information was sufficiently convincing to make it
more than probable that it was genuinely the skull of his
grandfather, and is prepared to accept it as such.'

A year after he had discovered it in the museum, and
four years after he had started on his enquiries, Twining
formally returned the skull to the reigning Chief. Much
publicity was given to this event and to the Governor's own
part in the recovery of the skull. Many glowing accounts were
written in many different languages by journalists and writers
but none perhaps was better written or more moving than
one written by an African schoolboy in Tanganyika in his
school magazine.

The Wahehe people hold Sir Edward Twining, the Governor of Tanganyika, in high esteem, for he worked hard
to return the skull of Chief Mkwawa who was the Chief of
the Hehes.

The Governor went to Germany to see if it was true that
the skull of Chief Mkwawa was still there. He discovered
it was there, but it was difficult to find because there were
so many skulls. But he was given a picture of it and came
with it to show to the Hehe people who could identify
it. The Hehes agreed that the picture was the skull of
Chief Mkwawa. As a result the skull was brought back to
Tanganyika.

The Wahehe prepared a beautiful house to receive the
skull and arranged that the handing-over ceremony should
take place a mile away. As the day approached all the
Hehes went to Kalenga and waited for the holiday.

Early on the morning of the 19th June 1954, all the
people were waiting for the Governor. Many of the Hehes
had very big spears and guns. While they were waiting
for the Governor they were enjoying native dances.

At eleven o'clock sharp in the morning, the Governor
arrived at Kalenga. He began to tell the history of Mkwawa
in English. When he finished Mr. Gaudensio Malanga-
lilalso began to tell the history in the Hehe language. Then
the Governor presented the skull to Chief Adam Sapi.

Chief Adam Sapi thanked the Governor very much. After that, when the Hehe saw that the skull was presented to their Chief, they shot their guns and shouted loudly to show how glad they were. Then at half past eleven the Governor went to Iringa.

At twelve sharp Chief Adam Sapi entered the Land Rover and was driven very slowly towards the house where the skull was to be put. The Hehes, who numbered about 30,000 followed him. When they arrived at the house, Chief Adam Sapi entered with the skull.

Then he allowed his people to enter the house one by one to see the skull.

The Hehes danced all the next day. After that they returned to their homes. The holiday was at an end.

Twining had been appointed Governor of Tanganyika for the usual period of five years. His term of office was due to expire in June 1954 but it had already been announced in advance that his appointment had been extended for another two years. There were few either in East Africa or in London who did not believe that it was a wise decision. Tanganyika had suffered in the past from lack of continuity as far as governors were concerned, and although Twining had in fact been quite seriously ill in 1952 his energy and catalystic powers were, as he pointed out himself in a probing letter to the Colonial Office, not yet quite extinct. There may have been some who wondered whether Twining's style of governorship was one that could be continually repeated, and whether it was entirely suited to the sort of problems that were likely to arise in the coming years. If there were, they tended to be younger post-war people who were not consulted rather than older more established men who were: for them, as for most people, Twining was still the man for stability and confidence. Moreover Twining's second term coincided with the appointment of Mr. Lennox-Boyd as Secretary of State for the Colonies. Alan Lennox-Boyd is remembered by a large number of persons of different races and conditions as a man of ability and wit, of restless energy and drive, and of an engaging and sometimes dangerously disarming amiability. His impact on colonial affairs and on

Tanganyika between 1954 and 1959 was very great.

Twining had in general a poor opinion of politicians whether they were white or coloured and whether in Britain they belonged to the Conservative or the Labour party. His letters to his mother right back to his Army days had been laced with scathing comments on politicians. Some were general, and some were very particular. But for Mr. Lennox-Boyd he had nothing but praise. 'He has great charm of personality, a good and quick brain and an excellent memory: and we met with complete agreement on everything.' Like Twining himself, Lennox-Boyd was very good with people, and he took a great deal of trouble, whether in his office or in his house in Westminster or on organised visits to Ascot and the Derby, to make his many visitors from the colonial Territories feel accepted and at ease. Together he and Twining made, as far as Tanganyika was concerned, a formidable combination both of personality and policy.

Lennox-Boyd had been to Tanganyika before as a junior Minister but his first visit as Secretary of State was in October 1954. One of his main objectives was to work out changes in the country's constitution. Although Twining had, as has been explained, early on set up his two constitutional committees under Charles Mathew and Professor Mackenzie to consider what changes should be made, and both had long since submitted their reports and recommendations, no changes had actually been made to the Constitution except for one which, as it happened, suited Twining himself very well. He had never liked presiding over meetings of Legislative Council and he was glad when he was relieved of this 'loathsome task' by the appointment of one of the European Members as Speaker. All the Governor now had to do was to make the rough equivalent of Speeches from the Throne. It was in such a speech on the 20th of April, 1955 that he outlined the changes which had been made with the agreement of the Secretary of State. The main difference was that, in place of a previous theory of racial parity which gave the African and Asian communities together the same number of representatives as the Europeans, there was equal representation for all three groups. In the new Legislature the thirty representative Members were therefore made up of ten Africans, ten Asians and ten Europeans. There was still a majority on the Government side of the Council, but fourteen of those who accepted the Government whip were persons chosen on their merits from all three races. For the first time some of the Councillors were women. Although none of the representative Members had achieved their positions by election, they were drawn on a broad representative basis from embryo constituencies consisting mainly of the eight Provinces and the urban concentration of Dar es Salaam, and the possibility of holding elections in the future in certain areas was, Twining announced, being examined. There were no representative Ministers but the unofficial members of the Executive Council were to be invited to 'associate themselves with and take an interest in the affairs of certain Departments'.

The changes generally followed the recommendations which had been made by the two constitutional committees when they reported in 1951 and 1953. At the time the recommendations had been regarded by many European settlers and business men in East Africa as going too far and too fast, and by most politically minded Africans and Asians as a substantial and reasonably satisfying advance. When he endorsed them in the early fifties Twining tended to be regarded by the former as a dangerous radical, and by the latter as a fair and liberal-minded man. In the interval between the endorsement and the date on which the recommendations were given effect, things had however changed. The local Europeans had for the most part accepted the inevitability and even the justice of some change and had come to regard Twining as a strong and stabilising influence. Most Asians and probably a majority of Africans still regarded the changes as a reasonable temporary measure, but in the year before the new Constitution was introduced two things in particular had happened which produced an element of open African opposition. The first of these was the founding by Julius Nyerere in July 1954 of the Tanganyika African National Union; the second was the visit of the third United Nations visiting mission in September and the publication of its report at the beginning of 1955. Nyerere and TANU would no doubt have opposed the 1955 Constitution in any case but their criticisms were encouraged and sharpened by the support and the widespread publicity given to them by some members of the mission. Twining had always gone out of his way to help these United Nations missions and make them feel welcome, and he was disappointed, if that is not too weak a word, to find that on this occasion some of its members seemed determined only to see and hear what their sympathies and prejudices had led them to expect. Nyerere's own criticisms and the way in which he expressed them when he went to New York were a good deal more reasonable and restrained than those put forward, for example, by Mr. Mason Sears, the American member of the visiting mission, but they were enough nevertheless to show that, even if, as Nyerere affirmed, he and the Government of Tanganyika were following the same stream in the same direction, they were travelling on opposite banks and at different speeds. Twining's idea of a multi-racial government was based on his belief that Tanganyika could only achieve the economic strength necessary to become politically independent by using the combined skills and resources of the Europeans and Asians and the Africans. He also believed that the experience and expertise of all three races would be needed if the country was to have sufficient trained staff available when it came to independence. His concept of parity through equal racial representation was based on the conviction, shared by many experienced and liberal-minded people of all races, that it was a fair reflection of the contribution which each of the three races was making at that time to the political and economic life of Tanganyika. 'Although,' Twining said in his speech on the 20th of April, 'I do not consider this to be by any means perfect, I do think that it suits the conditions of Tanganyika at this stage of its progress, and is likely to continue to be the best arrangement for a long time to come. It ensures equal representation by all three races, and diminishes the possibility of domination by any one race. It provides the best means for representation of the three races on which Tanganyika depends to examine the problems of the territory on an equal basis.'

To Twining 'parity' and multi-racial representation were

more than temporary political expedients. They were a new attitude of mind. When he arrived in the country the general practice was that while Europeans and Asians and Africans dealt with one another amiably enough in the office-hour periods of government and business, they did not as a rule mix socially or go to one another's houses. There were exceptions of course but those who did not follow the usual practice tended to be regarded as unusual, even as eccentrics. Twining did his best by example and by teasing and by exhortation to break this practice down. He invited Africans to stay at Government House and he mixed people of all races at his official receptions and at many of his more informal parties too. This may not seem much in the way of progress now but in East Africa in the early fifties it was a considerable and courageous advance.

Nyerere appreciated what Twining was doing, though he once made the comment that asking an African in for a whisky and soda did not solve all his political problems. His main criticism however was that the multi-racial approach was out of place in a country which was so predominantly African, and that the Twining version of parity could not be sustained by any practical argument against the logic of arithmetic—'25,000 Europeans, 70,000 Asians and 8 million Africans'. This at any rate was how he expressed it to his more sophisticated audiences and to his growing number of friends and supporters in Britain and America and India. Speaking as a demogogue in Tanganyika it was naturally 'Africa for the Africans' and 'One man, one vote'. The slogan on the banner was Uhuru—a Swahili word derived from Arabic meaning the liberty of an emancipated slave. Nyerere was a politician and a nationalist, and he had to use the language of politicians and nationalists if he were to survive, but in more private talk he admitted that most of Tanganyika was not yet ready for elections and that the country could not reasonably expect to be independent for another twenty-five years.

As differences went between the governors and the governed in colonial territories in the middle fifties, the gap between TANU and the Tanganyika Government did not look unbridgeable. With a man as liberal and friendly and as good at personal relations as Twining on the one hand, and a political leader as amiable and moderate and reasonable as Julius Nyerere on the other it seems surprising, with the benefit of hindsight, that they could not achieve a meeting point or at least a *modus vivendi* at that time. Several attempts to bring them together were in fact made in 1954 and 1955 through intermediaries both in the Colonial Office and in Dar es Salaam. The reasons why they failed were not perhaps all on one side.

When Julius Nyerere emerged as a political leader with the foundation of TANU in 1954 he was thirty-two, a quiet slight man with a quick brain and considerable talent as a speaker. Twining recognised these qualities and sought to enlist him as an ally. He appointed him as a temporary Member of Legislative Council, and when early in 1955 Nyerere resigned his position as a teacher in order to leave himself more scope for political activity, Twining unobtrusively arranged for him to be offered a post in a large European commercial firm to save him from the embarrassments and pressures of poverty. While Twining recognised that Nyerere had certain qualities, he didn't think that he had enough driving force and ruthlessness to make a successful nationalist leader. He tried to get Nyerere on his side but he did not to start with take him very seriously. Nor did he regard TANU then as truly representative of African opinion. Its appeal, he knew, was limited to certain areas and it was lacking in organisation, funds and lieutenants who matched their leader's qualities. There were also some other things about Nyerere and TANU which made Twining less inclined than he might otherwise have been to try and come to terms with them. The major differences in policy and timing could, one feels, have been dealt with by negotiation and compromise: it was the way in which some members of TANU behaved and the things they said which rankled and barred the way. One thing which particularly upset the Governor was the way in which they tried to humiliate and undermine the position of the tribal authorities and chiefs. Another was the acts of hooliganism and rudeness which some supporters of TANU directed at anyone, European, Asian or African who did not subscribe to their opinions or,

in some cases, to their party funds. The thing which upset
Twining most was perhaps the least ill-intentioned of their
offences. Judith Listowel, whose book is sympathetic to Nyerere and TANU, explains that

> at TANU's first National Executive meeting the members,
> hopelessly untutored, had passed a resolution refusing to
> acknowledge the Queen's sovereignty over Tanganyika.
> Nyerere did not realise the implications of this resolution,
> or understand the importance which the Governor would
> attach to it being passed ... When European friends ex-
> plained to Nyerere the enormity in British eyes of the
> TANU resolution, he wrote to the Governor assuring him
> that it would be withdrawn and explaining quite truth-
> fully that he did not think it would ever come to the
> Governor's attention.

Twining was a man who felt very strongly about loyalty
and royalty, and despite the offer to withdraw the resolution,
which Lady Listowel says was ignored, it was something, it
seems, which he neither forgave nor forgot.

Although Nyerere may have been ready to retract some of
TANU's earlier indiscretions and to offer compromises on
method and timing, there was always perhaps at the back of
his mind the realisation and an instinctive awareness that his
best chance of establishing himself as a politician and a
national leader lay in opposition rather than agreement.
There may have been times when he wanted to work with
Twining and his administration because he realised that
their intentions and ultimate objectives were much the same
as his own but he knew that if he did so too openly and too
often the leadership of TANU would pass into less patient
and more grasping hands. If Twining had to quarrel with
Nyerere to retain the confidence of the tribal chiefs and the
European and Asian producers of wealth and investment, so
Nyerere perhaps at this stage had to quarrel with Twining in
order to keep himself in his political saddle.

Although Twining was more concerned with politics and
questions of constitutional development in his second term
of office than in his first five years, that did not mean that he

TANGANYIKA: THE MIDDLE YEARS 255

neglected what he still thought of as his main concerns as Governor—the development of the country's resources; the establishment of a firm foundation of local and regional government on a multi-racial basis; and constant travelling to meet people and to see things for himself. One of the things which particularly interested him at this time was fostering co-operative associations through which African farmers could not only increase their yields by the purchase of better seed and fertilisers and by the communal use of agricultural machinery but also undertake the marketing and grading and even the processing of crops like cotton and coffee and rice which had formerly been largely in the hands of Asians and Europeans. Nearly 200 such co-operatives had been registered by the middle of 1954. It was a progress of which Twining was very proud though he was not so pleased when some of the co-operatives started to extend their activities into what he regarded as the less practical and less productive fields of politics. If these political excursions vexed him, as they often did, he would ease his feelings and refresh his optimism by paying visits on his travels to the various kinds of schools which were proliferating in all parts of Tanganyika—government schools, Native Authority schools, schools run by a bewildering multiplicity of Christian Missions, by the Muslim and Hindu communities and by other voluntary agencies in this field. Twining gave encouragement to them all, and although he would have preferred more schools to be run on non-racial and unsectarian lines, he made each one that he visited feel that it nevertheless had his special blessing. His own inclination was towards technical and agricultural education. This, taken with his occasional complaint that the cost of maintaining students at the new East African university at Makerere was £740 a year 'which is more than double the cost of educating a boy at a Public School or a University in England', earned him a reputation in some circles of wishing to discourage the more academic educations which produced the graduate teachers and the lawyers from which politicians in colonial territories were apt to come. It was one thing for later independent African Governments to have similar inclinations in educational policy: in a colonial governor it was bound to be interpreted as bias. Twining was nevertheless proud of the achievements of his administration in education and often referred in his public speeches and his private boastings to the fact that five and six times more was being spent on education than when he arrived in Tanganyika, and that more was now spent in each year on African education alone than the total budget of the government thirty years before. He didn't add, though others did, that these brave figures still came to an annual expenditure of less than five shillings a head; but it was of course as much a reflection on the poverty of Tanganyika's own resources as on the policies of its Government that even these small figures were only made possible by grants and loans from the British taxpayer.

Although Twining was inevitably mainly involved in matters which were intended to help the people and especially the Africans of Tanganyika to stand on their own feet in the competitive political and economic conditions of the twentieth century, he always retained a soft spot and a special sympathy for those who for one reason or another could not or would not adapt themselves to such conditions, people like the elegant semi-naked Masai and the Barabaig, and the quiet self-contained Gogo who preferred their own simplicities of custom and belief and dress to the sophistications of imported cultures. He took their side and fought their battles with equal zest against the persuasions and pressures of missionaries, government officials and African politicians, and earned from them as a governor an affection and respect which was normally reserved for their favourite District Officers. Twining had many interests and he espoused many causes in his time in Tanganyika but there were some things which he preferred to leave to his wife; nor did Lady Twining's close concern for those things which interested her or which she felt it was her duty to pursue in any way diminish with the years. Sometimes as before they travelled separately and visited different places and did different things. Even when they travelled together different schedules for them were usually arranged which sometimes presented problems both of an official and a domestic nature both to the officials who received them and to their wives. Things were always apt to happen when Twining went on his travels and his wife

Sir Edward Twining as Governor of Tanganyika: inspecting a guard of honour on arrival at Dar es Salaam, in 1949 and (*below*) a tribal farewell at Dodoma in 1958.

Tanganyika: The Lodge at Lushoto.

The multi-racial society: Sir Edward Twining watches Princess Margaret receiving a bouquet from an African, an Asian and a European child.

often had the same effect. When they travelled the same route things had a disconcerting habit of happening in different places at the same time in one and the same parish.

Despite all this travelling and all this activity Twining's medical advisers were still concerned about his weight. He now weighed about sixteen stone, and although bulk can be an asset to a showman or an actor playing a Falstaffian part, it can also be a hazard to good health. Some instructions on diet which were given to him at this time clearly had this point in mind. Some of them went further in precision perhaps than the directions of most Governors' doctors would have gone. After detailing what he should eat (lean meat, rabbit, fish, liver, tripe, etc.) and what he could have if he liked (mostly vegetables and fruit plus 'sour pickles, water, soda water, non-sweetened mineral waters'), the instructions become more restrictive.

3. You may have *one very small piece of bread* three times a day, each piece not exceeding one ounce—this may be toasted after weighing.

4. You may have *half a pint of milk*—not cream—daily.

5. You may have *NOTHING ELSE WHATEVER*. Please note that this means NO—Butter, margarine, oil, fat, sugar, jam ... [and twenty-seven other items ending with] ... alcohol (beer, cider, wine, spirits).

'You will,' the instructions ended on a cheerful note, 'find adherence to the above instructions surprisingly easy.' It doesn't seem however, from what one hears, that this optimism was well based. Nor did these restrictions cramp his exuberance and style in other ways, particularly when he was on his travels. In the notes which he sent to the Chief Secretary after a tour of the Southern Province in 1954 he had this to say about one of its more sleepy places.

Its motto should be 'From decadence to decadence'. Please look up my notes on my last safari there in September 1953. I thought I had made it abundantly clear and, in fact had given directions that certain things were to be done at once without any further delays and without the attitude of supreme indifference to some of our more humble Districts which one finds in certain Departments. I do not mind opposition to my views and proposals if they are put up in a reasoned way but I will not tolerate being ignored. The Governor's orders are the Governor's orders and are to be obeyed, and woe betide anyone who disregards them.

There were other examples of the Twining style of governing in these notes. At Lindi he opened 'a monument to the absurdity of the Dar es Salaam bureaucracy in the form of an elaborate and expensive new hospital which will undoubtedly lead to the resignation of any sensible Nursing Sister who goes there unless provided with a pair of roller skates'.

He also paid another visit to Newala where the success of the pilot scheme to pump water up the escarpment led him to endorse the first stage of a more ambitious scheme to pipe water to various parts of the plateau. Experience of the groundnut scheme tempered his enthusiasm with pragmatic caution, and he would only agree to support one step at a time, and that only after taking second opinions from financial and technical experts from the United Kingdom. His own contribution to the plan was the idea of giving the Makonde what he called a 'share in the equity'. The first stage of the new scheme was estimated to cost about £300,000 and the idea was to repay a loan by means of a compulsory water rate which would entitle those who paid it to a ten-shilling share which would earn them a dividend once the loan had been repaid. In this way Twining sought to give the Africans on the plateau a vested interest in the scheme and so ensure, if European logic applied, that it was a success. If it was, he promised, the second stage of the scheme would be carried out. God and the Governor, the message implied, help those who help themselves. The Makonde cheered him to the echo; but some of them still went on sending their women on the long journey to the bottom rather than pay a penny to buy it at the top. It was cheaper and, they argued, it also kept the women out of mischief. On such rocks the best-laid schemes can founder as, in the end, this one did.

The Governor made many other journeys too in 1954 and

1955. He went to Mtwara to open the new port and the railway linking it to the undeveloped country in the south. There were deep-water berths at Dar es Salaam and Tanga to be inaugurated, drilling for oil on Mafia Island to be looked at, a hydro-electric scheme at the Pangani Falls to be formally completed. There were the development schemes in every part of Tanganyika to be visited to see for himself what progress was being made to turn areas which had for centuries barely produced enough to keep their inhabitants alive into expanding sources of wealth and progress and content. 'Our aim,' Twining said in one of his speeches then, 'is a growth rate every year of eight to ten per cent.'

In the summer of 1955 Twining went on leave again to England. He spent a month on the Continent wandering alone, as he usually did, in Denmark and Holland, in Austria and Germany and Switzerland and France. As he pursued his crown jewels and regalia in the museums and courts of Europe, and listened to his music, and ate and drank the things he liked, and slept in the afternoons, he was perhaps entitled to look in the mirror each morning and allow himself a smile. He had just had his first grandchild. His elder son was happily married and doing well as a District Officer in Uganda. His younger son William had got a First in Law at Oxford and there was talk of him sitting for a Fellowship at All Souls'. And he himself had been asked informally, a little bit too informally, he thought, if he would stay on as Governor for another two years when his second term of office came to an end in 1956. He hesitated but in the end, he told his mother:

> I acquiesced. I think probably it is in the best interests and I shall be happy to do so. There is nothing that succeeds like success but I hope I shall not outstay my welcome and witness a deteriorating situation. But I think that we can hold the situation.

Those who reappointed him in London, and those who welcomed his reappointment in East Africa shared these feelings and these beliefs. They thought that Tanganyika had a long way to go before it would be self-sufficient and ready for self-government. They believed that there was still a lot that Twining, and only Twining perhaps, could do to give the country a sound foundation of economic strength and inter-racial local government, and to use his experience and prestige to put the brake gently but firmly on those who wanted to go too fast. There were others in both places who doubted the wisdom of asking Twining, or any Governor, to stay, in such a quickly changing world, in the same place for as long as nine years. Whether it was right that he was offered the extension, and whether it was right that he accepted it, were questions which it was easier to answer afterwards than at the time.

Tanganyika : the end

1956 WAS KNOWN TO journalists in Tanganyika as 'the year of the Princess'. In April Twining told his mother, with his usual mixture of filial consideration and gubernatorial discretion, that by the time she got his letter 'a certain announcement will have been made'. The news was that Princess Margaret would pay a visit to Tanganyika in the autumn. Royal visits usually require a long period of gestation, and in this case the six months between the conception of the visit and the arrival of the visitor was fully taken up with the pangs of pregnancy and the difficulties of labour. It didn't take long to draw up the outline of a programme which would enable the Princess to see as much of the country and as many people as possible. The trouble was that the thousand and one details of time and place and people could not be settled and arranged until the outline had been approved.

The Royal visit [Twining wrote two months later] is giving us a few headaches as we cannot get the programme fixed. The Princess is easy enough but the staff is difficult. Perhaps it is natural when one remembers that there are 12 in their party plus 6 or 7 in our party and 55 journalists plus 1½ tons of personal royal baggage.

In the end the Governor sent someone to London to sort things out, and followed this up with a visit to Clarence House himself when he went on leave again that summer. A further complication was that a new wing was being added to Government House at Dar es Salaam, and it had to be ready on

time to accommodate the royal party. Some idea of what this
complication meant is given in notes written afterwards by
Lady Twining 'in the hope that they may be of some use to a
Governor's wife who has to organise the domestic side of
another Royal Tour'. The note in question was short and to
the point. 'Avoid if possible any structural alterations or additional buildings within twelve months or more of a Royal
Tour so as to get over the settling and teething period and
the last minute rush. Contractors' and Public Works' dates of
completion should never be believed and up to a hundred
per cent additional time should be allowed.' In the end the
last workman left in the afternoon before the Royal party
arrived and a number of voluntary helpers had to be called
in to tidy up.

When everything had been arranged—the routes, the
transport, the accommodation, the events and who should
and who should not be invited to attend them—there was
still the question of rehearsals. Twining was determined that
everything should go like clockwork and he attended many
of the rehearsals himself. A week before the Princess was
due to arrive he wrote a final pre-visit letter to his mother
who had clearly taken a keen interest in the way her son
had managed things. At Mwanza, he told her:

we spent the whole day rehearsing except for an hour or
so for the formal opening of a Jamat Khan, a sort of
Indian Community Centre. The next day to Arusha with
a full programme of rehearsals and the following morning
to Moshi where likewise we went through every detail.
In the afternoon we flew to Dar es Salaam where we had a
warm welcome ... May has done wonders and the new
wing, though not ready, is looking very well. Last night we
rehearsed the State Banquet. 90 people attended, mostly
substitutes. It went surprisingly well although all the flaws
were shown up. I have been to two other major rehearsals
and have six more this week. But an 'atmosphere' is building up. The decorations are being erected and are very
elegant and everyone is having their hair done and buying
new clothes. It is all a bit of a strain but quite fun, though
I shall not be sorry when it is all over.

On the 8th of October at ten a.m. Princess Margaret arrived
at Dar es Salaam in the Royal yacht *Britannia*. After a long
full day of rather dutiful events there was the State banquet
in the evening. That night Peter Twining wrote a quick
letter of his first impressions to his mother, and dealt in it
with certain points on which, it seems, she had expressed concern after reading some of the English papers.

So far everything has gone remarkably well and
H.R.H.'s captivating charm has cast a spell on us all. The
elaborate opening of the dock ceremony was almost perfec-
tion. The processional drive through 5 miles of streets
evoked a sincere, warm and happy though quiet welcome
from an immense gathering of people—possibly 250,000.
Africans consider it rude to make a noise in front of the
great. But there was no doubt of the genuineness of their
friendly reception ... I have seen no sign of bad character
or rock an' roll. I imagine it was the vile press, 60 of whose
representatives are here and I addressed them for an hour
last night. They are really the most impossible people ...
In the car or sitting next to her at ceremonies she is easy
to talk to, with a quick wit and views of her own. She runs
through the part with dignity and grace although she is
tiny. But 11 days of it are going to be a great strain for all.

Ten days later Princess Margaret left Tanganyika for Nairobi by air to complete the rest of her tour. Those who were
there say that when the time came to say goodbye both
Princess Margaret and Sir Edward Twining seemed close
to tears.

During her visit to Tanganyika Princess Margaret travelled
about 1700 miles. She saw or was seen by something like half
a million people at the ceremonial occasions and on the
tours that were arranged for her. At closer quarters she met
15,000 Africans, Asians and Europeans at various functions
and shook hands with more than a thousand. She did all the
things which Royal visitors are supposed to enjoy, visiting
schools and hospitals, welfare centres, Girl Guides, Boy Scouts
and a sisal experimental station. She did a number of things,
visiting a diamond mine, a game reserve and attending tribal

dances which clearly pleased her very much. Whether she
did things for pleasure or out of duty she managed to look
cool and poised and very pretty. Above all, observers say, she
looked happy.

The Press [Twining told his mother] could not understand how I managed to keep H.R.H. amused. She always
seemed to be laughing and this led to all sorts of distorted
things. Actually I had a fund of simple little stories which
tickled her fancy ...

One of these stories, according to the *Daily Mail*, was that
when the then Prince of Wales visited Uganda in 1929 it had
been arranged that as a gesture he should sit on one of the
African rulers' ceremonial thrones. The throne was made of
wood and it was kept for safety in a special hut made of grass.
When the door of the hut was opened it was discovered that
the throne had been eaten by ants. Twining is alleged to
have ended the story with the moral that 'people who live in
grass houses shouldn't stow thrones'. It was a spoonerism to
make any Princess laugh, and although Twining admitted
sadly at the time that the story wasn't true, there was certainly
a flow of other less sophisticated stories which, he ended his
letter to his mother, 'tickled her a lot. I have had a charming
letter from her, a copy of which I enclose.'

It was indeed a charming letter and it was by all accounts
most well deserved. If Princess Margaret found Sir Edward
Twining a gay and entertaining host, he found her and
treated her as something between a favourite daughter and a
fairy-land princess. And if Princess Margaret found Tanganyika an exciting and happy place, people of all races there
certainly seem to have given her a moving and enthusiastic
welcome.

The reaction of most people in Tanganyika to Princess
Margaret's visit was spontaneous and emotional but it did
not have any noticeable political effect. Soon after the end of
the Royal visit, Julius Nyerere flew to London on his way to
New York. He went, among other places, to the United
Nations. Questioned there in the Fourth Committee, which
concerns itself with the freedom of colonial territories, he

said, 'It is difficult to specify a date in such cases but I think
that Tanganyika should be independent in about ten years
time.' This was somewhat less than the period of twenty-
five years which he had mentioned earlier but it still seemed
to many critics of colonialism in the United Nations as an
over-moderate and over-modest estimate.

There were others however both in London and in East
Africa who honestly believed that so early a date was precipitate and unrealistic. Even so, the Secretary of State, who
saw Nyerere on his way through London, felt that he might
have been able to reach an understanding with him as he
had with other nationalist leaders, if it had not been for
the Governor's less hopeful and less enthusiastic attitude.
Twining still did not look on Nyerere or TANU as serious
threats to the gradual, multi-racial policies to which he was
committed. Although he knew that TANU under Nyerere's
leadership had increased in popularity and strength, he did
not think that it had yet become a properly organised or
truly national movement. At the end of 1956 it claimed to
have a hundred thousand members but even this was only a
little over one per cent of the population. It was strong in
the Eastern Province, particularly in the urban area of Dar es
Salaam. It had made considerable progress too in the Lake
Province where, as Andrew Maguire explains in his admirable
book *Towards Uhuru in Tanzania*, it had built on the foundations laid by the Tanganyika African Association and the
Sukuma Union in the early fifties when they had attracted a
large rural following by calculated and well-organised exploitation of real as well as imaginary grievances against the
Indians and Arabs who controlled the buying and processing
of cotton, and against the irksome if well-intentioned mass of
rules and regulations which were thought necessary in order
to achieve the objectives of the Sukumaland Development
Scheme. No one likes rules and regulations at the best of
times but the least popular in any country are those which
academic experts use to direct practical farmers how to cultivate their land and look after their cattle. As Maguire puts
it, 'It was not a difficult task to link the aspirations of the
more sophisticated elite for freedom with colonial rule with
the desires of the ordinary rural Sukuma to be free from

rules which prevented him from cultivating his land as he saw fit'. In other parts of Tanganyika, however, TANU had made less headway, and Twining and his more conservative advisers were confident that wherever it operated it could be either ignored or countered or contained. As for Nyerere himself, he seemed to Twining then, and for some time afterwards, to be 'a lonely and unimpressive figure', hard-up, ill and under pressure from his family 'to give up politics and earn a decent living'. The Governor was still inclined to think of Nyerere as a gentle idealist who, because of his quick brain and power of eloquence, was being used by a bunch of hard-faced, 'riff-raff' men and women to further their own quests for power and money. He was to make one more attempt to come to terms with Nyerere but for the moment he was more inclined to concentrate on other things.

Although Twining supported and may indeed have proposed some of the statutory and administrative measures which were taken in 1955 and 1956 to contain and restrict the activities of TANU, he was by temperament and instinct more interested in finding more positive solutions. It was his duty as Governor, perhaps his first duty, to maintain law and order but using force to eliminate breaches of the peace did not, he knew from Ireland too, eliminate their causes. Realising that where it had succeeded TANU had gained support 'by emotional appeal to African nationalism and exploitation of grievances real or imaginary', he called, in instructions issued to his administrative officers, for 'understanding and heart-searching on the part of government', and for the removal of real grievances. The trouble was that however much Twining and his administrative officers were in sympathy with many of TANU's aims, the fact that it often sought to achieve them by attacking the chiefs and the established Native Authorities meant that it had to be treated sometimes as subversive. When it came to the emotional appeal of TANU to African nationalism, Twining sought to channel this into what he called 'local and tribal patriotism'. This meant pushing ahead with his plans to associate ordinary people with the chiefs in the management of their own affairs through a pyramid of inter-racial local authorities based, as in England, on the equivalent of parishes and rising through boroughs and rural districts to the equivalent of counties. On a national level he tried to counter the influence of the entirely African, and as he saw it racist TANU by fostering the creation of an inter-racial political party called the United Tanganyika Party, a sort of conservative party with liberal views which he hoped would appeal to moderate men and women of all races. He used all his powers of persuasion to induce a number of capable and influential Africans, Asians and Europeans to join and get it off to a good start. Some did so, it seems, more as a personal favour to a governor whose good intentions they respected than because they believed that it was likely to become an effective political force.

Another reason why Twining felt secure in his attitude to Nyerere and TANU at that time was that he was sure that what he was doing was right. He was encouraged in this belief by the knowledge that he had the confidence and the support of the Secretary of State, and that the policies he was pursuing had the blessing not only of members of both parties in the British Parliament, but of elements not usually sympathetic in the United Nations as well. Speaking in the General Assembly in October 1955, Mr. Krishna Menon, the often fiery representative of India, went out of his way to mention 'the name of Sir Edward Twining who stands out as a great apostle of the working out of the principles of the Charter for establishing a multi-racial community in his Territory, and of implementing the purposes of the Trusteeship Agreement.' Twining had his critics of course both in Britain and in Tanganyika but his belief in the rightness of what he was doing was beginning to be tinged perhaps at this period with a touch of arrogance, a sense of infallibility and an unwillingness to listen to contrary advice. He coined the word 'unocracy'. Unocracy, he would say, is the best form of government: government, he meant, by me. It wasn't all in jest. He felt that he knew, with an almost Cartesian certainty, what was good for people. It wasn't only the people of Tanganyika who felt the impact sometimes of this attitude.

The letters which Twining wrote to his mother in 1957 give an impression of a man moving busily but happily and easily along the last stages of a long and successful journey.

There is certainly no lack in them of action or incidents or personalities. Government House at Dar es Salaam and the Lodge at Lushoto were as usual full of visitors. Some were well-known people like Field-Marshal Auckinleck and Prince Aly Khan whose names and characteristics were carefully listed for his mother's interest and re-telling. Others were 'incredibly uninteresting people whom I did my best to avoid'. In January he set off on 'the most comprehensive safari I have ever made' covering seven out of Tanganyika's eight Provinces. In May he had '100 engagements in 30 days'. In July he flew to Egypt to attend the Aga Khan's funeral as Britain's representative, and in October, his statistical mind worked out that he had travelled a total of 10,000 miles, most of which were taken up with an official visit to the Belgian Congo and a wide-ranging tour of his own territory with Mr. Lennox-Boyd. Nor was there any shortage of family news. His wife was busy with a Red Cross visit from Lady Limerick, and with the inter-racial Council of Women which she had started in 1954 mainly to improve the education and standing of women in African society. His son William became engaged to a girl of whom he much approved. Evelyn Du Buisson came out on another visit. There was no mention in his letters of politics or Julius Nyerere or of TANU.

There were in fact increasing signs in the first half of 1957 that the Governor's estimates both of Nyerere's standing and of TANU's strength were becoming less and less realistic. When Nyerere returned from New York he was greeted by very large crowds and with great enthusiasm. When he travelled about the country his meetings were massively attended. He went to New York again soon afterwards for a meeting of the Trusteeship Council. When he got back the crowds were even bigger and the enthusiasm more intense. The impact of his carefully reasoned and moderate speeches at the United Nations and his increasing international reputation had the effect, too, of making his own position as a national leader in Tanganyika more secure. Although he was still talking of independence as something that Tanganyika could not hope to achieve in less than a decade, his increasing success and self-confidence led him to press for quicker and bigger concessions on matters like elections and franchises and African representation. Twining tried to hold the position at first by imposing restrictions on Nyerere's speech-making and on TANU's activities in certain areas, by correcting their mis-statements and misrepresentations in his public speeches and in Government broadcasts and publications, and on occasions by the less justifiable and less effective methods of ridicule and abuse. By the middle of the year however Twining seems to have come to the conclusion that he ought to try a different course. In February the United Nations General Assembly had called for independence for Tanganyika at 'an early date', and he knew that another visiting mission was due to arrive in the territory in August. Ghana's independence in March had also had a galvanising effect which was by no means confined to West Africa. The Governor had already appointed one member of TANU, the able and ambitious Paul Bomani, to Legislative Council, and at the end of June when Nyerere came back from America, Twining offered him a similar appointment. Nyerere accepted, and so later in the year did two other of his supporters, Rashidi Kawawa and George Kahama. In this way Twining hoped to persuade Nyerere and TANU to pursue their objectives by constitutional means. For a time it seemed that he had succeeded, although there were of course some elements in TANU who still preferred the more direct and exciting methods of disturbance and subversion and intimidation. Twining also offered Nyerere a post of assistant minister as understudy to one of the senior British officials who, somewhat to their surprise, found themselves after years of unobtrusive civil service carrying the less familiar and more public titles and functions of ministers. Similar appointments were offered to four other Africans, an Asian and a local European. After some hesitation Nyerere refused the offer, partly it seems on the advice of a cynical and experienced European friend in Kenya who warned him that 'any man who accepts office without power is committing political suicide', and partly perhaps because all the other Africans who were offered and accepted these apprentice posts were chiefs or ex-chiefs and known to be supporters and admirers of the Governor.

It was a disappointment but no surprise to Twining that Nyerere refused the appointment. He expected indeed that sooner or later Nyerere would find a time and a reason to resign from Legislative Council, and that he and his party would boycott the elections which were to take place in certain areas in 1958 and 1959. In this instance he was partly right and partly wrong. Nyerere did resign from Legislative Council but he decided in the end to urge that TANU should take part in the elections. Although he gave other reasons for his resignation, the two decisions were perhaps not entirely disconnected.

Twining seemed at the end of 1957 to have been disturbed but not disheartened by the way things were going. On the political side he felt that after going through a difficult period he had in the end 'regained the initiative' by a mixture of firmness and concessions. On the economic and financial side, although the country was having difficulty in balancing its budget and in raising the funds needed to keep its economic development in step with the increasing pace of political advance, he was still able in his speech to Legislative Council in September to give some impressive figures of increases in the production of crops and minerals during the period of his administration. He was concerned however that some people were unwilling to invest money in the country because of uncertainties about its political stability in the future. His changes of mood, and his occasional and a-typical moments of indecision, were reflected in uncertainties and changes of mind about his own future.

In August he told his wife, who was in Ireland for William's wedding, that he could see that

from all accounts there is likely to be very strong pressure for us to stay on including from Africans and probably even from Julius. But it will need a very strong appeal to one's sense of duty to do so and frankly I now long to get out and settle down to a new life. Moreover as things are going the situation should be such that we leave in a blaze of glory and in an atmosphere favourable to my successor. You need not be anxious about their being any danger. There is none. We are still held in a rare regard, respect and affection. The abusive letters come from Europeans...

When later he learnt that there were nevertheless movements towards the appointment of a new governor, he gave his opinion on the policies and the qualities which would be needed in the future.

The next few years are likely to be very crucial for the territory and it is therefore of great importance that its affairs should be guided by somebody with the right qualities ... On the political side it is likely to prove desirable to have a slowing down of the pace of progress rather than advancing it. This will have to be handled with great tact, diplomacy and strength. There is likely to be considerable progress made in the development of Local Government institutions which ... should become well established in advance of political development at the centre. It is also probable that the system of Provincial autonomy will be introduced which will in effect mean the re-organisation of the whole of the government structure.

But the greatest emphasis of all will be on economic development. Therefore what is needed is a man, not with a brilliant record, but with steady common sense, willing to take a strong line when necessary, but having at the same time a real sympathy for African aspirations. He must be a good administrator and should have a bent for economic development. I have found during the last $8\frac{1}{2}$ years that the position of the Governor has changed markedly and he is expected to be less authoritarian than he was, particularly now that the Ministerial system has been introduced and a great deal of the responsibility has been off-loaded on to the shoulders of the Ministers. Nevertheless his role is one of great importance and in fact the burden is much greater now than it was. It is essential that he should know the country thoroughly and should be well acquainted with the problems of every area or even district. He must be good at man management. While I do not regard it as essential for him to have had African experience, this is certainly a valuable asset as is a knowledge of Swahili...

The Secretary of State must have received this advice with a mixture of amusement and affection. He knew Peter Twining very well by now, and no doubt recognised certain familiar features in this portrait.

At the end of the year when the name of the new Governor and the date of his arrival had been decided, Twining told his mother that he and his wife had

an exercise—almost a game—about the future. On Mondays and Tuesdays we dote on the delights of England, the land of our birth and all the sentimental attachments. By Wednesday and Thursday the thought of no servants, the penal taxation and the awful winters drives us to house agents in Nairobi where we would at least live in an environment we know, could take some of our servants and work for the interests of E. Africa. By Friday and Saturday we think Nairobi too close to Tanganyika and our nostalgia would be unsettling. So we look to Salisbury and Southern Rhodesia where an attractive job is being dangled. But it is a country new to us, we do not approve of the policy there and the landscape is ugly. Sunday, as it should be, is a day of rest so we do not discuss it. But by Monday we are back talking of England again.

Sir Edward Twining and his wife left Tanganyika in the middle of June 1958. Much of their last six months in the country was spent in saying their goodbyes. They had both done a great deal of travelling in their time in Tanganyika. They had grown attached to places, and had interested themselves in many things. Some were big, general things, development schemes, mining, agriculture, irrigation, water supplies, schools and hospitals. Some were small, particular things, a well in some dry forgotten village, a dispensary in a remote mud and wattle hut, an African child with a sore on his leg in a place that they had once visited. They had met a large number of people, chiefs in leopard-skin cloaks, Indians and Arabs, administrative officers and their wives, Africans who went naked and Africans in shirts and shorts with serious, bespectacled faces. Peter Twining and his wife had had nine years of travelling and duties and repetition but they were

Farewell to Tanganyika, 1958: the Governor saying goodbye to friends at Lushoto and (*below*) to tribal chiefs at Morogoro.

Sir Edward and Lady Twining in London for the Queen's Coronation in 1953.

not the sort of people who forgot, or would not take the trouble, to say goodbye. They put or hid their feelings in different ways. May Twining wrote:

We had a very busy week last week and continued this farewell tour. We left Mwanza on Monday and had a great send off from the aerodrome, school children and officials, then a busy day in Tabora where Peter had a grand baraza, very colourful and the big Chief Fundikira's special warriors in white robes and red and green turbans escorted him to the car. Then next day we had another big send off from Tabora with the band and the warriors again. Then next day to Maswa in Sukumaland where there was another huge baraza and dances and a party and many schools out on the road to welcome Peter. Back to Mwanza where I sponsored a nun getting the O.B.E. and the guard of honour cheered Peter. Then a huge lunch with the Chopra's and I had a busy afternoon opening a Mothercraft Centre and attending a women's tea party of nearly 100 women of all races who had come to say goodbye... I hate all these farewells and it's hard to realise that we shall not come here again...

Twining himself was more laconic.

We certainly have had a very compact safari. May finds the emotional strain of the goodbyes rather trying. The barazas and receptions are full of adulatory phrases in wordy speeches. But there have been good turn outs and most friendly welcomes with a variety of presents...

The presents were something of a problem and he sought advice from London on what to do with them.

I have received literally hundreds: they vary from the traditional presents given by Chiefs and Native Councils to mementos of various occasions like opening a building or laying a foundation stone or to commemorate some special occasion, and lastly to mark their joy at our departure. They have taken the most varying forms and we have

rooms full of spears and shields, bows and arrows, lion-
mane and leopard-skin headdresses, emblems of fertility,
basketware, beadwork, embroidery, agricultural imple-
ments and various bric-à-brac. Then there are shelves of
trowels and locks and keys, usually made of base metal but
dipped in silver sometimes sufficiently thick to take a hall-
mark. Although I have cut a lot of tape I have however
only received one pair of scissors. [He finished up his letter
by saying that] I have always felt that these things are best
left to the good sense and judgment of the Governor concerned and he must decide in which case any offence would
be caused if the gifts were not retained and making sure
that he would not be subject to public criticism about any
item he did keep. I seem to spend a good deal of my time
at the moment persuading people not to give us things but
all these gifts emanate from a traditional custom or as a
token of real friendship.

Twining had a feeling for traditional custom and a talent
for friendship. Many among the thousands of Africans, Asians
and Europeans who came to see him and his wife off when
they left Dar es Salaam by boat on the 16th of June had had
experience both of this feeling and this talent. They had had
experience too of another Twining quality. As one person
put it in a small, spontaneous private letter, 'as well as being
a great privilege it has been fun knowing you.' There were
many, no doubt, who thought more seriously of his varied
achievements and of the progress which had been made under
his direction and his stimulus in almost every field of human
activity, but the feeling that was most common was that they
were saying goodbye not only to a big and warm and friendly
man but also to an era. Some of them had criticised or dis-
agreed with him. Some had not always liked his style. Others
were to criticise him more freely when he had gone. But
there were few among those who saw the Governor and his
wife off that day who did not look back afterwards on the
Twining period with nostalgia.

'Has Twining built something enduring,' *The Times* asked
itself in a leading article a month before his departure, 'or

will the heyday of his government merely be remembered
as "the good old days"?'

It is [the article went on] too early to judge. When he
stirred the country up out of its lethargy, he stirred up
desires and aspirations which will be hard to meet. His
progressive paternalism could not in any case have isolated
Tanganyika from the African nationalist movements developing to north and south. Recently he had concentrated
on preparing for the next phase by the introduction of an
electoral system. He has always tried to keep one jump
ahead of demand. But the pressures have mounted up
sometimes stronger and faster than could have been anticipated.

In the *Making of Tanganyika* Judith Listowel records
something which Nyerere told her in 1961 about the part
which Twining played in his movement towards independence.

Every nationalist movement must have something, or
somebody to fight against. Twining provided this foil for
us. Had he stopped me going round the country when I still
had to convince my people of the possibility of obtaining
Uhuru without creating a violent movement, things would
have worked out very differently. Had he given me complete freedom to go ahead without opposition, it would
also have been different, for we would have had no cause.
But he did the perfect thing: he opposed us, thus giving
us a foil: yet he only once barred me for three months
from speaking all around the country.

It is true that Twining eventually reached the point where
he opposed Nyerere and TANU but it was not, as is implied,
a purely personal opposition, and it was not done without a
number of good or at least understandable reasons. Twining
was certainly not alone in opposing TANU. He had the support, certainly to begin with, of many thoughtful and patriotic Africans as well as the more predictable backing of
most though not all Asians and local Europeans; he had the

support of most of his officials and advisers, and he had the support too, right to the end, of the British Government. If his policy and his attitudes were mistaken the errors were at least broadly based, and many who criticised them afterwards did so, one suspects, with the fervour and the certainty which so often accompanies the benefits of hindsight.

The opposition to Nyerere was based not so much on his objectives as on his methods and his timing. Twining himself, more perhaps than some of those who supported him, was in sympathy with Nyerere's broad aims—eventual self-government and narrowing the gap between rich and poor. The main difference between them was over the speed with which the first of these aims could be accomplished. Nyerere was a realist, he knew that it would be a long time before there were a sufficient number of Africans, able, trained and experienced enough to run the country on their own, but as a nationalist leader and a politician there had, in Tanganyika as in politically more sophisticated countries, to be a difference sometimes between what he thought and what he said. Twining was a realist too but as a governor he was less inhibited. He simply did not believe, from what he had seen and what he had heard, that the Africans of Tanganyika would be ready to run the complex and expensive machineries of a central government for many years to come. To hand over political power in such circumstances was to him as wrong as to appoint a man for shop-window purposes to a post he could not fill. He thought it was his duty therefore, as he said in his last speech to Legislative Council, 'to see that the pace is set at a speed which is suitable to local conditions and circumstances and not to give way to the clamour of those who, seeking to retain the loyalty of their supporters, sometimes make exaggerated demands incompatible with the realities of the situation and which they themselves know to be unrealistic.' He may have been less willing than others to let the inexperienced learn by their own mistakes, and more reluctant to test his estimates of capability against actual performance, although many of the Africans who have since proved their worth in Tanzania and elsewhere owed their first opportunities to Sir Edward Twining. He may have been influenced sometimes by the prejudices of his background and the incredulities of his generation, but it was not a lack of sympathy which governed his step-by-step approach or any disagreement with the rightness or the inevitability of what lay at the end of the road.

Another reason for Twining's opposition to TANU was economic. He still believed right to the end of his time in Tanganyika in one of the basic principles of the Twining period, that before a country could become independent its resources should be so developed that it could raise enough revenue to meet the costs of governing itself and providing its own social services. Stability and confidence were the catchwords he had used to attract the external capital and skills which were needed to achieve this development, and he was disappointed, and sometimes more than disappointed, when some of TANU's statements and actions had or threatened to have the opposite effect. He summed up his attitude just before he left. 'The exploration which is going on today should tell us within a few years whether we have mineral deposits capable of being profitably mined. If this should turn out to be so, we must, as the Secretary of State indicated when he was here last year, make sure that the conditions are right to attract the capital required which it is hoped would certainly run into many millions of pounds and, to quote his words, "ensure that to the normal hazards of mining are not added the abnormal hazards of political instability".'

In so far as politics and economics were concerned Twining's attitudes to Nyerere and TANU were mainly based on argument and reason. Because of this the differences between them could perhaps have been resolved as such differences were bridged by other Governors elsewhere. Some of Twining's attitudes however were more emotional, and it was these more than anything else perhaps which in the end made co-operation between him and Nyerere impossible.

In the first place Twining became more and more offended and upset as time went on by the attitude of Nyerere to the tribal chiefs. For reasons which from their point of view were sound and logical, Nyerere and TANU were determined to undermine the established position of the chiefs and eventually to destroy them. They wanted to build a nation: the tribal chiefs represented divisive, often mutually antagonistic forces. They wanted a popular, if not what we in the West regarded as a democratic, society: the chiefs were for the most part hereditary rulers and, despite the progress made with elected or representative tribal councils, still largely autocratic, almost feudal. Nyerere and TANU wanted to make a fresh start: the chiefs, it seemed to them and often with good reason, belonged to the past. Twining had however, so to speak, thrown in his lot with the chiefs. They were part of his administration. He aimed to base his whole system of local and eventually central government on them. He even had ideas of persuading them to form their own political party and of making them into the nucleus of a moderate, conservative Second Chamber. Apart from this he liked their style, he had always been attracted by the regal and the traditional in dress and manners and in speech. Many of them were his close friends. A more pragmatic man than Twining might, when he saw which way the wind was blowing, have abandoned the chiefs and allied himself with the new forces. Peter Twining's nature would not let him act like that. His reaction may have been more emotional than rational but if this was a fault, it was an amiable fault. The sadness of course was that most of the chiefs were coming to terms with Nyerere, secretly at first and then, towards the end of 1958, more openly. One cannot blame them. Twining was leaving Tanganyika. Twining was the past. They had to go on living there, if they could, in the future.

What however offended and upset Twining most was the hostile attitude eventually adopted by TANU to what he always referred to as 'my administrative officers'. In this case perhaps the attitude of TANU was less logical and more Machiavellian. It is true, as has been explained, that once TANU started to attack the chiefs and to disrupt the development schemes, the administrative officers were put in the position of having to treat it as subversive however much some of them may have admired Julius Nyerere and sympathised with his aims. Many too were disgusted, as Nyerere often was himself, at the way some of his adherents behaved. It is true too that the administrative officers were the closest and most tangible manifestations of what TANU had come to think of, as a result more often than not of external suggestion rather than local observation, as an objectionable colonial rule. But if ever, in Twining's philosophy, a debt was owed by one people to another it was the debt owed by the Africans of Tanganyika to these administrative officers. Some, Twining knew well, were owed more than others, just as he knew too that there were other servants of the Government, African and Asian as well as European, who had also made valuable professional and technical contributions to the slow, often discouraging process of trying to help the people of Tanganyika to stand on their own feet in what was to most of them a new and unfamiliar world. Twining had once been an administrative officer himself. He knew something of the pains and the frustrations as well as the satisfactions and pleasures of their work. Twining was above all a District Officer's governor. When TANU and in the end Nyerere himself attacked them, abused them and tried to undo their work, he became beyond compromise and reconciliation, and was glad to go. One of the last acts of the Twining regime was to prosecute Nyerere for criminal libel against two District Officers.

When Sir Richard Turnbull arrived in Tanganyika as Governor in July 1958 he found a political system and a style of government in a process of disintegration. Most of the checks and balances, the antidotes and the alternatives devised or proposed by Twining were discredited or in disarray. Turnbull quickly saw that there was now no alternative to TANU except, for a time perhaps if that was what was wanted, a policy of containment and repression. He looked at the forces at his disposal and saw that they were very small. Twining was not a repressor and the country was not equipped for repression; he had spent the money in a sense on development schemes and hospitals and schools. Turnbull made his judgment of what he could expect in the way of support from the Government and public opinion in Britain in meeting the cost and the consequences of using force. He came to terms with Nyerere and with TANU. He was a realist and a very clear-headed person but he had other reasons too of a less pragmatic kind for seeking a compro-

mise. He was also a different sort of man. Twining liked his
music loud and warm, emotional and soulful. Turnbull's
taste was for the cooler and more analytical attractions of
the string quartet.

Tanganyika achieved independence in 1961. Twining in
his time had moved in that direction as fast, as he saw it, as
he could. Turnbull, to use his own phrase, had moved as
slowly as he dared. Yet the fact remains, the sad fact in view
of all that Twining did for Tanganyika and how much he
cared for the country and its people, that when later President Nyerere used to ask Mr. Malcom Macdonald 'And how
is my Governor getting on?' it was not Sir Edward Twining
he was thinking of but Sir Richard Turnbull. There were
other criticisms too of Twining as a governor after he had
gone and Tanganyika started to move at an accelerated pace
to self-government and independence. There were those who
said that not only had political progress been too slow and
that Africans had been trained in insufficient numbers to
take the place of Europeans but that even the economic structure of the country, to which Twining had attached so much
importance, was inadequate or shaky, and compared un-
favourably with what had been achieved elsewhere. The
mood at that time was critical no less in Britain than in
Africa but there were some who kept a sense of perspective
and still recognised a debt where it was due. When Nyerere
became Chief Minister of Tanganyika in 1960 Twining
wrote him a letter which evoked this reply.

My dear Lord Twining,

It was very kind of you to write and wish me well in
our new responsibilities. Although, as you say, we did not
always agree on methods and timing I never considered
you my enemy or an enemy of Tanganyika. For all I know
this very fact that we did not always agree may have helped
us to reach this important stage we have reached in the
manner and the short period in which we have reached it.

The changes have taken place very quietly and we are
all most gratified. Our only complaint is the usual complaint: because we do not throw stones, we do not have
the headlines in the world press and this lack of publicity

is a disadvantage to us when we try to raise funds for our development schemes. We still prefer the Tanganyika way!

yours very sincerely,

Julius K. Nyerere.

When the following year a date was set for Tanganyika's independence 'amid scenes of great rejoicing and many sincere expressions of goodwill and friendship to all those who have made this great day possible', an official telegram was sent to Twining from Dar es Salaam to say that 'we could not let this occasion pass without sending to you our acknowledgment of the part which you yourself have played in preparing Tanganyika and its people for their future role as an independent member of the Commonwealth.'

12

Retirement

THE TWININGS ARRIVED back in England on the 9th of July. Their last port of call was Gibraltar where the Governor, General Keightley, encouraged by one of his officials who had served in Tanganyika, contrived a surprise to cheer and charm a man of Twining's exuberant and all-embracing nature. The births, marriages and deaths of Gibraltar's apes had for many years been carefully recorded, and each new arrival given a distinctive name. When he learnt that the latest arrival was to be called Edward, Twining was delighted: it was not every visitor to Gibraltar who was honoured or who cared to be honoured in this way.

There was another surprise for him in London. The Secretary of State was there himself to meet him. The ship had docked during the night, and Mr. Lennox-Boyd came out for breakfast. Afterwards, in the privacy of the cabin, he stretched himself out on the bunk for comfort and told Peter Twining that it was proposed to recommend him for appointment by the Queen as a life peer. The next day the matter was more formally and exactly broached in a letter which reached Twining at his house in Godalming in an envelope marked 'Personal and Confidential' at the top and 'Prime Minister' at the bottom. Mr. Harold MacMillan wrote:

> I have it in mind to submit your name to the Queen with a recommendation that her Majesty may be graciously pleased to approve that the dignity of a Barony of the United Kingdom for life be conferred upon you.

The style as well as the offer pleased Twining very much.

He had a feeling for form and an appetite for distinction, and he accepted the honour with alacrity and pride. As the news was not to be made public until the 24th of July he had to keep it to himself, but it was a fortnight of modest concealment and sphinx-like smiles which he seems to have enjoyed, and for which perhaps he had over the years acquired a special talent. He had certainly had some experience of keeping secrets of this kind but this had the additional attractions of being both unusual and unexpected. Only one other colonial governor had in living memory been made a peer on his retirement, and that had been eleven years previously when Sir Arthur Richards had been made Lord Milverton of Lagos and Clifton. Another distinctive thing about Twining's peerage was that he was in the first list of life peers to be created.

The Life Peerages Act of 1958 was the culmination of many years of good intentions and of spirited argument about how exactly they should be realised. The idea of course was to get away from the hereditary principle which many found offensive, and to appoint instead men and women who had achieved distinction in various ways in the hope that their experience and wisdom would add weight and talent to a Second Chamber whose value was being increasingly questioned. Even those who disliked any suggestion of lowering the tone of the House of Lords by introducing an element of merit, supported the idea because they realised that it would help the survival of something which might otherwise disappear. The Act may have fulfilled most of the intentions but it did not by any means end the controversies. As *The Times* said in a leading article at the time:

The first list of life peers and life peeresses under the new Act is respectable and, for all that it is in so many ways historic, not very exciting. Intellectual eminence is honoured in the person of Mrs. Wootton; long service to the State in the House of Commons in Sir Ian Fraser and Sir Robert Boothby; eminent proconsular achievement and wisdom in Sir Edward Twining; and the contribution of women to the public welfare in Lady Ravensdale and Lady Reading. Where all the fourteen have earned preferment on their merits, it is a pity that some have been labelled as nominees of the Leader of the Opposition ... Peers should be created, and especially a new class of peers, for their personal distinction and independent capacity to contribute to the collective wisdom of Parliament. Once seated there, they are free to give their support to any party which can hold their allegiance; but they should certainly not enter the House under any suspicion that they are controlled from outside by an invisible Whip.

Twining avoided this element of controversy by becoming a crossbencher. This has since become a generally accepted custom for public servants who are made life peers but at that time it seems to have been largely a matter of personal choice. Twining had never had any great enthusiasm for party politics and being a crossbencher left him free to go his own individualistic and, some thought, occasionally perverse way. Twining's was not in any way a political appointment, nor was he made a peer just as a reward for his own long and distinguished service. Life peers were expected to serve rather than adorn, and each appointment had a purpose. In Twining's case it was to bring his experience of colonial administration in the field to bear on the discussion of overseas affairs in Parliament and to represent the views, the interests, the hopes and the grievances of the Service to which he had belonged. His appointment was in a sense meant as much as a compliment to the Colonial Service as to himself personally, and Twining, one feels, would not have wished it any other way.

This serious element did not however by any means prevent him from enjoying the more immediate pleasures of being made a lord, and of sharing them with his ageing but still delighted mother.

Thank you [he wrote when the news was published in the papers] for your characteristically charming letter. We have been inundated with telegrams (60) and letters (over 100) to say nothing of telephone calls. It is quite a business answering them. We lunched with Alan Lennox-Boyd today and he thought it was a very good idea to call myself

Lord Twining of Tanganyika. So I have written to the
Governor to clear it there. One also has to take an English
title of some place where one had a house or some associations. I should like to have taken Westminster but that
would not have been allowed so as we have owned Rede-
hurst for twenty-seven years I have written to the Mayor
asking if he minds my taking Godalming. I am seeing
Garter King of Arms about it on Tuesday afternoon.

Later he sent her a dialogue of his visit to Garter Principal
King of Arms which, like many of his stories, was intended
more to entertain than to record what actually took place.
His meeting and his subsequent correspondence with the
College of Arms, with Garter himself and York Herald and
Rouge Croix Pursuivant, were in fact conducted with for-
mality and decorum on both sides but he still could not resist
a life-long habit of embroidery when it came to giving an
account of them.

His account is headed 'E.F.T.'s Introduction to the House
of Lords', and starts with the visit to Garter Principal King of
Arms.

G. Good morning. Glad to see you. What title do you wish
    to take?

E.F.T. I thought Lord God of Godalming would be quite
    appropriate.

G. Pshaw. Pshaw. Pshaw. Really quite impossible. Quite
    impossible.

E.F.T. Of course but I was only joking.

G. You should not joke about such important matters.

E.F.T. Sorry Sir.

G. Well what title do you really wish to take?

E.F.T. Well I should like to keep to the family name.

G. Twining. Twining. That sounds all right, you can
    get it round your tongue. You have a country seat I
    suppose?

E.F.T. Oh yes, situated at Godalming, but I want to sell it.
    I should like to call myself Lord Twining of Tanganyika.

G. Quite impossible. Quite impossible. It would be very
    wrong. You don't own the place do you?

E.F.T. For the matter of fact I did for nine years. I was longer in Tanganyika than Lord Mountbatten was in Burma. Lord Robins calls himself of Rhodesia.

G. I know. I know, but quite wrong. There is no such place, it's a Federation or something.

E.F.T. Well besides my own feelings I think many people in Tanganyika would like it and the S. of S. strongly approves.

Long pause

G. Well if you insist you can call yourself Lord Twining comma of Tanganyika (how do you spell it by the way?), and of Godalming in the County of Surrey.

E.F.T. Thank you but I think I should first get the formal approval of the Governor and of the Corporation of Godalming.

G. Quite unnecessary. Your seat is at Godalming isn't it?

There were several other fascinating details to be arranged before he could use his new title and be formally introduced in the House of Lords. One was the question of a Coat of Arms. He had already been through the complicated and expensive process of evolving Arms when he had been made a G.C.M.G., and all that was necessary to satisfy the College of Arms and the Editor of Debrett was the addition of a coronet. His Arms and Crest were based on genealogical research carried out by his father and continued by his brother, but his Supporters, as the animals up the side of the arms are called—'on the dexter, a crested crane, on the sinister, a giraffe both proper'—fitted in well with the African part of his new title. Another detail was the acquisition of a peer's Parliamentary Robe which he had to wear for his formal introduction to the House of Lords. As, apart from this, robes were only worn on ceremonial occasions like the State opening of Parliament, he originally thought of hiring one from Ede and Ravenscroft who kept a small discreet stock for this purpose. A new robe, 'of scarlet cloth, lined white with rich gold lace and mock ermine fur bars' cost sixty-five guineas at that time, but when the new Lord Twining learnt that they had a second-hand robe trimmed with real ermine for sale at forty-five guineas the temptation was too much for him. He sold off his G.C.M.G. mantle to the Order of St. Michael and St. George to cover the cost of this happy extravagance.

His formal introduction in the House of Lords had been fixed for the 22nd of October. As there were so many new peers and peeresses to be dealt with on this singular occasion a special meeting of the House was arranged for the purpose. He had been asked to go for a rehearsal in the morning with the two peers who were to act as his supporters at the ceremony of introduction. One was Lord Thurlow, a former regular soldier who had commanded a Brigade in East Africa in Twining's time, and the other was Lord Chesham whose father had done much to encourage Europeans to settle and farm in Tanganyika.

The ceremony itself in the afternoon he described in the sort of throw-away style which he knew would both please and slightly shock his mother.

I went to the Moses Room, robed and was photographed. I was fourth. In we went, Black Rod (Sir Brian Horrocks), the Earl Marshal (the Duke of Norfolk, who had lunched well), Garter resplendent in his tabard, Lord Chesham, E.F.T., and Lord Thurlow at about four paces interval. In turn we bowed to the throne, at the bar; in turn we bowed to the throne, at the table; in turn we bowed to the throne, at the Woolsack. I then knelt on one knee to the Lord Chancellor and handed him my Writ of Summons, and Garter handed us my Letter Patent which we patted. I arose and moved to the table where the Clerk of the House read the beautifully illuminated Letters Patent which contained a mistake describing me as Governor-General of Tanganyika. He then read the Writ of Summons and in a loud voice I took the Oath and unlike the others kissed the Bible. Then at the end of the table we in turn bowed to the throne, in turn we bowed to the bar and bowed to the throne and then with my supporters and Garter we went to a back bench. Sit down, said Garter, and put on your hats. Get up, said Garter, take off your hats and bow to the Lord Chancellor. Sit down, said Garter, and put on your hats (cocked hats). Stand up, said Garter, take off your hats and bow to the Lord Chancellor. Sit down said Garter, and put on your hats. Get up, said Garter, take off your hats, bow to the Lord Chancellor and don't sit down or put on your hats again. We obediently followed the directions and the Lord Chancellor, a sinister-looking figure in black and wearing a tricorne, sat on the Woolsack trying hard to get his short legs on the floor and raised his hat and bowed back at us. Then we went out. At the table in turn we bowed to the throne. At the Woolsack in turn we bowed to the throne. I shook hands with the L.C. who made some polite remarks. Finally we retreated from the House behind the throne and returned to the Moses Room and disrobed. I returned to the House and took a seat.

Then when it was over I was introduced to some notabilities, including the Duke of Buccleuch, the Indian Marchioness of Winchester and others. They all tried to proselytise me to join the Conservative Party but I remained neutral. Then I was given a huge red box containing my Letters Patent and home we went.

'Home' now was Ashley Gardens in Westminster where the Twinings, having sold their house in Godalming, had taken a flat. Ashley Gardens is a series of blocks of flats of late Victorian architecture, sandwiched, in a manner of speaking, between the Roman Catholic cathedral of Westminster and the Army and Navy stores, but the important thing as far as Twining himself was concerned was that it was in a part of London which he had known, on and off, all his life, and where he felt that he belonged. 74 Ashley Gardens itself was a spacious first-floor flat with large rooms, high ceilings and long corridors. For a couple who had spent most of their adult lives abroad with plenty of servants and in official residencies maintained by the Public Works Department, the size of the flat presented a number of practical and domestic problems. Although these problems were eased by the employment of a resident housekeeper, it still left residues of household duties which Lord Twining sometimes felt he ought perhaps to share. A photograph which appeared in a London paper showed him doing the drying up in shirt-sleeves and apron but in practice, it seems, he preferred to confine himself to 'doing the things the Butler did', like cleaning the silver and doing the wine. If there were any question of doing less portly duties after dinner he was apt to excuse himself by saying it was time to turn down the beds. He was not a domesticated man. One thing however which he always did was to make the early morning tea. The milk was always put in first with the precision and the gestures of a ritual though he knew that this practice was more a question of history than of taste. When tea originally came to England the china of those who could afford it was too delicate and fragile to risk the impact of hot water and it was for this practical reason that the milk was put in first. No sugar was allowed to spoil the flavour; even tea cosies were frowned on in some Twining households as they were supposed to prolong the process of infusion. When the tea was made to his satisfaction he would take it in to his wife, and for an hour they would talk, as they had always done at this time, or one would talk and the other would listen. He worked in the mornings in his study on his still considerable correspondence or on his crown jewels but he usually went out to lunch at one or other of his clubs. He had been made a member of the Athenaeum under special rules designed, it was said, for governors and bishops but he still preferred the less hushed and less academic atmosphere of the United Services Club to which he had belonged since its amalgamation with the Junior version of his Army days.

In the afternoons he went to the House of Lords. He liked the ten minutes' walk between his clubs in Waterloo Place and the Houses of Parliament, and the ten minutes' walk home at the end of his working day. It was exercise enough now for a man of his weight and size and age: and the walk back at half past five (the Lord Chancellor, it was said, used to apologise if proceedings went on beyond that hour) took him, if he went that way, past his father's old church and within sight of the place in Vincent Square where he had been born. The church is not a pretty church and the vicarage site is now part of the Westminster College of Technology but there must have been other satisfactions in passing them on his way from the House of Lords to his expensive flat in

Ashley Gardens. He was however a practical man and he usually went home by the more direct and less nostalgic route along Victoria Street. He didn't often go out in the evenings. He watered the flowers on the balcony and had a light supper and watched television. *Harry Worth* was his favourite programme. He liked *Steptoe* too, and he watched *Dr. Finlay's Casebook* companionably with his doctor wife. He was usually in bed by nine or ten o'clock.

Twining seems to have enjoyed being a member of the House of Lords. It was pleasant to go in through the Peers' Entrance and be recognised and greeted by the policemen and the servants of the House, and to find in the cloakroom a special peg for his hat and coat and umbrella marked with his title and his name. He had always had a feeling for the past, and the stairs and the corridors of the House of Lords reek of history, the names on the panels and pictures and busts evoke the smells of schoolrooms and chalk and the cheap bindings of text books by Philip Guedalla and Tout. Even the underlings and the clerks as they go about their business have a faintly hereditary air. Inside the chamber the Lord Chancellor on his enormous bolster Woolsack keeps murmuring as the afternoon meanders on, 'As many as are of that opinion will say content, the contrary not content', like a priest seeking responses from a sleepy congregation in a language that no one any longer speaks. Like a number of other noble Lords, Twining found it as good a place as any other for his afternoon sleep.

There are about a thousand members of the House of Lords but the average daily attendance is considerably less. In spite of this, or because of it perhaps, the standard of oratory and debate is often very high. Twining was not an accomplished orator and he had little direct experience of the strategies and cut and thrust of parliamentary debate: his was the experience for the most part of a man who had had the protections and the advantages of speaking from the Chair to bodies of less gifted or less well-positioned men. His maiden speech however was well received even allowing for the courtesies and the compliments which are the custom on such occasions in the House of Lords. He had spoken about the work of the Colonial Development Corporation, of which he had considerable experience, and Lord Milverton, who phrases his praise with as much exactitude as his invective, remarked that 'he speaks with such great and recent authority on most Colonial problems that it will indeed be a pleasure to look forward to future contributions from him to debates in this House. The boisterous energy with which he has so successfully fulfilled the duties of his various offices will indeed be an addition to our debates, and we shall look forward to hearing from him frequently in the future.'

Twining's next speech was more controversial and less evenly received. In a debate on the Devlin Report on recent disturbances in Nyasaland he had said that he believed that the British Government was in good faith pursuing a policy of leading her colonial territories to self-government on a democratic Parliamentary basis. 'But,' he went on, 'if we are to succeed in Africa, the political leaders must play the rules of the game, and not for ever conspire to take short cuts by positive action, be it by civil disobedience or by violence. Such a policy shows political bankruptcy. We support democracy and not demagogy . . .' When he sat down Lord Latham stood up, and Hansard records the following brief exchange.

Lord Latham: My Lords, the noble Lord, Lord Twining, said that the Africans must be taught to play the rules of the game. Who settles the rules?
Lord Twining: I think they are well established rules.
Lord Latham: Established by whom?
Lord Twining: By us, my Lords.

Several of Twining's other speeches in his early years in the House of Lords reflect a similar philosophy. 'There have been criticisms,' he said in a debate on the Commonwealth in the summer of 1960, 'about our going too fast in the granting of self-government to these East African territories. The African National political leaders have not been slow to reply. They have replied quite sharply—that who are we to take an objective view as to when they are ready to look after their own affairs. They say that they are interested in self-government, not good government: and they say that if they make a mess of it it will be their own mess. I do not think that we should take these arguments too seriously, so as to allow them to affect our responsibilities in the matter. We have great responsibilities and we must ensure that the leaders with whom we negotiate are the real leaders —responsible leaders who have the backing of the people of their territories. There are other responsibilities: to see that if independence is to be real these territories have an economy which can raise the revenue to maintain them in a real, independent way: and for them to have an adequate number of staff available to run their countries.' He went on to develop a theme which was not by any means new in him but which was to play an increasing part in his thinking on colonial affairs as more and more territories reached the threshold of independence. 'Now I touch on a somewhat delicate matter. Various Ministers, in speaking about the future of the East African territories, have said that the constitutional reforms are to be based on the introduction of Westminster parliamentary democracy. I feel sure that we all agree with that. I think it is one of our most cherished institutions, and we want to offer them the best. But we must ask the question: will the Westminster model, when exported to African soil, work? I cannot resist the temptation to say that the export model has nothing in it which resembles your Lordships' House.'

He was concerned, with the genuine concern of a man who really cared about what happened to the peoples he had known and worked for, over the tendency of African leaders to think in terms of a one-party system in which there would be no place for a democratic opposition; about the prevalence of intimidation, particularly of hidden intimidation based in many parts of Africa on secret societies and witchcraft which, he said, was 'much more wide-spread than is realised by people who have perhaps not lived in these countries'; and about the threat to basic British juridical principles like the independence of the judiciary and respect for the Common Law. If his speeches on such themes seemed to some of his listeners in the House of Lords and elsewhere to be touched with a paternalism which was beginning to seem a little out of date, they were disarmed when he got up to speak on the Tanganyika Independence Bill in November of 1961. 'I saw the other day,' he said, 'that I was described as the last of the paternal Governors. Well, I am sufficiently old-fashioned not to mind being paternal, although I recognise that the worst feature of it that one is inclined to overlook is the fact that one's children are growing up.' He went on to pay tribute to his successor Turnbull's acceleration of the processes of self-government and independence. 'There were many people at the time who thought that the pace was too fast, but I am quite sure that the decision was a wise and courageous one and that to have tried to go at a slower pace would have jeopardised the goodwill that existed and would have led to difficulties, if not to disaster.'

This was generous and warm-hearted praise, and so too was his final tribute to Julius Nyerere. 'So in the space of forty-two years we have achieved our target and Tanganyika is gaining its independence peacefully without the recriminations and troubles which have undoubtedly been experienced in some other colonial territories. A great deal of the credit for this satisfactory situation must be given to Mr. Julius Nyerere, who is the undisputed national leader. He is a good Christian, a man of high principles and strong convictions, who has shown himself not only to be an outstanding political leader but also to be a statesman.' 'On January 9,' he concluded, 'Tanganyika will enter upon a new chapter of its history as a Sovereign State, and it is gratifying that she has applied for membership of the British Commonwealth of Nations. All of us who know the country and its people will wish them well, and I am sure that they will receive the good wishes of your Lordships' House.' For a man who had become such a controversial figure in the last stages of colonial rule in Tanganyika it was a good note on which to end.

Although Twining was disturbed by various things which happened in Tanzania in the next few years, he avoided the temptation in his public speeches of saying 'I told you so', and he remained hopeful, for most though perhaps not all of the time, that in the end the qualities of the people and of President Nyerere would enable the country to survive what he saw as growing pains and to fulfil the expectations expressed when it gained its independence. For many people these expectations meant that Tanganyika and the other ex-colonial Territories would continue after independence to develop on recognisably British lines within the political and economic framework of the Commonwealth. It was part of the philosophy of the Twining period that this would be so, and almost everything that was done was based on this premise. Twining soon saw however that this was unlikely to happen. He saw, as he said in one of his best and most empathetic speeches in the House of Lords, that the people of Africa wanted to build a society based on their own historical and cultural background and not 'as partners in the history and culture of a European mother country'. He saw that they wanted to be uncommitted either to the East or the West and, that their aim was 'to make Africa a third power in the world as soon as possible'. It is always easier of course to think objectively when one is not involved in the stresses and strains of keeping the peace, nor subject to the pressures and irritations of intimidation and abuse; it is interesting all the same to wonder what would have happened in Tanganyika in the last years of his administration if Twining had come to these conclusions earlier.

Although Lord Twining spoke in the House of Lords at one time or another about all the other countries in which he had served, Uganda, Mauritius, St. Lucia and North Borneo, as if to show perhaps that he did not forget old friends, his most forceful and moving interventions were on behalf of the Administrative and other officers of the Colonial Service. Their position in the last days of colonial rule and the first years of independence was difficult and exacting. It is not always easy for old hands to transfer power, or for new hands to assume it, with grace and good temper. Added to this was a nagging uncertainty about their future, whether to stay and serve new and often quixotic masters as many of them were invited to do, or whether to go at once while there was still a chance perhaps for them to start another life and another career in Britain or elsewhere. For men in their thirties and forties with young children particularly, it was often an agonising decision, a conflict of loyalties and fears, a teasing assessment of possibilities and probabilities. Twining presented these problems and argued the case for helping to ease them with the aid and the weight of genuine sympathy and first-hand experience.

Although he spoke on a wide variety of subjects relating directly or indirectly to what were or had been colonial affairs. Twining was not as effective in the House of Lords as some had expected. He never, it seems, quite mastered the specialised style needed for its debates nor did a wit or pungency which could so easily cover the span of a table at lunch or the distance between two arm chairs quite carry to the Speaker and the benches and the press gallery in the House of Lords. He might perhaps, it was said, have overcome these difficulties if he had been a more regular attender. He went to the House of Lords frequently, it was true, when he was in London: but for six months of the year, from November to April, he wasn't in London at all. He was in Kenya.

He and his wife had in the end solved the problem of where to live by buying a house at Karen on the outskirts of Nairobi and spending the winters there. The Secretary of State, when he learnt of this, was good enough to say that it would have the advantage of keeping Twining in touch with African affairs, but others concerned with the duties of life peers were not always so charitable. There was no doubt however that when he was in East Africa Twining did keep in touch both with people and with events, and he even used the knowledge and experience he gained in the winters to speak as a contemporary observer of developments in Kenya: once in one of his less serious moments he went so far as to declare an interest as a Kenya farmer on the strength of keeping a dozen sheep to crop the grass in his Nairobi garden. As time went on he may have become out of touch with some more recent political and economic trends and changes but he still knew a great many people of all races in East Africa. It was for this perhaps and for his genial and persuasive qualities as a chairman rather than for his knowledge of banking and finance and trade that he was employed and paid retainers by National and Grindlays Bank, The South African and General Investment and Trust Company and the large East African trading firm of Smith Mackenzie. He had a number of other interests and occupations too both in East Africa and in London, some of which were charitable or benevolent and unpaid, and some commercial. He was one way and another well provided for. By careful investment of his and his wife's capital and savings and his various employments after he retired, Lord Twining was, by the standards of those who serve the Crown, a comparatively rich man. He was generous and thoughtful for the embarrassments of those who were not as well off as himself, but he was careful of his money, and was apt to be sharp, and sometimes disconcertingly sharp with those who tried to abuse his generosity or stretch his hospitality.

The Twinings liked Kenya. They had a large, pleasant house and ten acres of garden, but they had plenty of servants including Ali, whom they brought with them from Government House at Dar es Salaam, and this left Lady Twining free to devote her energies and attentions, as she preferred, to medical and welfare work. They got up at six fifteen with the daily domestic ritual of early morning tea. Twining bathed and dressed and breakfasted at his own pace and pleasure. He usually worked in the mornings on his East African occupations or on crown jewels, and he sometimes went into Nairobi for lunch. He slept in the afternoons in a chair and in the evenings he went for a walk. They had a car and an African driver but they didn't often go out in the evenings. As in London, Twining was usually in bed by nine or ten o'clock.

Spending the winter in Kenya and the summer in London suited Lord Twining. Although he had a satisfactory fullness of occupations and interests and friends in both places and had evolved a way of life in each which pleased him, he was always glad when it was time to leave Kenya in April for England, and equally glad to leave England for Kenya in November. It was something to look forward to, twice in each year, and there was more to it than a change of climate. He was fifty-nine when he retired but he still had a nomadic streak, a craving for new pastures and for travel, a youthful optimism that the grass would be greener in other fields. He was able when he was in East Africa to satisfy these urges to some extent by visiting the branches of National and Grindlays Bank in Kenya and Uganda in his capacity as Chairman of the Bank's local advisory council but, because of rules restricting the activities of retired Governors which he scrupulously observed, he didn't go to Tanganyika. The only time he went back to Tanganyika was when he and his wife were invited to attend its independence celebrations in 1961. He made a brave show in his letters to his mother of the attentions he received, not least from his old African servants at Government House, but it was not in truth a return that he particularly enjoyed. He even managed when he was in England to extract a taste of safari from his chairmanship of the Victoria League by visiting the widespread branches of that organisation which cared, with a delicately balanced mixture of the patrician and the practical, for Commonwealth visitors and students in Britain. Twining's own main concern was with providing hostels for students, particularly Asian and African students, but he still found time to charm those whose preferences were for more traditional forms of hospitality like visits to Hughenden Manor and country walks. He paid regular visits too to the Ross Institute of Tropical Hygiene of which he was also chairman and where his bluff humour and capacity for by-passing customary procedures in order to get things done were much valued at a time when relations with the countries where tropical diseases occurred were changing as rapidly as ideas of how to deal with the diseases.

When even the variety of London failed to contain his moods he would go off to Europe and draw fresh substance and taste, like some outsize butterfly, from the hotels and restaurants and cafés of France and Germany and Italy.

The letters which Lord Twining wrote to his mother in 1961 and 1962 were gentle letters. When he was in London he went to see her regularly. He wrote too, small notes about the details of his next visit and the pleasures of his last, but most of the letters were naturally from Kenya. His mother was ill with the illnesses and discomforts of old age, and in much pain. Her elder son Stephen had just died. The letters were for comfort, short simple letters that could be read aloud by nuns to an old lady with headaches and bad eyes and replied to by dictation without too much stress of memory or concentration. He wrote about the weather and the garden, with news about the family and the household pets.

We are still looking for a dog [he wrote]. Any on offer seem to get snapped up quickly. There seem to be only two sorts—one which is so amiable that it licks everyone's hands including thieves and the other which goes for all Africans indiscriminately and bites their trousers. The owner of one we were offered had had to replace 12 pairs of trousers of the dog's victims. Very expensive! But not so expensive as a Great Dane we were offered which eats 3 pounds of meat a day ... There is little other news. It has not yet rained but otherwise we are quite happy in our peaceful atmosphere.

When it was nearly time for them to go to England he wrote saying that she should 'be patient and await our return with courage and faith'. The last letter from her younger son found among Mrs. Twining's papers was written from the House of Lords in April 1962.

My darling Mother, in the Underground I was worried about your clock and as I had to lunch at the Royal College of Surgeons which meant getting out at Holborn I popped into R. A. Miles and told them to get a clock and send it down by special messenger to-day. Young Miles (who is now not so young and is bald) took a personal interest and said he would do his best. So I hope it arrives and is suitable. It is a present from me. I know how miserable it is to be without a clock. If you want me on Friday I could come if they telephone early enough. But I will certainly come on Saturday. Meanwhile my very loving sympathy in your suffering. Your very loving son, E. F. Peter Twining.

She died soon afterwards when she was a few weeks short of her ninetieth birthday. Many people mourned her. Some of them were young, grandchildren, great-nephews and nieces who had visited her at the convent at Harrow. They went at first perhaps from a sense of duty but most of them went back again and again of their own free will to draw on her warmth and her vitality and her sense of humour, and on the strength and the stimulus of her character; but none had drawn on these qualities more, nor owed so much to them, as her youngest child Peter.

One thing which pleased Peter Twining very much was that his mother had lived to see the publication of his book on the crown jewels of Europe. What had started as a dilettante occupation when he was on a lonely station in Uganda had developed into an absorbing interest and an exciting and satisfying pursuit, and he had for many years planned and hoped that it would one day achieve consummation in the form of a published book. He had already had some interim achievements in this direction with two small shilling handbooks on the regalia in the Tower of London and Edinburgh Castle, which didn't do very well, and with a larger and more successful commentary on the English Coronation ceremony which appeared with timely timing in 1937. The reviews paid rather more attention to the illustrations than to the text largely because Twining made something of a coup by reproducing a unique series of photographs taken during the Coronation of George the Fifth. The *Guardian* however judged it 'a readable book', and the *Times Literary Supplement*, for whom no subject is too esoteric, said that 'while hardly a book that anyone will be tempted to consult for archaeological detail', for its own purpose, 'that of allowing the modern rite to be followed step by step, nothing better could be desired'. One cannot but admire the enterprise and the pertinacity which enabled him as an amateur living in the middle of Africa and with a limited academic education, successfully to enter such a specialised and scholarly field and to be sufficiently accepted in it to be invited, as he was, to write a series of articles for the *Goldsmiths' Journal* on orbs and sceptres and jewelled swords. These small books and articles were of course a long way short of his objective of a comprehensive and copiously illustrated book on the crown jewels and regalia of Europe but he went gaily and persistently on with his reading and his correspondence and his searches in the museums and courts and lumber rooms of Europe, and by September 1952 he was, as has been explained, far enough advanced with material and self-confidence to ask Batsfords if they were interested in publishing his book. His idea was that the book should be produced in time to catch the floodtide of interest in crowns and regalia which he thought might be released by the Coronation of Queen Elizabeth in the summer of 1953, and to extend its scope, with the help of that voracious traveller Sir Harry Luke, to cover the coronation procedures and regalia of such exotic kingdoms as Tonga, Brazil, Haiti, Ethiopia and the Mosquito Coast of Central America. Batsfords were both interested and intrigued, as much perhaps by the author as the subject, but it soon became clear that there was no possibility that either the author or the publishers would be in a position to complete the project in time for the Coronation. There for various reasons the matter rested until the spring of 1958 when Twining wrote again asking if, now that he was retiring and would have more time to finish the book, they were still interested in publishing it.

The aim of this book [he wrote in an accompanying note] is to provide a factual work of an almost encyclopedic nature on the history of European regalia and Crown Jewels from about the 4th to the 20th century ... The author of this work has been studying the subject and conducting enquiries and research for 27 years. He has had to obtain translations of works from 15 languages and has had to visit over 70 centres in 17 countries in Europe. He has had the opportunity of discussing points with a number of members of European royal families, with the Keepers of Crown Jewels and regalia in a number of countries, and with recognised experts...

The work is divided into two parts—the first, a series of essays on the different royal ornaments, and the second, 27 chapters dealing with individual kingdoms ... Inevitably the book is going to be a big one and it will probably be difficult to keep it down to less than 500,000 words. It will also have to be very well illustrated. The author has a collection of some 2,000 photographs from which to draw and it is thought that some 800–1,000 will be needed adequately to illustrate the work...

Although a large and expensive book of this nature may have a limited market, the fact that it deals with so many

different countries of course widens it and the author has
found considerable interest in the proposed book in many
countries and in many walks of life. The reigning and the
exiled royal families would all be interested as well as
many other heads of States throughout the world. It is the
sort of book which would appeal to the rich and would
find a place on the shelves of most of the great libraries
of the world. The jewellery trade, particularly in America,
would probably support it and there is quite a large body
of individuals who are either interested or collectors of
such books. It looks therefore as if it should be possible to
launch it as a commercial success.

Although Batsfords were indeed still interested they were
not entirely bewitched by the prospects of commercial success held out to them, and they made it politely but firmly
plain that their own balance of the probable costs on the one
hand and the probable number of purchasers on the other
meant that they could only publish the book if it was subsidised, and considerably subsidised, by the author. Twining
accepted this with the cheerful amiability and good grace
which were to characterise his relations with his publishers
and make him over the years one of their favourite authors.
He had realised, despite his good sales talk, that he would
probably have to pay some of the cost if he were ever to
see his work in print, but he was surprised nevertheless when
he discovered that the cost would be over nine thousand
pounds and that he had to bear all the risk. He was surprised
but he was not discouraged or nonplussed. He sold part of his
stamp collection for about seven thousand pounds to help
pay the bill, and he not unnaturally thereafter took a close
and very lively interest in the individual items which made
up the costs of printing and publication. He took a close and
lively interest too in the arrangement of the photographs and
the processes of editing. Publishers do not as a rule encourage their authors to take a detailed interest in such matters
but in this case they found Lord Twining's distinctive inter-
pretations of an author's rights and duties, both before and
after publication, a constant and endearing challenge; exhilarating most of the time, exhausting sometimes and always

fun. *A History of the Crown Jewels of Europe* by Lord Twining was eventually published in November 1960. It had 720 pages of text, 232 pages of plates with over 750 photographs: it weighed nine pounds and it cost sixteen guineas. 'Too heavy to hold, too dull to read and too expensive to buy', was how Twining himself described it, but the reviews were, on the whole, more kind. Some reviewers used the opportunity, as reviewers do, to air their own knowledge rather than their critical faculties or to point out small errors of fact with unnecessary relish, but the general consensus was, as Sir James Mann put it, that Lord Twining had produced 'a standard work which is unlikely to be superseded for many years to come'. Equally satisfying perhaps from Twining's point of view was that over a thousand copies of the book were sold and that he made in the end, when all the costs of publication had been met, a clear profit of over a thousand pounds.

The *History of the Crown Jewels of Europe* was only the first part of the magnum opus: there was a second part still to come on the regalia. Batsfords agreed to publish it on the same terms as before. It was a smaller book, but even so the production costs were nearly seven thousand pounds. Much of the research and the collection of material had already been done but there were still some more museums in Europe to be visited, more books to be read, more people to be written to and questioned, more cupboards and lumber rooms to be explored. In the next few years Lord Twining made several trips to the Continent. His appetite for research and for travel didn't seem to have abated. He threw himself into the journeys and the planning of the journeys with as much enthusiasm and attention to detail as he had done before. The only difference was that whereas he had in the past gone on these journeys alone, now he sought for company. He liked when he could to take one or other of his sons on these journeys, and he was very pleased when he discovered that they accepted his somewhat diffident invitations because they liked travelling with him and not out of filial duty. His affection for his family became less inarticulate and more familiar as he grew older, and as they perhaps grew less in awe of him. Sometimes he took someone else

of his sons' generation and treated them like sons, and expected them in turn to treat him like a father, that is to say,
as fathers were treated when he himself was a boy. They
were 'John' or 'David' to him and favoured companions on
his travels but they called him 'Sir' or 'Lord Twining' and
there were borderlines of familiarity which they quickly and
instinctively learned not to cross. He was a generous traveller. They went first class and stayed at the best hotels, and
his itineraries usually managed to include, as much for his
companions' pleasure as his own, visits to a favourite restaurant in Munich where they served roast quail and to the Coq
Hardi at Bougival near Paris where by a happy coincidence
Berlioz had lived for a while. He had always liked good food
and wine and he knew now from long experience in Europe
where his tastes could be indulged and shared. Another
reason why he liked to take a companion on his travels was
that he had a need for a listener and a questioner for his
talking. He was in his sixties, and he tended to talk more
and more about the past than the present or the future. He
had drafted some chapters of a somewhat apocryphal autobiography but he wasn't pleased with them and had put
them aside uncorrected and unfinished; but as he travelled
by train or by car through the middle parts of Europe—he
never went to the extremities of Spain or Russia—he achieved
in conversation a style and a vividness which he couldn't seem
to manage on paper. He talked frankly and disarmingly about
the mistakes which he, like any other man, had made
through the ordinary processes of human error, particularly
during the time when he was in Tanganyika, but most of
his reminiscences were about his early years, about his green,
gauche periods at school and in the Army and in Ireland. He
had often told the story of his capture of De Valera, a story
which became richly embellished with the years, but he
rarely talked about his experiences in the slums and brothels
of Dublin, and the effect, perhaps the traumatic effect, which
they had had on him. Now these too came out as if they were
secrets which he had kept to himself too long, things which
had been bottled up and grown bitter. He used words, harsh
physical words, which he didn't ordinarily use, he talked of
subjects which he usually never mentioned. He talked of his

childhood too, of those part happy, part envious years at Cowarne Court, the days of his boyhood in Westminster when he was awkward and slight, untalented and unnoticed and had a painful stammer. These however were only moods: for the most part he was still a most entertaining companion, relaxed, never dull, always it seemed in control of every situation.

He finished work on his second book in the summer of 1966. He went through the arduous processes of selecting and arranging the photographs, and of having his text extensively edited again, with the same attention to detail, the same passion for argument and the same sense of the ridiculous as he had shown before. He was sixty-seven. If he had begun to feel his age or the first symptoms of a physical unease he didn't let it show. He didn't speak in the House of Lords that summer, but he pursued his other interests with as much vigour and humour as before.

It was in Kenya that winter that Twining started to feel and to look unwell. At first it was just 'trouble with my waterworks', something that could still be made a joke of. By the spring when it was time for them to go to England he was seriously ill. He thought it was something to do with his gout: only his wife and doctors knew that it was cancer. *European Regalia* was published early in 1967. Even the reviews which were kind and which his publishers sent out to him with encouraging little notes failed to cheer him. He wouldn't even open the parcel which contained his own copies of the book. He left it unopened on the table by his bed.

He had an operation when he arrived in England and he spent some time in a nursing home, but when it was clear that there wasn't anything more that could be done he went back to Ashley Gardens and the devoted care of his wife and family. He didn't know he was dying, and people who came to see him in June and the early part of July still found flashes of the familiar spirit and laughter and wit, and of his kindness too: one of the last things he did was to go to great lengths to try and find a post in a bank for a son of an old friend.

Lord Twining died on the 21st of July. Not many people

knew that he was seriously ill, very few knew that he was near his death. The letters that poured in to Lady Twining from all over the world reflected shock, almost disbelief that a person who had been so full of life and the love of living could so suddenly disappear. Much sadness was reflected in these letters, much heartfelt and genuine grief but one note which comes through the formal expressions of condolence and regret is pride in having known him and pleasure in remembering what he had been like. Many graceful and generous things were said about Lord Twining after his death. Many, as one would expect, were tributes to his practical achievements in the territories where he had been or to the various bodies and organisations he served when he had retired, but the most moving were those which touched on his qualities as a man, and on the impact and influence which he had had on people. 'Twining,' *The Times* said in a long obituary, 'was one of the most remarkable of the postwar colonial Governors ... In manner he was bluff, boisterous and possessed of a schoolboyish sense of humour. A strong personality, of untiring energy, he gave a sense of purpose and direction to his subordinates and to ordinary people of all races in Tanganyika. His most notable achievements', the article went on, 'were in the field of race relations. By example rather than precept he succeeded in a remarkable degree in breaking down the social barriers between the three communities: and a happy and constructive period unrolled itself beneath his aegis...' Although the view from State House in Dar es Salaam from which President Nyerere issued his statement was naturally somewhat different, what was said about Twining as a man was remarkably the same. 'Lord Twining was Governor of Tanganyika at a time when the people of the country were organising to throw off the colonial yoke. However this did not, and does not, prevent Tanzanians from appreciating his qualities as a man: his personal kindness and his integrity were much appreciated, and he played a great part in preventing Tanganyika's freedom struggle from becoming imbued with bitterness...'

A memorial service for Lord Twining was held in September at St. Stephen's, Rochester Row. There was a very large congregation of official mourners, of admirers and of friends. They listened in silence and sadness at first, each with his or her own memories and nostalgias. The organ voluntary at the beginning was selections from Brahms and Berlioz. The hymn after the prayers was Kipling's *Recessional*: it had been Twining's own choice. The address was given by Viscount Boyd of Merton, who as Alan Lennox-Boyd and as Secretary of State had been one of Twining's warmest friends and most staunch supporters.

'This is a thanksgiving,' he said, 'for a life of gay and courageous leadership and service, and for a partnership between husband and wife which has brought much happiness and enrichment to countless people of different races in many parts of the world.

'We all have our special memories of Peter Twining. His powers of leadership, derived from energy, showmanship and a shrewd judgment of his fellow men, and a passionate belief that a governor should be known to his people and be accessible to them. His detailed knowledge of the territories in which he served. I doubt whether any governor spent a longer time on tour and he neglected no method, however novel, of making an impact. He loved people—all of them— the sophisticated of all races, and the humbler or less ambitious sort, who, as was said of the African caravan porters who walked with Speke and Burton and first saw Lake Tanganyika, "bore the future of East Africa on their heads, as day after weary day they trudged through bush and swamp to serve purposes beyond their comprehension".

'When he thought the Secretary of State was going wrong he said so in language no less vehement and picturesque than he used to certain visiting UNO Missions whose reports, as one newspaper said recently in a major understatement, "varied very much in quality"...'

People in the congregation began to relax, even to smile. They began to remember the happy things, the singular eccentricities, the special words and phrases he had used, the schoolboyish pranks and stratagems, the atmospheres which he generated wherever he went of stimulus and challenge and enjoyment...

Lord Boyd went on, 'Tributes to his memory have poured in; from his regiment, from the Colonial Service and from people of all races whom he served. The Prime Minister of Mauritius, "Ever grateful for his contribution to social development in our island". In St. Lucia, where he was Administrator, his name is still a legend. "He gave," a recent governor wrote, "new hope to the small islands when they were undergoing a period of apathy after the war. Everywhere his sense of humour and ebullience is remembered with affection."

'In North Borneo, more heavily devastated during the war than any territory in the Commonwealth, he had to create entirely anew the whole infrastructure, administrative and economic. He did this by energy and inspiration and, as another governor wrote, "This inspiration had in it not only morale but imagination, lots of ideas and vision. His departure left behind a feeling of desolation."

'And then to Tanganyika...'

As Lord Boyd spoke of Twining's years in Tanganyika some of those present who had served with him there fought to conceal the lumps in their throat. Others had equal difficulty with reminiscent smiles. Yet what they remembered or were reminded of made it difficult for them to remain as unemotional as most of them had been brought up to be, and when at the end of the service the organ poured out the loud, proud, exhilarating sounds of 'Ngoma', the Tanganyika police march which Twining himself used to conduct wherever he could with such happy unorthodoxy, they came out of the church touched quite unashamedly with the emotions which this great, gay man had stirred in them in a nostalgic period of their lives which one day others too perhaps will remember with the pride and the understanding which it deserves.

Appendix

I have not included any post-nominal decorations in this list for fear of overloading it with initials and of giving it too hierarchical a look: nor have I mentioned separately the wives of men to whom I have talked or written although many of them have given me much valuable information or advice. For these omissions I tender my apologies.

The Rt. Hon. Lord Aldington
Mrs. Dorothy Anderson
Robin Baily
Dr. John Baker
Valentine Baker
Professor J. C. Beckett
Walter Bell
John Birch
Sir Robert Black
Sir Kenneth Blackburne
Peter Bleakley
Sir Michael Blundell
John Boles
Lady Bolitho
Wilfred Bourne
Colonel T. J. Bowen
The Rt. Hon. Viscount Boyd of Merton
Sir Alan Burns
John Chant
Mrs. John Chappell
Bernard Cheeseman

I. C. Chopra
Henry Clark, M.P.
Mrs. L. Clemens
Lady Clifford
R. G. P. N. Combe
The late Dr. W. S. C. Copeman
Sir Beresford Craddock, M.P.
Sir Frederick Crawford
Sir Julian Crossley
J. O. C. Dalton
Rev. W. W. Davidson
Michael Davies
F. E. Degazon
Miss Evelyn Du Buisson
William Du Buisson
E. W. Ellison
Cyril Ehrlich
R. F. Evans
The late Mathew Fortescue-Brickdale
Canon Adam Fox
Sir Arthur Galsworthy
Sir Ronald Garvey

Canon R. M. Gibbons
Colonel W. H. Godfrey
E. B. Gordon
Sir Garnet Gordon
J. G. D. Gordon
Sir William Gorrell Barnes
Mrs. Bramwell Graham
Sir Arthur Grattan-Bellew
Geoffrey Gray
Tony Grier
Col. J. R. Hall
Miss A. N. Hamersley
Dr. K. Hazareesingh
Sir Ralph Hone
Mrs. Michael Hope
W. M. Howitt
Sir Bruce Hutt
Dr. W. F. Jepson
Abdulla M. A. Karimjee
P. N. Kavuma
Marjorie Kenyon
Capt. G. King
Capt. H. Kite
John Kisch
General Sir Gerald Lathbury
Colin Legum
Sir Lawrence Lindo
The Rt. Hon. Earl of Listowel
Sir Francis Loyd
Sir Ivison Macadam
Michael McCoun
The Rt. Hon. Malcolm Mac-
    Donald
Sir John Macpherson
T. L. M. Marealle
John Margetson
Philip Mason
Rt. Rev. David Mathew
Rev. Gervase Mathew
C. I. Meek
Lord Milverton
John Moffett
Peter Molloy

M. J. B. Molohan
Sir Leslie Monson
Mrs. Sydney Moody
Sir Owen Morshead
Lt.-Col. H. Moyse-Bartlett
Ian Norton
Roger Norton
Miss Thelma Nye
Paulo Odong
Professor Roland Oliver
Dunstan Omari
Antonio Opwa
Mrs. Lindy Orlebar
John Peel, M.P.
N. C. Pickett
A. H. Pickwood
Andrew Pike
Sir Theodore Pike
Douglas Pirie
General Sir William Platt
Sir Charles Ponsonby
H. Pook
Sir Hilton Poynton
Sir Philippe Raffray
Sir Seewoosagur Ramgoolam
Richard Rathbone
C. A. L. Richards
G. Robertson
Mrs. Helene Rogers
Sir Philip Rogers
Col. W. A. Rolleston
E. G. Rowe
Mrs. P. Rowntree
Rt. Rev. Neil Russell
John Shaw
Col. G. W. I. Shipp
J. F. Sinclair
Sir George Sinclair, M.P.
Miss Alison Smith
Dr. Teresa Spens
G. H. T. Spring
Sir Robert de Stapeldon
Sir John Stow

Basil Stubbings
Sir Rex Surridge
Frank Sykes
John Tawney
N. G. F. Taylor
Stanley Thompson
Robin Thorne
The late Maj.-General Lord
  Thurlow
Miss Mary Trevelyan
Sir Richard Turnbull
Gordon Tunze
Lord Tweedsmuir

Mrs. Georgina Twining
Hon. John Twining
Lady Twining
S. H. G. Twining
Professor Hon. William
  Twining
S. A. Walden
H. B. Watney
David Whatley
Lt.-Col. E. T. C. Wilson
Brig. C. P. G. Wills
Oliver Woods

Short Bibliography

Sir Samuel Baker, *The Albert N'yanza, Great Basin of the Nile*
Sir Michael Blundell, *So Rough a Wind*
Edward Braithwaite, *Iouanaloa: recent writings from St. Lucia*
B. T. G. Chidzero, *Tanganyika and International Trusteeship*
Sir Bede Clifford, *Life of a Proconsul*
Sir Andrew Cohen, *British Policy in Changing Africa*
George Eggleston, *Orchids in the Calabash Tree*
John Fothergill, *An Innkeeper's Diary*
Sir Ralph Furse, *Acuparius*
Stephen Gwynn, *De Valera*
Stephen Gwynn, *Ireland*
Maxwell Hall, *Makan Siap*
Thomas Hodgkin, *Nationalism in Colonial Africa*
Harold Ingrams, *Uganda*
James Joyce, *The Dubliners*
Agnes Newton Keith, *White Man Returns*
J. M. Lee, *Colonial Development and Good Government*
Judith Listowel, *The Making of Tanganyika*
Malcolm MacDonald, *Borneo Peoples*
G. A. Maguire, *Towards Uhuru in Tanzania*
Dorothy Middleton, *Baker of the Nile*
Sir Philip Mitchell, *African Afterthoughts*
T. D. Murray and A. S. White, *Sir Samuel Baker*
Julius Nyerere, *Freedom and Unity*
Cyril Pearl, *Dublin in Bloomtime*
James Pope-Hennesy, *Verandah*
James Pope-Hennesy, *The Baths of Absolom*
J. E. Smith *St. John the Evangelist, Westminster*
Maj. C. H. Stigand, *Equatoria—the Lado Enclave*
Michael Swan, *Island of the Swan*

K. G. Tregonning, *A History of Modern Sabah*
Evelyn Waugh, *A Little Learning*
Philip Woodruff, *The Guardians*
Carlton Younger, *Ireland's Civil War*
History of East Africa, Volume I edited by Gervase Mathew and Roland Oliver. Volume II edited by Vincent Harlow and E. M. Chilver

Index

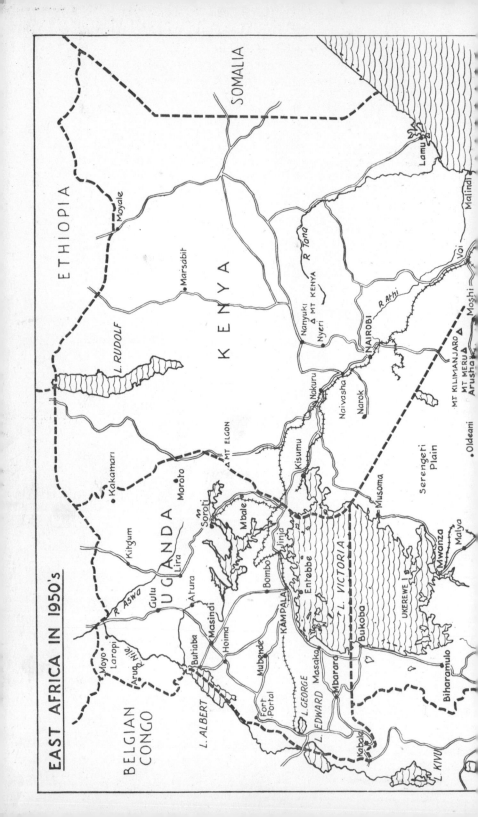

EAST AFRICA IN 1950's